# KILLING
# JOHN WAYNE
## THE MAKING OF
## *THE CONQUEROR*

## Ryan Uytdewilligen

Guilford, Connecticut

An imprint of Globe Pequot, the trade division of
The Rowman & Littlefield Publishing Group, Inc.
4501 Forbes Blvd., Ste. 200
Lanham, MD 20706
www.rowman.com

Distributed by NATIONAL BOOK NETWORK

British Library Cataloguing in Publication Information available

**Library of Congress Cataloging-in-Publication Data available**

ISBN 978-1-4930-5847-1 (cloth : alk. paper)
ISBN 978-1-4930-6331-4 (electronic)

∞™ The paper used in this publication meets the minimum requirements of
American National Standard for Information Sciences–Permanence of Paper
for Printed Library Materials, ANSI/NISO Z39.48-1992.

# Contents

Dedicated to Karen, my favorite aunt, my writing cheerleader,
and my biggest role model.

# PART THREE: AFTER

# Acknowledgments

Just as there was a vast team that brought *The Conqueror* to the screen in 1956, many helped bring *Killing John Wayne* to the page. Thank you to my cousin David Rosfeld, who was the first to turn me on to the unbelievable *Conqueror* legend. Thank you to my rock star agent, Brenna English-Loeb, who championed the story to be told and guided the book throughout its publication journey. Thank you to publisher Rick Rinehart of Globe Pequot/Rowman & Littlefield for saying yes and sharing the story with the world as well as the brilliant team of editors who made the manuscript what it is. Thank you to Natalie Luvera, curator of the National Atomic Testing Museum, and researcher Bruce Church for contending with phone calls and e-mails and pointing me in the right direction for nuclear information.

Thank you to the fascinating collection of information preserved by the Atomic Heritage Foundation. Thank you to the work and passion of authors who have come before me, particularly Richard B. Jewell, author of the mesmerizing *RKO Story*, and Scott Eyman, author of *John Wayne: The Life and Legend*. Without your work, I would be lost. Thank you to the John Wayne Cancer Foundation for your help and all the great work that you continue to do.

Thank you to Turner Classic Movies for fielding a plethora of pesky inquiries about dates and data. Thank you to my partner, Mariana, for taking the first read and putting up with obsessive conversations about John Wayne and enduring his most awful, terrible, shockingly bad but oh-so-fun-to-watch movie over and over again.

I'm not sure who to thank for my obsession with Howard Hughes, but I'm sure the credit should go to the man himself, living such a fascinating and indescribable life that occupies most of my attention span.

Thank you to all of the movie buffs and cinephiles who kept the story alive all these years and who have taken an interest in this book!

And to anyone who worked on *The Conqueror*, whether as an actor, an extra, a caterer, or an extra pair of hands, thank you and condolences to you and your family.

# Prologue

Gloria Swanson twirled her spidery fingers as she craned her head back in pure theatrical flair. With an assurance to Mr. DeMille that she was ready for her close-up, the washed-up star ushered with her the 1950s.

Brando then chewed the scenery in pure method madness, screaming "Stella!" at the top of his lungs. Bright blonde and curvy Marilyn Monroe assured all the ladies that "Diamonds Are a Girl's Best Friend," while Bogie and Hepburn drifted through jungle aboard the *African Queen*. Gene Kelly danced with a lamppost in the rain, Jimmy Stewart watched a murder from his living room, and James Dean screeched to all the parents of the world that they were tearing their teens apart.

What a time it was for moviemaking . . . a time of popping color patterns, lavish lives, and classic after classic. A time fresh from war, when folks of every age sought excitement and escape by visiting their local movie theaters. A time when the tired cogs and pulleys that held the film business together, the studio system, broke loose. The 1950s would bring the Golden Age of Hollywood to a close.

And there, at the cinematic center of it all, stood a man who embodied the spirit—the very essence of America's twentieth-century history, values, and culture. Topped with a ten-gallon hat, adorned with a neckerchief, and paired with a trusty horse for over half his roles, the legend had the general public convinced he was a real cowboy. His approach to acting was just that—a one-trick pony who honed the hero guise like no others before.

Having graced the screen in more than one hundred pictures by the end of World War II, he still insisted that he just put on his costume and did what he was told to do. Whatever the method, the image stuck as soldiers, impressionable youngsters, and near-relics of the real Old West looked to the steady conservative icon for hope and most certainly national pride. Pitted against Hitchcock thrillers, Doris Day romps, and Charlton Heston biblical epics, Marion Mitchell Morrison emerged as the decade's number one box office draw.

Yes, John Wayne—as he became professionally known—was the biggest movie star during the brightest era for film. How then could the Duke have starred in the greatest disaster ever put on celluloid?

Much has been rumored about the colossal failure that was *The Conqueror* (1956), but never has the story been accurately written down from beginning to end. It has absolutely become one of Hollywood's wildest urban legends, passed down from guilt-ridden studio heads and kept alive through circles of the most dedicated of cinephiles. It was partially swept under the rug and occasionally recycled as trivia tidbits. Many seem to know the legend, but only a handful of dedicated Wayne fans have actually seen the film.

Rest assured, you would be hard-pressed to find another flick that makes you cringe like each frame of this manages to do. Every fact unearthed from the "making-of" just adds another layer of erroneous judgment into the harebrained mixture along with cringe-worthy subtext to each scene. The whole thing feels like a slow-motion car crash that was doomed from day one. So perhaps, in a way, *The Conqueror* has redeemed itself by becoming a better story than the movie itself could have ever hoped to be.

How does a bad film get made anyway? Few people, if any, get into the motion picture business hoping to make something terrible. Yet it does seem like Hollywood churns out more stinkers than gold. The first step naturally lies in the writing—the carefully crafted instructions for the movie. Bad instructions, bad results. Or the team could be embarking on the filmmaking journey for all the wrong reasons, such as oodles of cash. An actor could be miscast in a part or guided under the wrong direction, thus plainly coming across as bad, bad, bad!

*The Conqueror* began with all of these mistakes and then plunged its poor players toward near destruction. Extreme heat, desolate conditions, and even panther attacks plagued the shoot. Add eccentric billionaire, aviator, and occasional picture producer Howard Hughes into the mix as the head of RKO, and there was simply no way to win.

It was these misguided moves that drove the entirety of Hollywood and the picture business to the brink. Beneath the glistening array of freshly filmed classics was the weary studio system. Aging moguls had staked their claim since before the invention of sound and had been around the block a time or two; they also carried firm beliefs in how picture production should be done.

The old Hollywood republic keenly stepped up to fight the arrival of television armed with bloated period pieces, which cost an arm and a leg to produce. The excuse was to attract viewers out of their homes for more astonishing star-driven entertainment. At first, the sights and sounds succeeded, but the out-of-touch sugary escapism of the latter 1950s wore out its welcome rather quickly.

Behind the scenes, troubles have only been further exposed and condemned in modern times. Howard Hughes used filmmaking as a way to exploit young starlets, a hobby in which he was hardly alone. There was just too much of everything harmful driving production and too many people blindly saying "yes" to those in possession. *The Conqueror* could be argued as the first real domino in the collapse of the original moviemaking process. Without it, we may have never seen the likes of Coppola, Spielberg, or Scorsese arrive during the new wave movement of the 1970s.

On the darker side of the 1950s, far away from the decade's cinematic circus, came the life-annihilating threats of the Cold War. After the United States dropped "Fat Man" and "Little Boy" over Japan, the world was forever altered with the looming panic of a nuclear attack. The Soviet Union, with its opposing Communist views, perfectly etched itself into a villainous rival for the United States to loathe and fear. Nuclear testing in desolate southwestern landscapes was deemed a must for survival. These were the very same landscapes where exotic stories set in faraway lands could be made.

The dismal cherry atop this story acts as a stark reminder of how dangerous film production and this cruel world can be. Beyond the outlandishness of a chaotic production came years of pain, heartbreak, conspiracy, madness, and death.

Could John Wayne be blamed for the critical thrashing this film received? Could the blindness of Howard Hughes be constituted as murder? The absolute truth can only be speculated. This debate has turned *The Conqueror* into a disputed myth among film fans, film producers, citizens, and even the US government.

But it has been so long since 1956, the questions will almost certainly never get their answers. Advocates still vie for justice. Audiences still scratch their heads in confusion. No matter the opinions, the author would still like to give condolences to any family members and friends who lost a loved one who worked on this film and those in the desert towns of the American Southwest who continue to see others succumb to cancer.

Through articles and studies, the work of biographers, and the mouths of residents from Utah, the story survived. For those desperate to get a glimpse of the wreckage, trying to find a decent copy of the film can be quite a journey. But when you do find it, the pieces are all right there–a culmination of everything right about fifties' filmmaking–bound and gagged by everything that was wrong. American pride and Communist paranoia transformed into a backfiring elephant in the room.

So honestly, just how bad can the thing really be? Few have made it through the runtime with a straight face. Even fewer have learned about its legacy with a dry eye. In today's social justice climate, a film like this would never see the light of day or be shot in the manner in which it was shot. But, as we so often hear when defending once-beloved classic artworks, it was a different time. Surely, this spectacle was on a different planet altogether.

Here you have Wayne, standing in Mongol makeup as fierce warrior Genghis Khan in all his glory. In his flat drawl, he proclaims, "I feel this Tatar woman is for me, and my blood says, take her," while laying his gaze on a sprawled Susan Hayward.

It must have been sheer cosmic misfortune for Duke and Howard Hughes to meet. In the decade of Elia Kazan dramas and Vincente

Minnelli musicals, dusty Westerns and imported masterworks from Japan, the Duke and Hughes gave us *The Conqueror*.

Don't say I didn't warn you.

# PART ONE

# BEFORE

# 1: Tale of Two Titans

To say eccentric billionaire, aviator, and occasional moviemaker Howard Hughes was having a busy few years would be an understatement. Tasked with constructing spy planes for the US Air Force in World War II, Hughes's aircraft company promised to deliver one hundred XF-11 aircrafts, designed and tested personally by the infamous owner himself. After three lagging years of no output, Hughes finally piloted the first prototype, tail number 44-70155, on July 7, 1946.

An oil leak midflight caused one of the propellers to reverse pitch and swiftly lose altitude. In an attempt to land on the Los Angeles Country Club golf course, Hughes destroyed the rooftops of three upscale Beverly Hills houses, setting fire to the final one while shattering, contorting, and then finally setting the aircraft–and himself–ablaze.

Hughes was barely saved from the flames by a marine sergeant who happened to be nearby. He suffered a crushed collarbone, cracked ribs, third-degree burns, and most impressive of all, a crushed chest, which collapsed his lung and completely shifted his heart to the opposite side of his chest cavity. When brought to the hospital, he was given a 50/50 chance of survival, but he managed to cling to life, claiming to benefit solely from the natural life-giving properties of freshly squeezed orange juice. Miraculously, he walked away from the incident months later with his trademark mustache covering the only visible scars on his upper lip.

Howard Hughes was back in the sky by April 5, 1947, testing his second XF-11 design, which finally flew without issue. Despite the belated success, the program was cancelled, which proved to be an exhausting embarrassment for Hughes and his entire company, having labored on the project for almost half the decade. Hughes was subsequently called upon to appear before a Senate War Investigating Committee to answer for his undelivered airplanes–including a plywood monstrosity professionally known as the H-4 Hercules.

Scorned as the *Spruce Goose* through plentiful media play, the pet project of Hughes and cargo shipbuilder Henry J. Kaiser was developed to transport materials to Britain, thus bypassing German seafaring blockages. Contracted in 1942 and constructed mostly out of wood to conserve precious metals, the Hercules also never took to the sky; its requirement of government funds was contentiously examined by Senator Owen Brewster and a very Hughes-hungry panel.

Hughes snapped a furious rebuttal at the climax of his heated and highly publicized hearings by stating the Hercules would indeed take flight. "Now, I put the sweat of my life into this thing. I have my reputation all rolled up in it, and I have stated several times that if it's a failure, I'll probably leave this country and never come back. And I mean it."

At a cost of $23 million (nearly $300 million adjusted for inflation), it was one of the United States' most expensive aviation projects. Stretching 319 feet and 11 inches, the Hercules possessed the longest wingspan in the world. The weight was more staggering, totaling 250,000 pounds on its own while the structure could carry 150,000 pounds of cargo.

Trucked piece by piece to Long Beach Harbor, Hughes did indeed fly the *Spruce Goose* for one mile on November 2, 1947, a mere seventy feet above water. Though the flight lasted for twenty-six seconds, it was still considered a victory for Hughes, proving his plane operational and deserving of government funds. The definitive case against him would be dismissed by the end of that same year. True to his word, Hughes remained a US citizen for the remainder of his life.

In any other person's entire lifespan, just one of those extravagant activities would be enough to define them and cast their legacy into immortalization. For some, the bruises earned and lessons learned would be enough for them to dust off their shoulders, call it a day, and retire. But the sudden acquirement of a mass conglomerate . . . commander of a dream factory . . . a movie studio, for anybody, would have been a whole other unimaginable fantasy altogether.

The billionaire had just gone from near-death plane crash to a potentially detrimental national Senate hearing and finally to flying the world's largest boat. In anyone else's life, none of those events would be imaginable, nor would the fact that the next move would be to own one of the most profitable Hollywood landmarks. But for Hughes, this gargantuan life-altering business mistake would merely be just another Tuesday.

RKO stood for Radio-Keith-Orpheum and became RKO Productions, Inc., on October 23, 1928, after the marriage of a small silent-era studio and a decaying vaudevillian theater company. David Sarnoff of the Radio Corporation of America (RCA) gained control of Joseph P. Kennedy's Film Booking Offices of America (FBO) and the Keith-Albee-Orpheum theater chain in an attempt to capitalize on talking pictures by finding an outlet to exploit his new sound recording system, the photophone. Legend has it this deal was shaped and slurped inside a Manhattan oyster bar.

With those three integral aspects acquired–the innovative technology of the day, a production space to shoot projects, and theaters to present the work–RKO was brought into the world with all the necessary components for a prosperous beginning. The RKO Forty Acres, a five-hundred-acre backlot in the desolate San Fernando Valley, would soon become an iconic pop culture hub sprawling northeast from Melrose Avenue and Gower Street. Advertisements announcing the studio's arrival in Hollywood proudly claimed "A Titan Is Born."

It was said to have been Sarnoff, by the way, because of his background in the radio business, who suggested the iconic logo with the broadcast tower beaming atop the entire world.

The business floundered through its beginnings until the acquisition of the moderately successful Pathé Exchange–another production and distribution chain–secured the studio's future with an established newsreel operation and a Culver City backlot. *Syncopation* and *Street Girl* became RKO's first two out of thirteen releases in 1929, both of them musical hits that capitalized on the recent invention of sound.

RKO released *Cimarron*, an epic Oklahoma-set Western that earned the fourth Academy Award for Best Picture despite losing the studio a significant amount of cash. Profit be damned, the studio had officially arrived, just in the nick of time, as the movie business took a more defined shape.

The studio system was becoming a solidified moviemaking machine in the very moment RKO became a reality. In the late twenties and early thirties, the leaders of the industry emerged with a bona fide formula that transported motion pictures from a mere road show fad to the absolute entertainment staple for the masses.

Each juggernaut staked out a piece of land where whole worlds past, present, and future could come alive through the right paint, fabric, and stage fixtures. The rapid expansion of these studio lots was revolutionary–dedicated spaces covering all aspects of cinema and made for these dream factories to come together to form, essentially, small filmmaking communities.

Moguls with money contracted directors and writers and most certainly pleasant-faced actors to stick with that particular studio. No one was free to just bounce around and work where they wanted to. Everyone had an obligation to fulfill and paid a flat rate no matter the project. As star power and recognition rose, this tactic was a significant reason why the big studios stayed in business and became as powerful as they were; they could ride on the backs of their celebrities all the way to the bank.

Each company got a boost in legitimacy with daily coverage from growing tabloids and magazines like *Variety*, as the Academy Awards proved to be the stuff marketers' dreams were made of. Combine that with the desire for escapism from the American working class during the Great Depression, and the Golden Age of Hollywood became nearly unstoppable.

Now, sure, there were a few small start-ups that were able to produce a handful of pictures every year; but Hollywood belonged to "the majors." Most had been cobbled together during the silent era and had already weathered a few storms of total industrial reform. Talkies, of course, changed everything, killing the way those studios operated. But they survived.

Each major studio, nicknamed the "Big Five," carved out a niche, rising up by clinging to defined style and specialized genres. MGM produced lush, bright, and expensive musicals and comedies, while 20th Century Fox opted for a more melodramatic approach.

Paramount Pictures was known as the most "European" studio, as it developed a more diverse roster of ethnic stars and worldly settings. Warner Bros. billed itself as the studio for the working class and notably churned out more realistic entertainment and gritty gangster films.

The fifth movie studio that rounded out the Big Five during this incomparable era was unexpectedly RKO. Their lucky formation dealings and early Oscar win truly drummed up enough good fortune, catapulting the company far beyond comparisons of the competing minor studios of Universal Studios, Columbia Pictures, and United Artists–otherwise known as the "Little Three."

Shifting through changing presentation titles beginning with RKO Pathé and then Radio Pictures–officially sticking with RKO Radio Pictures from 1936 onward–the studio's niche market was a tad more complicated than its four established competitors. Barely on the cusp of thirty, burgeoning producer David O. Selznick was hired to transform RKO's mediocre output into an array of consistent gold. He delivered, instituting more directorial control, which proved to be attractive to more auteur-driven talent.

Important figures passed through RKO's walls at the time, including John Barrymore, Cary Grant, and Katharine Hepburn; the latter legend has been credited with launching the studio almost singlehandedly. Hepburn's very first starring role in George Cukor's *A Bill of Divorcement*, her first Oscar-winning role for *Morning Glory*, and one of her most celebrated roles in *Little Women*, all arrived in the span of one year, 1933, through RKO. Her 1938 Howard Hawks–directed screwball comedy, *Bringing Up Baby,* with Grant remains as one of cinema's most beloved laugh-a-thons from that era.

By far, RKO's most prominent picture then, or at any moment of its entire existence, would be Merian C. Cooper's *King Kong*. Selznick backed the jungle-set monster movie, which catapulted original scream queen Fay Wray into stardom, set the standard for miniature model work and stop-motion animation, and jump-started an entire creature-feature genre of its own. Against a $675,000 budget, *King Kong* earned RKO a substantial profit of $5.3 million ($100 million adjusted for inflation) at the box office.

Cooper picked up where Selznick left off as he exited RKO to work for his father-in-law, Louis B. Mayer, over at MGM. The midthirties saw immense stabilization through an array of diverse output, including eight toe-tapping Ginger Rogers and Fred Astaire musicals between 1934 and 1939. The duo actually became RKO's largest cinematic draw, particularly with the highly lauded hits *The Gay Divorcee*, *Top Hat*, and *Swing Time*. Charles Laughton's performance in *The Hunchback of Notre Dame* and the sexually charged horror *Cat People* also stand out as cinema classics gifted to the moviegoing world by RKO.

Industrialist Floyd Odlum, touted as "possibly the only man in the United States who made a great fortune out of the Depression," swooped in to buy up 50 percent of RCA's stake in the studio during this pivotal upswing. As one of the wealthiest American men throughout the 1930s, Odlum made a career, much like Hughes, as an investor–additionally holding stock in Convair, Northeast Airlines, and Transcontinental Air Transport, Inc., through his Atlas Corporation firm. The Rockefeller brothers bought a smaller stake in the company at around the same time.

RKO's boom ignited with these high-profile financial controllers alongside production chief Samuel Briskin's decision to distribute Walt Disney's cartoons. The deal began with Disney's first animated feature and what ultimately became the second-highest-grossing picture of the decade, *Snow White and the Seven Dwarfs*. This single industry-altering moment was arguably RKO's highest point in existence.

The trouble that put the studio on rocky ground always seemed to stem from the very method that kept it alive: a hunger for variety. While its rivals produced grand-scale stories with a noticeable stamp, little about RKO was recognizable beyond its worldly logo and periods of a futuristic Art Deco atmosphere. And unlike the other companies, which had extra years that helped them operate like well-oiled machines, RKO struggled to stay consistent.

After Disney's deal, their bread and butter became distribution deals, which kept them afloat but did nothing to define them as content creators. Samuel Goldwyn, who helped initiate MGM, established his own self-titled production company and released twenty-one films through RKO–starting with *The Little Foxes* in 1941 and culminating with *The Best Years of Our Lives* in 1946. They were all films associated with RKO, but at much too far of an arm's length to truly solidify it as a major production house.

Twenty-five-year-old Orson Welles struck the deal of the century at the turn of the decade with RKO; studio head George J. Schaefer immensely enjoyed Welles's controversial *War of the Worlds* broadcast. Welles was promised a two-picture deal that gave him a then-unheard-of freedom of complete artistic control and the opportunity to write, act, produce, and direct. Schaefer's reasoning for the extravagant contract was to attract publicity and steer the studio toward more creative endeavors. The result was *Citizen Kane*, a hit with critics and historians for its editing and narrative innovations (which took real-life inspiration not only from newspaper publisher William Randolph Hearst but also from Howard Hughes).

*Kane* ultimately lost money at the box office due to its tumultuous overdrawn production and then a denial of significant advertising opportunities by an enraged Hearst himself. With Welles's second film, *The Magnificent Ambersons*, a commercial dud, RKO's investors began to fear the risks the studio was taking, which resulted in Schaefer's and Welles's dismissals.

RKO wobbled its way along for most of its life after *Kane*, relying more heavily than its competitors on B movies. This, in turn, may have saved a buck but tarnished its reputation. Entertainment assembled for under two hundred thousand dollars made up at least one-quarter of its yearly releases–most of which have been long since forgotten. That output and the fact that RKO had the right movies but at the wrong time seemed to damage the studio time and time again.

Along with *Kane*, the perennial Capra holiday classic, *It's a Wonderful Life*, flopped, bankrupting subsidiary production company Liberty Films, which produced only two projects with RKO before dissolving. The fantasy film starring James Stewart was loathed by many critics and was financially hurt by a mass release several weeks after Christmas. Somehow, it managed to earn five Oscar nominations against Goldwyn's *The Best Years of Our Lives*–curiously making 1946 one of RKO's most awarded years of existence.

Potentially fruitful endeavors such as the embrace of television should have helped, as RKO was the first major movie studio to produce their own content for the new medium with the release of the one-hour drama *Talk Fast, Mister*. Executives took a few trips down south to Mexico City, where the studio helped establish Estudios Churubusco with businessman Emilio Azcárraga Vidaurreta. Perhaps the most erroneous act of all was that there were just too many film fingers in too many non-film pies.

Another undeniable aspect that hurt RKO's chance at long-term stability was the fact that there was no identifiable mogul at the helm. Fox had Darryl F. Zanuck. MGM literally had their Mayer. The first father figure who shepherded the company along, Selznick, returned only to lease a portion of the studio for his own productions. The reining boss after Schaefer became Charles Koerner, who, to his credit, kept RKO on high ground but produced nothing of note. His motto, "Showmanship in Place of Genius: A New Deal at RKO," was a direct attempt at washing their hands of the *Citizen Kane* production woes by vowing never to be "too creative."

Given more time to build on this model, he would have provided the studio with its closest shot at success (much to the chagrin of cinema lovers). Koerner instead died in February 1946, leaving a string of chiefs and presidents, most importantly Dore Schary, in charge and plummeting RKO toward uncertainty. It seemed as though the right person would never come along at the right moment to raise the studio to its full potential.

The earliest nails in the coffin came when the British government imposed a 75 percent tax on foreign films, an act that severely sliced revenue just as the bright new glow of television stole audiences faster than expected.

McCarthyism took hold in late 1947, causing the iron fist of the House Un-American Activities Committee to strike down on Communism, feared to be rising within Hollywood's midst. Contracted actors and producers that were, even in that moment, a box office draw for RKO were let go for having any believed Communist ties.

Then there was the major crackdown on the process of block booking, one of the studio system's cornerstone dealings to rake in high-profit earnings. Up until this point, major studios additionally owned a large portion of the theater chains that screened their movies. Studio-owned chains were typically charged low rent while A pictures—the more desirable products with bigger budgets, recognizable stars, and in most cases more built-in hype—were then sold to independent chains in packages through an all-or-nothing basis. In other words, if you wanted to show *Casablanca* at your theater, you were going to also have to screen *King of the Zombies* to make it happen.

Small chains were forced to rent and screen less desirable output to acquire the right to show a studio's higher-quality work—a process that certainly benefited RKO's excessive B movie slate. The low-budget releases were almost always guaranteed a profit until *United States v. Paramount Pictures, Inc.* found they and the rest of the major Hollywood studios were guilty of breaking antitrust statutes. The practice was outlawed, and studios were forced to split off their theater chains by the end of the decade.

By this time, the Rockefellers had sold off all their stock. Initial owner and operator David Sarnoff walked away from his involvement with RCA. It was Floyd Odlum who had gained a controlling interest in the company through his Atlas Corporation, a capital formation and investment firm. He took the role of production chief in the early part of the 1940s and was involved with occasional creative decisions. Before the wave of uncertainty, he had sold roughly 40 percent of his shares to cash in on RKO's seemingly endless success. By the end of 1947, Odlum decided he had endured all he could take of the unpredictable film business and put his remaining 25 percent on the market.

The most befuddling fact that comes from this great blunder in history is that Howard Hughes had seemingly turned his back on the picture business to obsessively focus on airplanes—a move many around him saw as his true life's calling. Hardly an adult at eighteen, Hughes had found his way in both businesses after he inherited his father's drill bit company in 1924 in the wake of both his parents' deaths. Equipped with disposable millions in his pocket, Hughes's plan of action at first was to drop out of Rice University to marry Ella Botts Rice and haphazardly pursue a career as a professional golfer.

What the young Mr. Hughes truly desired, however, was a career in the motion picture business—a bug that never could truly be traced beyond the fact it was one of the fastest-growing industries in the world. That, and the fact that the moving pictures were just so fabulously larger than life.

Hughes moved from his home in Houston, Texas, out west to Los Angeles, where he took his inheritance and started producing almost immediately—making connections through his screenwriter uncle, Rupert Hughes. He converted the Caddo Rock Drilling Company, a subsidiary of his father's Toolco, into his very own Caddo Productions.

Hughes put up $80,000 ($1.1 million after inflation) for the little-seen *Swell Hogan* in 1926, starring and directed by matinee idol Ralph Graves, a move that saw little advancement or return. Much to the worriment of his remaining family, Hughes produced a second movie, *Everybody's Acting,* a hit that made up for the losses and then some.

His next effort as a producer was insignificant though fascinating by any era's standards: *The Mating Call* in 1928 told the silent story of a WWI vet who vows vengeance on the KKK after finding his wife having an affair with a Klansman. *The Racket*, a film noir about a police captain busting a bootlegger, immediately changed Hughes's fortune. It was nominated for "Outstanding Picture" at the very first Academy Awards in 1929. His earlier war-set comedy, *Two Arabian Knights*, also won Lewis Milestone the now-defunct award of "Best Director of a Comedy" that same year.

Now a proven hit-making machine, Hughes had many cozying up to him, with some agreeing he was the man with the "Midas touch" in Hollywood. Others apparently referred to him as "the sucker with the money" behind his back.

"This is a business," Hughes assured the press. "The purpose of a business is to make money. If it happens to make art, too, that would be secondary and accidental." He was also known for assuring folks that he intended to make the biggest motion pictures ever seen.

Above all, Hughes desired control—creative control that allowed him to sink his teeth and all of his available cash into a unique and distinctly Howard Hughes–made project. The 1930 epic *Hell's*

*Angels* gave him the chance to write, direct, and truly showcase his passion. The aviation war epic told the story of two brothers who have passionate affairs in the midst of joining the Royal Flying Corps. Hughes employed nearly 150 pilots to work on the picture and bring to life some of the most realistic dogfight sequences ever put on celluloid.

Under the advisement that these shots would look even better with cloudy skies as a backdrop, Hughes often grounded the entire fleet for days or weeks on end just to capture more stimulating movements. He was involved in a serious crash when test piloting one of the planes used for his big climax. He entered an uncorrectable tailspin but walked away with a skull fracture. Three pilots and a mechanic were not so lucky, succumbing to injuries acquired while filming the chaotic final scenes.

Although *Hell's Angels* was conceived and shot as a silent movie, Hughes shocked Hollywood when the influence of *The Jazz Singer* caused him to halt production–halfway complete at that point–to remake the film into a talkie. Altogether, the mammoth production stretched on for two and a half years. In pursuit of crafting what the relatively inexperienced Hughes self-described as "the greatest epic ever seen," he discovered and signed platinum blonde Jean Harlow and threw a massive opening reception at Grauman's Chinese Theatre, one of the largest red carpet star-studded affairs of the time.

At a cost of $3.95 million ($77 million in modern terms), the production ballooned into the second most expensive movie ever made in that period, narrowly trailing behind *Ben-Hur: A Tale of the Christ* (1925)–or at least that's what legend would have the public believe. Hughes claimed the fact was merely a public relations stunt to drum up interest, and costs merely hovered around what would have been the $2.8 million mark.

Arguably, the man's greatest contribution to film came with the same frantic stroke to remain relevant in Tinseltown when he took more of a backseat approach. Hughes additionally produced the screwball comedy *The Front Page* and the violent Al Capone–inspired mob thriller *Scarface*, both hits with critics and audiences, which would be remade into celebrated hits decades later. Unexpectedly, those projects signified the end of his film efforts for more than ten years as he disbanded the Caddo Company and pocketed his career as a producer in a sudden snap decision of competing passions. Left dusty and forgotten, Caddo would never be touched again.

Hughes instead took up flying, working as an assistant pilot for American Airlines under the pseudonym Charles Howard; it was his ploy to learn all he could about the emerging industry that fascinated him more than the movies.

In 1932, Hughes formed Hughes Aircraft Company as a division of the Hughes Tool Company; he appointed his right-hand financial manager, Noah Dietrich, to be in charge. Hughes designed and piloted the sleek and streamlined H-1 Racer in this period, breaking the world landplane speed record at 352.29 mph in 1935; he ran the aircraft's fuel down, later crashing into a beet field, where he insisted, "She'll go faster."

In 1937, he began to buy a controlling interest in TWA; in 1938, he set another monumental record by personally flying around the entire world in ninety-one hours. To commend his aviation efforts, Hughes was awarded the Congressional Gold Medal in 1939.

Unsuccessfully developing the Hughes D-2 and the Sikorsky S-43, with the latter crashing into Lake Mead and killing two employees onboard (Hughes managed to walk away unharmed), he unexpectedly made his return to film with a second directorial effort through a new self-titled production company. He made a heavily panned Western called *The Outlaw* (1943) starring Jane Russell.

Filmed in 1941, few could explain what exactly drew Hughes back other than the obvious pursuit for money and possibly an unshakable sexual obsession. Above all else during production, Hughes feared Russell's breasts were not being properly showcased to their fullest advantage, leading him to specially rig an underwire push-up mechanism sewn into the actress's brassiere–a precursor to the push-up bra. The Hollywood Production Code Administration did not approve of Hughes's "indecent" mammary shots and ordered half a minute cut. Released for one week in 1943, *The Outlaw* was retracted due to public outcry and moral concern and was eventually redistributed by United Artists in 1946 to mixed reception.

Next, Hughes struck up a friendship with celebrated comedy auteur Preston Sturges and formed a third production company, abandoning his latest one-picture venture, Howard Hughes Productions, to start California Pictures.

A string of celebrated works, including *The Lady Eve, Sullivan's Travels*, and *The Palm Beach Story*, made a proud Sturges desire complete control. The handshake deal with Hughes in 1944 established him as the only writer-producer-director in Hollywood behind Charlie Chaplin; the billionaire became Sturges's financier.

The result was *The Sin of Harold Diddlebock*, a poorly reviewed college-set comedy filmed on the Samuel Goldwyn lot and starring retired silent film icon Harold Lloyd. Hughes apparently ran a company-wide contest, offering $250 to anyone who could come up with a shorter name. He quickly took the film out of circulation and away from Sturges, re-editing it himself and releasing it under the name *Mad Wednesday* three years later. The two had a falling out and dissolved California Pictures over the muddled period piece *Vendetta* (1950).

The aviator was no stranger to RKO at the time of the buyout. Amid his 1929 divorce, Hughes had a playboy reputation linking him to actresses contracted to RKO in the 1930s, including Katharine Hepburn, Fay Wray, and Joan Fontaine, not to mention persistent bisexual relationship rumors that linked him to men like studio stars Cary Grant, Errol Flynn, and Randolph Scott.

Being as well connected as he was and due to his abundance of friendships with various movers and shakers, he got to know the inner workings of RKO a time or two, sizing up the business all along.

After his flirtation with the film industry during the middle of the decade, it was evident RKO was the one place willing to let him claw his way back into the business once more. Seeing three of his own production start-ups fail to gather any steam, the easy acquisition of a fully loaded superpower of a studio must have had him salivating.

Floyd Odlum must have seen something of himself in Hughes when he came knocking at the investor's door. Word has it the two never officially met, and Odlum did all of his major negotiating from a phone long enough to reach his swimming pool. The two were among the richest businessmen in the country, both by investing in airlines and plane manufacturers then major movie studios.

Whatever he did, Hughes made an impression, beating out obvious contender Joseph Arthur Rank, a British film industrialist with decades of ownership experience, for ownership.

With the expertise of Noah Dietrich negotiating for half a year at his side, Hughes spent $8.8 million ($94 million) to acquire Odlum and his Atlas Corporation's 929,000 shares on Tuesday, May 11, 1948.

With all other investors holding less than a 25 percent block of the studio's stock, controlling interest fell to Howard. He was now in charge, the moviemaking puppet master that he always desired to be. RKO finally received a dedicated and somewhat seasoned leader, a father figure to steer the studio toward the right path through sensible business models and a healthy desire for some creative risk-taking. At the most manipulable and malleable point in its existence, the shaky studio, one of the Big Five players in Hollywood, RKO, became the property of Howard Hughes.

A Hollywood urban legend grew into a well-spun ball of yarn that Hughes never stepped foot on the RKO studio lot on which he spent a fortune. Many executives have attested to this fact, not once seeing him take a trip down the halls. Others claimed he came in once: right after the deal with Odlum was officially struck. Hughes did stop in the RKO hallways to take a welcoming tour. Partway through, he turned to the staff and plainly instructed them, "Paint it!" before walking out.

# 2: Hughes at the Helm

The RKO takeover was flogged around Hollywood as the "biggest move since 20th Century bought Fox," a transaction that had occurred back in 1935. Always the public relations whiz, Hughes more than likely sparked this claim himself. Whatever awe and wonder business insiders and studio competitors may have been dazzled with by the arrival of Hughes was washed away over a single weekend.

As his first major action as head of studio, Hughes began stripping RKO of just about everything and everyone who had kept it going through thick and thin over the past decade. Roughly eight hundred jobs were cut on a Friday, prompting tabloid headlines to skewer the mogul's business decisions and flog rumors that absolutely no one was safe from getting the boot come Monday morning. RKO president Peter Rathvon may have assured workers there was nothing to sweat, but evidently the newspapers' extravagant rumor-mill claims were absolutely correct.

Lower-level grunt workers—the film developers and promotions departments, layout artists, painters, set designers, even writers—got the ax. Hughes then began putting his paws all over prints: Films such as *Battleground* and *Bed of Roses* that were completed and set to ship to theaters were instead shelved. They had been specifically made by the morally inclined production chief Dore Schary, who had hoped to bring more social conscience and thought-provoking tales to the medium.

Hughes disliked the works, calling them "message pictures," a title that did not sit well with Schary. Neither of the two men had started off on the right foot; at their first meeting, Hughes directly asked Schary if he was a Communist. Schary had controversially stood up for his former employees wrapped up in the "Hollywood Ten" trials—a group of individuals who faced jail time after refusing to answer questions from the House Un-American Activities Committee on their alleged Communist ties.

"I'm an extreme Liberal," Schary responded in defensive gusto. As Hughes tinkered with and pulled apart every film RKO had in production, Schary had enough and quit just a month and a half after the new owner's arrival. As Ravthon followed, leaving RKO with hardly any voice of reason, Hughes appointed newbie Sid Rogell to oversee production.

The inflaming Communist question was certainly not just a one-off altercation either—Hughes made sniffing out Reds his number one priority. The man fostered a deep hatred of the Communist cause so much that he gave millions of dollars from his own pocket on the off chance there were one or two of them in his midst. The investigations put forth by the House Un-American Activities Committee had every studio head and owner biting their fingernails and cutting employees; Hughes turned RKO into his own private battleground against Communism.

A task force was established to interview and intimidate every RKO employee, regardless of rank or position. The shakedown reduced the list of workers even further; if an employee signified even a kernel of a Communist interest–in Hughes's view–they were let go. Anyone who earned more than fifteen hundred dollars a month had a file kept on them that detailed what they did with their money and where their interests allegedly lay.

Kemp Niver was Hughes's secret spy in the field and was dispatched to listen in on conversations and poke around for any lead that could link someone to a Soviet Union uprising. In fact, Hughes ordered his goons to give anyone showing displeasure with the way the US government operated an extreme warning or, in some cases, sent them packing. He would only refer to these firings as "leaves of absence" to the remaining roster of employees to keep from riling them up.

Hughes spared no expense to rid himself and the studio of any accidental Communist content that could tarnish either his or the studio's image. Reaching far past the borders of his own time, Hughes had the audacity to order that hundreds of credits of suspected Communists be removed from RKO films dating as far back as 1931. Filing cabinets filled with damning red ink kept tabs on just about anyone who so much as looked at the studio.

In that early ownership period, one of his first productions was a laughably melodramatic film noir blatantly entitled *I Married a Communist* as a means to test staff members' loyalty. Designed as more of a propaganda science fiction piece, the seventy-three-minute mess starring Robert Ryan and Laraine Day told the story of a former Communist Party member who is hunted down by an over-the-top interpretation of the political group. Retitled *The Woman on Pier 13*, the picture was released in 1949 and flopped with critics and audiences alike–a foreshadowing of the films to come.

Within the very first year of taking ownership, Hughes cut 75 percent of the entire studio workforce, grinding down the twenty-five hundred employees to a woeful skeleton crew of just six hundred. In a tumultuous period for all of Hollywood, Hughes's managerial actions raised the eyebrows of literally anyone following the saga. The method to his madness here was to save the studio by gutting the inner workings of its bloat, thus saving money by avoiding "unnecessary" salaries. To Hughes's credit, RKO did see a million-dollar profit in 1949–but the emotional expense was hardly worth the earnings.

Hughes did not see a single instance of tears, pain, or poverty stemming from his business model, because his RKO office was housed inside a rival studio, the Samuel Goldwyn lot, a few blocks away. With a desk, a chair, and a private screening room, the office remained cold and bare throughout its service life. Word around the office was Hughes deemed RKO to be far too unclean for him; meetings, casting sessions, and shooting would have to be done offsite if the boss was to be present.

A fairly strong case can be made for May 8, 1948, just three days before Hughes took control of RKO, as the day the studio system died and the Golden Age of Hollywood began to rust. The landmark Paramount case resulted in the outlawing of block booking; studios would have to end their monopolies and divorce their theater chains if they wished to stay in business.

The discussion had been dragging along for an entire decade until this do-or-die ruling was finally passed. Every member of the Big Five dug in their heels, fearing a full-on collapse was on the horizon. Each studio head claimed a profit could not be earned this way and that many of the movies, mostly low-budget B grades, would never get an audience if the studio could not control where and how the films were released.

From MGM's Louis B. Mayer to Paramount's Adolph Zukor, movie studio heads banded together to prove to the government that this was an entertainment execution waiting to happen. RKO happened to own the fewest theaters of the group but made the bulk of its funds through the block-booking process. As the new sheriff in town, Hughes should have cozied up to the rest of the moguls, but Hughes was never in the business–any business–to make pals and run anything predictably.

Instead, RKO was the first studio to abandon all of the fuss and enter a consent decree with the Justice Department. Hughes kept the production company, broke off the theater chain into its own distribution business, and proved to the moguls and stunned lawmakers that the move was more than feasible.

Forced to follow, every other studio begrudgingly sold off their theater chains, focusing solely on production and giving theater owners the freedom to choose what was shown. No production could be effortlessly slapped together anymore with over-the-top acting and subpar plots—quality was the only way a motion picture could find life. Because of that shift, the amount of films released annually was instantaneously decreased, doing away with disposable fluff made solely for the sake of having something to screen.

Howard Hughes's name was cursed by every other owner and studio head, still scratching their heads about how the quick and unexpected requirement was suddenly causing such monumental grief.

With RKO Pictures Corporation and RKO Theaters Corporation on his hands, Hughes felt his move would create a domino effect that would put all of the major studios on more of an equal footing with his own floundering company. In theory, the move should have worked; but Hughes, plain and simple, did not have his ducks lined up in a row.

Buyers for the newly formed distribution business, including Floyd Odlum—who apparently had a change of heart with the picture business—were chomping at the bit to acquire the selection of theaters. Hughes instead held on to everything for several years, extending divorcement deadlines further and further as his attention fell to minute production details that had never concerned him in the past.

The Hollywood Studio System instantly faltered as a result, exposing weaknesses that left it vulnerable.

Instead of a quest for overall production quality so RKO could hold their own against other producers, Hughes festered over the most intricate and unnecessary minutiae, driving his remaining crew completely mad. His executive assistant, William Fadiman, recalled that Hughes spent a great deal of time alone in his Goldwyn office learning how to cut and edit film just to bring himself up to speed with the technology.

"If it took ten days to do something anyone else could do in a day . . . he would do it in twenty. But he would master it by the nineteenth day," Fadiman said. "And it was his money, in this case, so he did what he wished."

Allying himself with graphic artist Mario Zamparelli, Hughes demanded to lower already low-cut dresses to show more cleavage on advertisements. He apparently spent half an hour discussing the thickness of a shirt to imprint in Zamparelli's mind what he wanted showcased. He studied and planned for hours just exactly how actress Faith Domergue's lips should be pursed on another poster.

Then there was his meddling with movies like *His Kind of Woman,* which was turned over complete, with Jane Russell and RKO's most fiery hopeful of the era, Robert Mitchum, in lead roles. At the turn of the decade, Mitchum was becoming one of the studio's last major stars standing—and fortunately was one of Hughes's better decisions.

The young, rebellious thespian had been caught smoking marijuana at a party during a police sting operation; one week in county jail and forty-two days at a Castaic, California, prison farm placed pressure on Hughes to drop Mitchum from his RKO contract. Instead, Hughes slipped reporters a few bucks to place a victimized spin on Mitchum's arrest and immediately pushed *His Kind of Woman* forward to capitalize on the bad boy image, thus saving one of Hollywood's most riveting careers.

Months later, Hughes stalled this very production, demanding that a new ending be shot and that character-actor Vincent Price have his role in the story expanded. Refusing to comply, director John Farrow was replaced with Richard Fleischer, thus dragging on nonconstructive production meetings for nearly two years and sinking an extra $850,000 of the studio's money into a project that ultimately flopped.

Perhaps some could excuse the fact that Hughes was making deals with none other than himself to profit on and give his personally produced projects—*The Outlaw, Mad Wednesday,* and *Vendetta*—another run. They did manage to churn up some ticket sales and add to a sparse production slate. But few could ignore his absolute disruptive obsession with anything to do with the female form.

It is completely impossible to name all of the people Howard Hughes went to bed with during the course of his life–the rumored "selection" of partners would completely fill this story and then some! Recognizable figures linked to Hughes in the 1940s alone included Ava Gardner, Lana Turner, Rita Hayworth, Ginger Rogers, Jean Simmons, Virginia Mayo, Zsa Zsa Gabor, Carole Lombard, Marlene Dietrich, Ingrid Bergman, Blanche Sweet, Barbara Pepper, Phyllis Brooks, Barbara Stanwyck, Barbara Hutton, Bette Davis, Norma Shearer, Andrea Leeds, and Cyd Charisse, to name a very few.

That doesn't account for the many men Hughes was rumored to have kept hidden from the tabloids plus the bevy of nameless starlets. Each dreamer was suckered into a contracted trap motivated by nothing more than an insatiable lust. Their chances at fame were slim to none.

As a studio head, Hughes made it his legitimate business to view reels of young hopefuls looking to make their Hollywood mark with a silver screen career at RKO. In most cases, he auditioned them personally or flew them out for a talent meeting. But after only a short time in power at RKO, he had signed small armies of actresses to personal contracts–one hundred thousand dollars seemed to be the going rate. They and their careers were indebted to the producer, and they had to be ready at his every beck and call.

Three picture deals were drafted for those who were told they'd be cast when "acting promise was exemplified." Furnished apartments were supplied to those under contract so Hughes could keep them close and quiet and have them at his disposal. When difficulties arose, such as when one of his no-name contracted actresses Rene Rosseau was found dead as a result of suicide in a Hughes-gifted apartment, nothing came of the tragedy; he carried on without batting an eye.

He did spontaneously wed *Mighty Joe Young* (1949) star Terry Moore through the services of a sea captain aboard a boat. Desiring nothing more than her virginity, Hughes apparently destroyed the ship's logbook, causing the nuptials to be questioned for years to come.

"He'd have his hands full with one or two beautiful women," Moore remembered, "and he'd see someone else and want her also."

For the women who had the audacity to turn him down or resist his advances, the billionaire would go out of his way to unleash a special kind of hell, all heightened with help from his studio.

Jean Simmons stated that out of retaliation for cutting her hair shorter than Hughes liked, he instructed director Otto Preminger to treat her terribly and have her forcibly slapped for a scene. When she was offered the Audrey Hepburn Oscar-winning role in *Roman Holiday* while under contract at RKO, he refused to loan her out so she wouldn't be able to take the coveted part.

Ida Lupino and Jane Russell, the latter held under a personal ten-year contract to Hughes, were forced into sexually exploitive roles and truly awful films. Jane Greer was kept on contract and paid twenty-five hundred dollars every week just so she couldn't work with another studio. Her career eventually fizzled—all because Hughes allegedly took offense to the fact that she was happy raising a family.

Susan Hayward was busy climbing the Hollywood ladder for most of the 1940s through B pictures and supporting roles. Hughes actually came across the actress early on in her career on a blind date arranged by mutual friend Ben Medford. She cooked Hughes a chicken dinner and refused to do anything more with him that night; the two instantly disliked each other and went their own ways. Hayward married actor Jess Barker in 1944; Hughes kindled and stoked a burning resentment toward her, waiting for his opportune moment to exact revenge.

On screen, Hughes's arrival marked a noticeable shift in RKO's more risqué content; films like *The French Line* had Jane Russell flaunting a musical number called "Lookin' for Trouble," in which she giggled that men "can be short, tall, or elooooooongated . . ."

The Breen Production Code board grew very tired of Hughes's antics by the turn of the decade, taking issue alongside the Catholic Church on just about everything the "indecent" producer released.

Sid Rogell and Sam Bischoff contended with routine three-in-the-morning phone calls from Hughes, who believed in natural sleep—a process of working continuously until he physically felt tired and ready to go to bed rather than going to bed at a set time. This practice resulted in days and nights spent at his office with intermittent naps on the floor sprinkled in. Rogell, who preferred sleeping during the night, quit his production chief position after barely one year of enduring the complete disregard for working hours. Bischoff held out a little longer but fled in 1950, leaving the production chief position vacant.

This growing exodus had no bearing on their boss whatsoever; Hughes never took the blame or reevaluated his behavior when others began to leave. Meetings could only be held inside vehicles due to his fear of being secretly recorded. The same meal had to be brought to him every day: a steak, peas, mashed potatoes, and an ice-cream sundae. Eventually, the man that could afford to have any feast he so desired consumed only frozen TV dinners.

Those close to Hughes commonly stated that his obsession with his personal well-being, and certainly his fear of germs, stemmed from his near-fatal XF-11 crash. There was no consoling him when he found himself inside the same room as obvious dust particles, disruptive bits of fuzz, and other near-microscopic particles that most people would never notice. Conversations were abruptly stalled and meetings frequently halted so Hughes's peculiarities, such as a lengthy handwashing break, could be attended to.

The stress of heading RKO, TWA, and Hughes Aircraft Company surely weighed heavily on his thoughts; the billionaire began experiencing occasional fits of repetitive phrases stuck in an ugly replay like a broken record. A far-too-late diagnosis may have pointed to obsessive-compulsive disorder; but Hughes's apparent codeine addiction didn't help his muddled mind, either.

Film release dates were pushed, actresses were traded and tormented, and nearly the entire staff roster was gutted on a whim; but everything continued to operate his way. Hughes was just being Hughes; and if you couldn't get behind the man's zeal or industrial potency, it was impossible to find a reason to like him.

Rest assured, the studio owner was in plenty of "good" company when it came to using his business as his own personal playground. Darryl F. Zanuck, over at Fox, ordered up starlets like dinner from a menu, having them escorted straight to his office in room service fashion by a troop of equally keen assistants. Louis B. Mayer stuck a fifteen-year-old Judy Garland on a harmful diet packed full of amphetamines, referring to them as only "pep pills," when casting *The Wizard of Oz*. MGM producer Arthur Freed allegedly exposed himself to a twelve-year-old Shirley Temple. Harry Cohn at Columbia, otherwise known as "King Cohn," had ties to organized crime and took inspiration from Italian dictator Benito Mussolini.

So, Hughes was not alone in his intimidating, assaultive, disruptive, meddling, obsessive, counterproductive, pedophilic, disrespectful behavior. For poor RKO, the fact was that Howard Hughes had to one-up his competitors by doing absolutely everything grander in every possible way. Perhaps his extreme flamboyancy was heightened just to outdo the legendary sins of the rest of the shameful Hollywood pack.

Before Hughes took over RKO, hardly forty-four thousand television sets stood in American households—most of them concentrated around New York City. Only two years after Hughes gained control, six million TVs were dazzling families all across the country. Roughly 10 percent of the nation had the glowing gizmo in their living rooms. But just as with the introduction of sound and color, the picture business was told not to worry. But the numbers—and history of other erroneous fad claims—said otherwise.

*Howdy Doody*, *Texaco Star Theatre*, and *The Jack Benny Show* laid the groundwork for the variety pack of programming to come. By the time October 15, 1951, rolled around, the movies didn't stand a chance. *I Love Lucy*, the mold for all sitcoms to follow, made the square box one of life's absolute necessities. Comedienne Lucille Ball was ruining everything movie moguls had worked for.

The film business as a whole was suffering thanks to an onslaught of behind-the-scenes issues and lagging box office numbers. Studios were struggling to divest themselves of their theater chains while losing big-name stars amid the community witch hunt and opportunities to start their own production companies.

The year 1949 is often looked upon as one of the worst years in the business; aside from Oscar winner *All the Kings Men*, Tracy and Hepburn rom-com *Adam's Rib*, Cagney classic *White Heat*, and film fanatic fuel *The Third Man*, there wasn't much to remember.

Lucky for Hughes, he did manage to distribute one of the top ten grossing pictures of 1949 through no efforts of his own. Much to the crew's delight, he had no production input and essentially waltzed in just as the picture was being completed. The John Ford Western *She Wore a Yellow Ribbon* would be RKO's saving grace in the wake of complete turmoil.

At an unusually high budget of $1.6 million ($17 million in modern day), the American historical epic illustrated the efforts of Captain Nathan Brittles following the fall of George Armstrong Custer at the Battle of Little Bighorn. The costume-heavy cavalry epic raked in $7 million domestically ($160 million after inflation) and was one of the last RKO-associated films to do so.

Not without the occasional moment of savvy, the boss didn't take too long to pinpoint the movie's appeal. The star player was coming off one their most beloved Western roles in *Red River* (another bizarre Hughes saga best saved for another day) and found himself suddenly skyrocketing to the very absolute top of the popularity charts. Hughes pounced, spying an in with America's number one star, and began wheeling and dealing his way to save RKO from the brink of disaster. He had found the perfect ticket to glom onto and at any cost necessary.

Yes, much to both men's delight, the career and popularity of *She Wore a Yellow Ribbon*'s indisputable star, John Wayne, were on the verge of exploding like an atomic bomb.

# 3: Wayne of the West

Marion Robert Morrison was born May 26, 1907, in Winterset, Iowa. The town was so small and docile, Morrison's birth actually made the local paper; though, to be fair, his mammoth weight of thirteen pounds certainly was notable. Named in honor of a relative who fought in the Civil War, the Morrison clan would move west to the Southern California town of Glendale, where father, Clyde, took a job as a pharmacist.

After giving birth to another son, his parents decided they liked the name Robert and couldn't run the risk of confusing their boys by using it twice; Marion's middle name was swiftly replaced with

Mitchell. Furthering the cutesy alliteration, which paired nicely with his typically feminine first name, Morrison seemed to suffer the same problem Johnny Cash immortalized in the song "A Boy Named Sue." Morrison was teased about the title for most of his childhood, a bother that served him well in developing an assertive, tough-guy image.

He preferred to go by the nickname bestowed on him by a local fireman who often saw him marching down the streets with his large Airedale named Duke. It began as "Little Duke" but was simplified once the young whippersnapper grew into a towering six-foot-four-inch man.

Morrison was your typical all-American man's man—quiet and reserved but quick with his defensive fists or a thundering tackle in a football game. Academics also proved to be Morrison's forte—he was president of the Latin club and wrote columns for the high school newspaper. His early ambition was to head off to law school on a football scholarship, but a bodysurfing injury put the kibosh on his athletic ability. Raised in relative poverty, he couldn't afford college without a scholarship and was left with few options when rejected by the US Naval Academy.

Nabbing a job at Fox Studios thanks to his burly physique, nineteen-year-old Morrison earned thirty-five dollars a week as a prop boy, diligently lugging anything and everything around movie sets to wherever they needed to go. On occasion, one of the perks of the job was bit parts or standing in the background as an extra for a few silent movies in 1926 and 1927.

It was there he met longtime friend and collaborator John Ford, one of America's most awarded and celebrated directors in cinema history, while learning the ropes in the silent picture business and searching for his big break.

When director Raoul Walsh took notice of Wayne's striking good looks and sedulous strength as he lugged around set furniture, a Hollywood career was born. Never having taken lessons or said more than a few words onscreen, Morrison was cast in his very first lead role. He played trapper Breck Coleman, leader of a caravan of Mississippi settlers who embarked on a sweeping journey across the United States via the Oregon Trail.

Problems began right from the start. Morrison's flat, emotion-less delivery made it clear he had no prior experience. Then there was the problem of the budding star's collection of triple M's. In a meeting Morrison wasn't present for, Walsh and Fox Studio chief Winfield Sheehan batted around "Anthony Wayne," the name of a Revolutionary War general, as a possible replacement; it was deemed too Italian. Duke Morrison, his own suggestion, was felt to be too rough and risqué. John, however, was simple, strong, and memorable.

Marion Morrison was reluctantly assigned the role of a lifetime, John Wayne, and hurriedly debuted to the public. The public knew him by the simplistic two-syllable creation; he insisted his friends and coworkers just call him Duke or his given name.

Welcomed with a hefty ad campaign focused on American land-scapes and the arrival of a fresh big-screen hero, *The Big Trail* was released to dismal reception in 1930. Critics weren't quite sure what to make of Wayne, proving a path to sudden stardom wasn't as clear cut as he had initially believed. Yet a spark was ignited within him, and the new leading man continued to work, playing a mixture of athletes, college students, soldiers, a corpse, and, of course, plenty of cowboys throughout the 1930s.

Hollywood was at its peak love affair with Westerns; the histori-cal subject matter was fresh and relatable to most rural moviegoers, while the genre was relatively easy and cheap to produce. Wayne appeared in nearly fifty Westerns in that decade alone, many of them repetitive B movies churned out from strained "Poverty Row" studios Republic and Monogram Pictures.

Both studios specialized in low-grade action entertainment often assembled by the same crew and made with the same cast members in marginally different plot lines. Wayne had stumbled on steady work that paid well and cut his teeth on these shoestring projects, growing more comfortable in front of a camera as time went on.

He was reintroduced to cinemagoers in 1939, reteaming with Ford for *Stagecoach*—a film often regarded as the greatest Western of all time. Charting the path of a motley array of passengers traveling aboard a stagecoach through war-torn Apache country, the short, simple, heart-pounding classic breathed new life into the well-worn genre.

While flagging down the stagecoach, Wayne spun his rifle as the camera zoomed straight into his face for an intimately tight close-up. After mustering mystery and machismo into his stature, an off-guard expression mixed with wide eyes and a bead of sweat made for the perfect amount of vulnerability that launched Wayne to stardom.

Ford knew how to bring out the best in him as Wayne whittled down his own talents to a fine point that was able to pierce the American public deep in their hearts. Both would be pigeonholed to cattle drives and dusty saloons from the day immediately after *Stagecoach*'s release, but to them, it was worth it.

Offers poured in, and the freedom of choice allowed the legendary icon to continue placing the building blocks that led him to the top of the entire entertainment industry. Not bad for a fellow who apparently detested farm life growing up and wondered if his daily horse rides to school would ever serve him well.

"Don't act! React," Wayne advised when interviewers, critics, and fellow movie stars routinely pestered him about his wooden performance.

As the limelight grew brighter, so did both the praise and scrutiny of his talents, which time and time again he defended with the most banal and bashful of explanations. "I merely try to act naturally," Wayne explained. "If I start acting phony on the screen, you start looking at me instead of feeling with me."

The typical moviegoer in the 1940s lapped up his straitlaced performance, whether it was behind the controls of a fighter jet or the reins of a trusty stallion. His movies were made for a male audience looking for a quick hit of testosterone. Wartime saw a major shift in audience numbers with more masculine gangsters, private eyes, and gun-toting heroes stealing the screen. Wayne's escapist thrills provided the perfect answer for the exhausted army recruits and factory workers yearning for a break.

That's not to say women didn't find Wayne's looks appealing; he was cast as a high-society gambler in the romantic comedy *Lady for a Night.* No matter the genre, his line delivery remained unaltered, an annoyance many coworkers held against him.

His first director, Raoul Walsh, stated that the better description for his style was that he "underacts," a typically damaging route to take that Wayne felt he used to his advantage. Due to his discomfort for stepping out of his element and rocking the boat, Wayne brought only himself to the screen, a character he could trust would work. In forming the familiar traits people expected from the John Wayne image, calm and collected rodeo rider and stuntman Yakima Canutt provided the inspiration for how Wayne should walk, talk, and pull off certain stunts, such as falling to the ground from his horse.

Later advice to budding British actor Michael Caine revealed that Wayne's mastery was built on "talking low, talking slow, and not saying too much," which, when examined, is an apt description of his speech patterns. Unlike in theater, where performers are forced to project every emotion, Wayne felt the audience was already invested in the actor and would be put off if the correct amount of simple natural illusion wasn't struck.

The dry delivery drummed up a mixed bag of responses from Hollywood elite. Humphrey Bogart drew offense from Wayne's claim of merely standing in front of a camera and being told what to do, insisting he worked very hard to pull off a character. On the contrary, Katharine Hepburn felt Wayne was given an extraordinary gift of believing in his own traits and laying them out so casually for millions to see. John Ford obviously defended his partner, stating, "He's not something out of a book, governed by acting rules. He's not one of those method actors, like they send out here from drama schools in New York. He's real. He is perfectly natural."

But there was clearly something more to his appeal and acting talents than a reaction to an unfolding situation or another scene partner's lines—a characteristic that was not found in his contemporaries. Wayne was more confident and edgy than James Stewart's do-gooder shtick. He acted rougher than Henry Fonda, but he would never go to quite the dark antihero territory that Bogart and Cagney often showcased. Wayne could feel more alive and tangible onscreen than an often droll Gary Cooper and more blue-collar than a suit-and-tie-wearing Spencer Tracy. He was grittier than Gregory Peck yet more trustworthy than Robert Mitchum.

Wayne's appeal outdid most other Hollywood types at a time when macho cowboys and handsome faces were about a dime a dozen. His natural approach blended with his own personal style to provide something very fresh for the film screen that struck at the most opportune time.

During the 1940s, Wayne's filmography wasn't all that impressive let alone recognizable to the most astute of cinephiles. Another ten years were spent defining, refining, and exploring with a collection of forgettable roles. Only this time, Wayne was almost always the leading man and the companies weren't just strained B studios Republic and Monogram. His persistence and growing presence allowed the actor to be lent out for bigger and better productions over at MGM, United Artists, and RKO.

Through the mid-to-late forties, Wayne appeared on loan in a total of six RKO features, most notably the rodeo romance *A Lady Takes a Chance*, World War II POW drama *Back to Bataan*, and the South America–set epic *Tycoon*, where he played an obsessed contractor building a mountain railroad tunnel.

With the rah-rah attitude of American patriotism during World War II, a celebration of everything made in the country and every notion of pride was heightened. Wayne, a lifelong Republican, embarked on a United Service Organization (USO) tour to the southwest Pacific, visiting hospitals and entertaining troops with a variety of live shows, including a few performances where he apparently let go of his underacting to sing a few tunes.

Back home, Wayne led the charge by publicly asking people to donate reminders of America to the men overseas; anything from cigars to radios and even thank-you letters were encouraged. Wayne also backed the formation of a conservative Hollywood group, the Motion Picture Alliance for the Preservation of American Ideals, in 1943. This was a place where he found friends within the industry and emerged as a vocal supporter of right-wing politics.

Tossed together with his corresponding movie roles and a boom of flag-waving public spirit, John Wayne's growing celebrity was almost a given. Everything about Wayne felt like the impeccable image for the country in that moment in time, with many beginning to point to his ideals, rippling physicality, and historically steeped film roles as a celebratory image of the United States of America itself.

Wayne's road to Hughes's RKO was partially paved by director John Ford, fashioned during a quest for more artistic freedom. Ford's unpredicted success coming off *Stagecoach* rooted him as one of the most prestigious figures ever to grace the picture business. Starting with *Young Mr. Lincoln*, also in 1939, his faithful adaptation of John Steinbeck's *The Grapes of Wrath* quickly followed.

The plight of the Joad family traveling from Oklahoma to California in search of work during the dust bowl earned Ford a Best Director Oscar at the Thirteenth Academy Awards. The very next year, he earned the same award for *How Green Was My Valley*, a traditional drama exploring similar themes only this time with Welsh miners. It was and has since been revered and reviled for catapulting RKO's *Citizen Kane* out of every coveted category.

Ford became the first director to hold that one-two punch honor for seventy-five years. Several years prior, his win for *The Informer* further added to his prize collection, thus making Ford the most decorated director ever and all in the span of seven years. Even more impressive was the fact that he created such visually stunning efforts with only one eye: Ford famously stuck a black patch over the poor performer on his left side to cope with a botched cataract surgery.

Such masterful storytelling abilities and critical fanfare quickly had Ford, like seemingly everyone else in Hollywood, yearning for more control—a freedom the contracted director-for-hire institutions of the studio system didn't allow.

Spending the early part of the decade shooting World War II documentaries, Ford returned to fiction with one major goal: to form his own production company and have his own say. In 1940, he informally created Argosy Pictures with former RKO production chief Merian C. Cooper and resurrected the pet project in 1947, transforming it into a full-fledged business.

The first film made under the Argosy banner was *The Fugitive*, a Mexican-set thriller starring Henry Fonda and a Ford regular,

Mexican treasure and Wayne's pal Pedro Armendáriz. Cooper's connection led them to RKO, where a distribution deal was struck to share the costs and profits fifty-fifty. Arrangements like these had been done by studio heads and a few producers like Cooper before, but there was hardly a filmmaker responsible for creating their own content. That was all new, and Ford was leading the charge. As part of the contract, RKO agreed to release two more of Argosy's works.

An eight-year hiatus ended when Ford reteamed with John Wayne for film number two, *3 Godfathers*, a riveting three-men-and-a-baby-type tale that had Wayne, Armendáriz, and Harry Carey Jr. caring for a dead woman's child in the desert. The third Argosy film was monumental for all parties involved; *Fort Apache* paired Wayne (having the movie-making year of his life) and Fonda to tell the story of two vastly different leaders and their treatment of a Native American tribe.

Not only was it one of the first films to present an authentic and sympathetic portrayal, it was also the first of Ford's informal "cavalry trilogy." Next in line was *She Wore a Yellow Ribbon*, which is where Howard Hughes came in.

For most people, it's bizarre to imagine Howard Hughes and John Wayne being in the same room together let alone becoming collaborative partners. Their backgrounds were different: one rich and one poor. Their relationships were different: Wayne married his first wife, Josephine Saenz, at the age of twenty-six, while Hughes balked at any sort of commitment. Their overall pop culture images, fan bases, and fashion styles seemed to be polar opposites. But the truth of the matter was the pair were actually friends; they were familiar with each other through the hobnobbing nature of business.

When Wayne married his second wife, Esperanza "Chata" Baur, Hughes personally flew the newlyweds to Hawaii on what may have been the first civilian flight to the islands after the war ended. Their Republican views, mixed with their cemented stance against Communism, provided plenty for the two to bond over—plus there was a mutual love for Westerns.

At a time when Hollywood openly leaned left against the ravages of war, conservative screenplays, and the painful implications of the blacklist, Wayne and Hughes had more in common to chit-chat about than one might at first think.

"Duke's one of the few surefire box office things left in Holly-wood," Hughes said of the actor at the time of his RKO takeover. Wayne remarked how he liked the way Hughes unapologetically commanded the crew of his studio.

Peaceful beginnings seemed like they were in the cards, but the Hughes/Wayne collaboration kicked off with a copyright lawsuit. *Red River*, directed by former Hughes collaborator Howard Hawks through his own burgeoning little production company Monterey, was a smash hit and a career-maker. Hughes felt differently.

RKO's billionaire boss was not involved with that film, but he objected to a line of dialogue—"Draw your gun"—insisting those words and the entire climactic end sequence had been stolen from his own film *The Outlaw*.

The battle of the two Howards ensued at an advanced screening, where the similarities were first noted mere weeks before an already delayed release. Hughes took Hawks to court and demanded that *Red River* be cut. Hughes emerged victorious because *The Outlaw* predated *Red River*, and Hawks had been heavily involved with that turbulent production before quitting partway through.

It was agreed that six minutes would be cut on almost the eve of *Red River*'s release; this was a dismaying and rushed move to keep the picture on schedule and in theaters. Since three hundred prints had already been shipped to the southern United States, editors were deployed to trim the story.

Wayne was simultaneously sent to offer an olive branch to Hughes, who was more than delighted to meet with the star. His visit managed to help cool the man's temper. Months later, Wayne was called to massage his Howard-Hughes-whispering skills when *She Wore a Yellow Ribbon* was in danger of heading down a similar path. The studio head had been given a taste of just what Hughes was capable of: The ability to stop a rival's motion picture release was a potent skill to have up one's sleeve.

When Argosy's distribution deal was technically up at the time of *Ribbon*'s completion, Hughes licked his lips and wondered what he could squeeze out of the predicament.

Ford feared that his film would struggle to get a theatrical run and fail to earn his young production company a profit. The movie had been coproduced with RKO's blessing before Hughes arrived, so he would have had little grounds to stop it beyond impeding its debut. But with the unpredictable RKO studio head in charge, anything was possible, even if harming the release was a positively foolish business move done to pound his chest.

Wayne certainly wanted his mentor to succeed in his Argosy Pictures endeavor, plus he knew the film they had on their hands was an absolute winner. Wayne stated on numerous occasions that *She Wore a Yellow Ribbon* was his most favorite movie in which he had appeared, so he wanted to get it out to the public at just about any cost.

On top of the *Red River* lawsuit and a loyal desire to help out a friend, Wayne felt he owed RKO for the previous work they had given him. Grateful to the "Poverty Row" studios that launched his career, the actor grew tired of jogging from studio to studio, hustling for better roles to land. RKO had treated Wayne fairly beforehand and still, at that point, seemed like a positive place to pick up a juicy part.

Finally, there was Wayne's own desire for control. Seeing Ford's success, Wayne thought his own production company might lead to more creative and fruitful projects. Above all, the actor desperately wanted to dramatize the events of the Alamo onscreen; the epic 1836 battle for Texas lent itself beautifully as Hollywood blockbuster material. Fitting with Wayne's cowboy image and the cavalry stories he and Ford were currently enjoying telling, the project certainly seemed like an appropriate venture for the moment. Wayne had it in his mind that he would produce, direct, and star in the movie.

Hughes and Wayne got to talking about RKO. They discussed Argosy Pictures and the merits of *She Wore a Yellow Ribbon*. They talked about John Ford and his role as the premier American filmmaker of the day. They talked politics and Communists and *Red River* copyrights and the fruits and foibles of having a Hollywood career. Hughes toyed with Wayne's idea for an Alamo movie, hinting, though never explicitly, that there could be an opportunity with RKO to one day produce the picture.

With all of these facets orbiting around the pair, the only logical result in both of their minds was to reach a deal–a deal to keep Argosy's productions on track to the big screen and a deal to give Wayne freedom he wasn't quite getting anywhere else. Through an informal un-exclusive agreement, Howard Hughes and John Wayne moved to smooth over any squabbles from the past and step forward to support each other.

Hughes released the hugely successful *She Wore a Yellow Ribbon* without interference and considered helping with *The Alamo*, while Wayne lent his growing celebrity status to three RKO productions in return. They shook on it and immediately went to work.

# 4: A Deal Most Disastrous

*Jet Pilot* was a kernel of an idea that had been incubating inside Hughes for at least four years. His fond memories of the *Hell's Angels* shoot were well over two decades old, but the story stuck with him–as did his love for aviation. Hughes felt he could revamp the World War I fighter pilot story and make it modern, showcasing the Jet Age and how aerial combat had progressed.

Borrowing heavily from Ernst Lubitsch's snappy 1939 comedy *Ninotchka*, where Greta Garbo plays a Soviet spy, Jules Furthman's half-completed screenplay was acquired. The man had been responsible for a collection of classics including *Mutiny on the Bounty*, *To Have and Have Not*, and *The Big Sleep* as well as Hughes's own dud *The Outlaw*. The script was quickly written and shoved into Wayne's hands almost directly after they finished shaking over their deal.

*Jet Pilot* told the escapades of a sexy Soviet spy who travels to an American airstrip and defects, falling in love with a straitlaced air force colonel. Filled with gushy romance, cheesy one-liners, and on-the-nose observations, the film reserved a significant portion for daring aerobatics and dogfights. Wayne responded to the underlying theme of, well, the United States doing everything far better than they do in Siberia. Just as *Ninotchka* had done, *Jet Pilot*'s main motivation behind the Soviet defection was that the Russian character found consumerism and freedom of speech far too enchanting to return to her home country. Lubitsch's film managed to explore the topic of culture shock with a greater level of grace and subtlety.

At the height of his anti-Communist crusade, Wayne felt the movie could be a chance at making a political statement and act as something of a rebuttal to the Hollywood Ten. The actor accepted the role of Jim Shannon to kick off his three-picture promise to RKO; production thus began at lightning speed with principle photography happening in October 1949.

Wayne was quickly paired with twenty-two-year-old Janet Leigh at the infancy of her career. Leigh was just coming off of her first big hit, a remake of *Little Women* with MGM, and had been lent to RKO for the Robert Mitchum comedy *Holiday Affair*. Leigh accepted the role of Lieutenant Anna Marladovna, a move she would instantly regret.

The twenty-year age difference between the romantic leads was never questioned. Nor was the fact that Leigh and the other actors playing Soviets failed to don any sort of accent to differentiate them from the Americans. The actress's modern stylish hair and glamorous outfits were apparently okayed without an itch.

Seasoned director Josef von Sternberg was hired to work through little hiccups and shape Hughes's vision; the producer had to tend to other production matters at RKO and couldn't be heavily involved behind the camera. Von Sternberg later claimed that this was never the case; Hughes was on set almost constantly, watching production like a hawk. "I was told step by step, day by day, movement for movement, word for word, precisely what I was to direct," recalled von Sternberg.

When Hughes was not present, both Wayne and Leigh felt von Sternberg was authoritative, condescending, and undeservingly nasty to them and the entire crew. "I hadn't been exposed to that kind of arrogance. *Jet Pilot* was the first time I used a four-letter word on a movie set," Leigh said about the experience.

Even Wayne was getting annoyed with how the production was running. Exposed to the chaotic world of Hughes's RKO, the actor began clenching his teeth, holding back groans and frustrated mumbles, wondering just what he had gotten himself into. Still, Duke remained quiet for the *Jet Pilot* shoot, keeping his head down and trying to get the job done as quickly as possible.

When asked by Leigh why he hadn't stood up for himself or the crew against the tyrannical director, Wayne assured her it took all the restraint he could muster to keep going without a scuffle. "Honey, if I ever let loose, if I ever started on him, I'd kill the son of a bitch," Wayne said.

Hughes was heavily involved with the flying sequences, working with the Edwards and Hamilton Air Force Bases in California. He employed fairly substantial pilots to double for Wayne and Leigh, including Chuck Yeager, the first confirmed man to fly faster than the speed of sound. A B-45 Tornado bomber was used to do the physical filming while the innovative F-86A jet got its own showcase in the story, pulling off a series of thrilling aerobatic maneuvers.

The real novelty of *Jet Pilot* was the close encounters with actual jets zipping around the sky like a documentary, much like Hughes's other aviation-oriented plots. The producer butted in to ensure sequences were as exciting as they could possibly get via his vision and his vision only. Von Sternberg grew exhausted and left the project.

Filming wrapped in early 1950, but a scant amount of the material pleased Hughes. Slated for a release that same year, *Jet Pilot* was delayed as he ordered reshoots, replacing von Sternberg with producer Jules Furthman. The leads had already bolted in opposite directions to work on other projects, so it wouldn't be until the spring of 1951 that Leigh and Wayne could don their naval costumes again.

Reshot between January 21 and February 9, then again March 17 to April 2, the first Wayne/Hughes collaboration actually lagged behind their second project together, which was being filmed at the very same time.

*Jet Pilot* was further delayed when Hughes sent William Clothier to retrieve more aerial photography intermittently between 1951 and 1953. Clothier apparently logged over 200 hours in the air, flying more than 30,000 miles for the movie and shooting over 100,000 feet of Technicolor film.

The original budget was a fairly hefty sum of $1.4 million (roughly $15 million today), with $201,666 going into Wayne's pocket. Reshoots and further delays started bloating the total to upward of $3.9 million, a cost that was only reserved for gigantic epics, certainly not anti-Communist comedies. "They played with that footage like kids playing with toy trains," Leigh quipped, watching Hughes dismantle and reassemble the poor project countless times as both stars rose in celebrity stature.

By the start of 1953, Hughes grew tired and frustrated with his constant tinkering and shelved the project completely—a move that no doubt pained RKO's investors. The production company would have to, as they say, take a bath and cut their losses. Hughes had no qualms as far as bank account numbers went, only swearing to his lead actor that he'd get around to fixing it and releasing their collaboration sometime in the future.

With his paycheck deposited and one-third of his obligation fulfilled, Wayne didn't seem to mind that people probably wouldn't ever get to see *Jet Pilot* anyway.

The second Hughes/Wayne collaboration surely took the cake for the most peculiar movie title in Hollywood history: *Flying Leathernecks* nabbed its name from military slang. The word *leatherneck* had long referred to the stiff leather collars marines wore to keep their posture upright and neck erect, but few outside that realm would have been familiar with the term. Set during World War II at a marine corps base in the South Pacific, yet again the pair set off to make a plane picture.

Wayne had gone ahead with other projects, virtually unaffected with the delay of *Jet Pilot* as his career was taking off faster than any of Hughes's real-life jets ever could. In 1950, he unexpectedly earned his first Best Actor Oscar nomination for his role in *Sands of Iwo Jima*. The World War II Republic Pictures drama had Wayne playing a tough-as-nails marine sergeant preparing his troops for the notorious real-life battle over the Japanese island. Wayne felt his performance in *She Wore a Yellow Ribbon* was far superior and should have been the role to earn him the coveted statue. He lost to Broderick Crawford for *All the King's Men*.

Waiting for Hughes's second picture to come together, Wayne and Ford started a small campaign to get *The Quiet Man* going, the story of an Irish boxer returning to his hometown–an idea RKO balked at. Republic gave a muddled commitment to make the off-beat drama their next project but insisted their last cavalry movie come first. Wayne simultaneously poked and prodded Howard Hughes for any sort of detail on when *The Alamo* might possibly come together; there never was a definitive "yes" or "no" response.

Despite his illustrious status, Wayne's wheeling and dealing with Hughes was all for naught; RKO dropped John Ford's Argosy Pictures and refused to coproduce any further works. Ford's first Argosy film, *The Fugitive*, had racked up quite a debt; more than one million dollars was still owed to RKO, producer Merian C. Cooper, and Wayne himself. Ford sold *Fort Apache* and *She Wore a Yellow Ribbon* outright to RKO just so he could get his company back to ground zero.

The filmmaker quickly signed a three-picture deal with Republic so he and Wayne could finish their cavalry trilogy with *Rio Grande*, a film Wayne had hoped to count toward one of his RKO obligations. Retreading on the previous two films, *Rio Grande* was noticeably more rushed and ultimately the most unsuccessful of the three. Still, Wayne was again billed as the biggest box office draw that year, and the RKO split managed to postpone Argosy's curtain call.

With delay after delay, John Wayne found the time to star in the forgettable action-romance *Operation Pacific* in 1951, where he played a tough-as-nails submarine commander–a character also with the name Duke. Set against the backdrop of WWII and the events of Pearl Harbor, an ineffective torpedo that won't explode was the largest obstacle its plotline provided.

Wayne came off of the testosterone-heavy propaganda piece and went straight into *Flying Leathernecks* without blinking an eye. Hughes's war picture would be the third film in three years where Wayne played a stern war hero leading men to battle against Japan. In a way, the setup was unintentionally clever, forming another very loose trilogy of Wayne fighting on land (*Sands of Iwo Jima*), sea (*Operation Pacific*), and now sky (*Flying Leathernecks*).

There was no objection whatsoever or fear that he'd been type-cast coming from the actor. The role of, you guessed it, a tough-as-nails major–this time given the name Daniel Kirby–was just the kind of person he felt comfortable playing. Most likely, the banal role was accepted to Wayne's relief, knowing he was about to embark on another Howard Hughes picture; anything could happen and he needed all the familiarity he could get.

Writers-for-hire Kenneth Gamet and James Edward Grant were brought on to shape the screenplay while RKO producer Edmund Grainger oversaw production. The story, more specifically Wayne's character, was based on the actions and leadership style of flying ace and Medal of Honor winner Major John L. Smith. *Flying Leathernecks'* purpose was to dramatize the efforts of the Cactus Air Force on the Solomon Islands and the Guadalcanal campaign, an early retaliation effort for Pearl Harbor.

Nicholas Ray, who immortalized James Dean in *Rebel Without a Cause*, was the man picked to direct. Ray was one of RKO's fledgling directors under contract and was tasked by Hughes to work in a vast gamut of genres from Robert Mitchum melodramas to unused additional scenes for the period piece *Androcles and the Lion*. Ray would fair far better departing RKO; but in the early part of his career, Hughes had Ray by the scruff, apparently assigning *Flying Leathernecks* as another one of his loyalty tests to gauge a staff member's patriotism.

Ray stemmed from the new wave of Hollywood filmmakers, a group that included talents like Fred Zinnemann, Sidney Lumet, and patron saint of method actors, Elia Kazan. They recognized the art in what they were doing and saw room for raw emotion and authenticity to shine in an actor's performance. This approach often had directors overstepping their bounds in pursuit of extracting truth from a performer to reflect the painful realities of society right back to itself.

Ray was everything Wayne was not, nor was a run-of-the-mill Republican aviator flick the best-suited story for the man's background. The actor and director did not get along, with Wayne holding Ray's intensity against him and resenting the same left-leaning political view Hughes feared would corrupt his studio. "He was a much better actor than most people gave him credit for being, almost daily full of nice surprises," Ray said of Wayne. "But he was not flexible about himself."

Wayne's costar, Robert Ryan, was another RKO contract player who rose through the ranks of tedious roles to become an unlikely star. He was a direct rival, having joined the Committee for the First Amendment during the Hollywood Ten trials during Wayne's membership with the Motion Picture Alliance for the Preservation of American Ideals.

Ray cast him because he felt Ryan was one of the only actors in Hollywood capable of "kicking Wayne's ass." The two nearly put that theory to the test, almost coming to blows on multiple occasions because of ideological disagreements. "Wayne would close all political discussions with 'You're full of shit!,'" *Flying Leathernecks'* dialogue director Rod Amateau remembered.

Principal photography took place between November 1950 and February 1951 at RKO Studios and Camp Pendleton Marine Corps Base just outside San Diego County. *Flying Leathernecks* had the rare good fortune of having Howard Hughes being too occupied with other projects to be heavily involved; this was evidenced by the swift and generally painless production.

The billionaire festered over the aerial *Jet Pilot* shots, encouraging the use of actual footage from the South Pacific and fresh Korean War newsreels; everything was to be blended in with imagery filmed on set. Sparing no expense and ordering the picture be made in Technicolor, the illuminated realism of the documentary snippets also came in color and ended up heightening the overall spectacle of *Flying Leathernecks*. For all of Hughes's filmmaking faults, this was one of the first action war films released completely in color and an early pioneer in using real wartime clips.

Released on August 28, 1951, at a cost of $1.2 million (Wayne's paycheck ate up one-quarter of the whole budget), *Flying Leathernecks* managed to scrape back its losses and break even against mixed reviews. The film did garner the consistent criticism that Wayne and Ryan were significantly older than pilots who served in the marines, but as far as Howard Hughes controversies go, that minuscule bump was hardly a complaint.

*Flying Leathernecks* also earned the dubious distinction of being the first RKO movie to open with the ominous label "Howards Hughes Presents . . ." The egotist inside of him insisted that his name go before each title so that audiences knew exactly who was responsible for what they were about to see–a move Hughes had also pulled during the early and more independent era of his career. Fifteen more productions credited him as the film's presenter, each one making him regret the association more than the last.

Wayne brought up the possibility of doing *The Alamo*, and like clockwork, a disinterested Hughes blew the actor off. It would be months before Wayne got wind of anything happening over at RKO, only to be blown off again when he showed up ready to talk about ideas. Growing all the more impatient, he marched over to Hughes's Samuel Goldwyn office to see if the third production was ready to go. Vague as ever, Hughes assured him "he was working on the idea" and would let Duke know the very moment it was ready for him to read.

Hughes flipped through many scripts, picking and choosing almost everything that would go to camera at RKO. What he didn't green-light–projects left over from brighter, simpler days before he took charge–Hughes meddled with to bend into his personal taste. There were also times when the mogul would just rattle off ideas to production chiefs, assembling writers to take his fantasies and run with them. The billionaire lacked any free time to write his own work. Many never made it past the page; others like *Jet Pilot* barely made it past the editing room.

One such interest that seemed to have emerged out of thin air was an epic retelling of the life of Mongol conqueror Genghis Khan. There was no definable reasoning known . . . no proper lineage to trace back that thought . . . surprisingly, no planes necessary . . . just one day out of the blue, the request was made for a screenplay written about Genghis Khan.

The Mongol ruler, born Temüjin in 1162, had grown up in poverty and despair among a nomadic tribe that straddled their domain along the border of the Siberian forest. After his father was poisoned to death and mother kidnapped, Khan rose above his own brothers' ranks, killing one of them to take leadership over his people. Under his direction, appointing soldiers based on merit instead of lineage and establishing monumental institutions of free trade through the cohesion of the Silk Road, the Mongols took eleven million square miles of land in East Eurasia. All of it was obtained through shockingly violent measures in a minuscule forty-year span.

Historians and movie producers have long been intrigued by the legends of Khan, whose temperamental ruthlessness resulted in thousands of gory murders, acts of rape, and cannibalistic feasts. His involvement in shaping modern geography has been acknowledged and celebrated by some cultures. In most Western cases, Khan's genocidal methods have typically categorized him as a villain. Alarmingly but unsurprisingly, it was the allure of his overbearing leadership and unrestrained power that may have led Hughes to Khan's story.

Little information besides a couple biographical textbooks would have been accessible in 1950s America. *Genghis Khan: Empire of All Men* by Harold Lamb and Macmillan's *The Mongol Empire: Its Rise and Legacy* were just about the only popular texts a curious reader might have found. Khan's general place in history was certainly known, but the more intricate details, particularly when it came to his representation in pop culture, were not present.

Raping and pillaging were not suitable plot aspects that could be portrayed or mentioned in a motion picture, still under strict censorship laws, so Khan's story had been left untouched out of fear or just a lack of information.

The only film to touch on the Mongol's rise at that point was the 1950 foreign language adaptation from the Philippines plainly called *Genghis Khan*. The movie wasn't released in the United States until long after Hughes's own Mongol story began to take shape and was soon thought to have been lost for most of the decades that followed. Universal's 1951 *The Golden Horde*, meanwhile, had Khan and his army as merely an antagonistic subplot.

To make matters even stranger, Hughes had made almost no period pieces throughout his career, opting for more modern-day urban settings that would have been physically familiar. Only his Western, *The Outlaw*, was set in the mid-1800s as was his ill-fated Corsica-set drama *Vendetta*. Real-life figures like Al Capone and Doc Holliday served as inspirations for his stories but were never faithfully captured.

With John Wayne in the back of his mind, Hughes enlisted the services of British scribe Oscar Millard to do some poking around and draft a treatment, a detailed document outlining the story. The London-born screenwriter was in his midforties and only just breaking into the industry.

His work on the 20th Century Fox nun comedy *Come to the Stable* in 1949 opened the doors to Hollywood. His script for the James Stewart thriller *No Highway in the Sky* attracted Hughes's attention two years later. Exploring the themes of aviation design and pilot fatigue, that flick was obviously right up his alley.

Impressed with Millard, Hughes brought him on to do some script work on the Robert Mitchum projects *Angel Face* and *Second Chance*. In the midst of it all, Millard found himself nominated for a "Best Story" Academy Award in 1952 for the World War II thriller *The Frogmen*. From a resume standpoint, Hughes must have figured he had just put one of the best men in Hollywood on the job.

"I was, in fact, such an authority on Genghis Khan, that when I looked him up in the Britannica in the half hour before the meeting, I had trouble finding him because I couldn't spell his name," Millard later admitted.

Taking inspiration from old classical Shakespearian English (frightfully distant from a twelfth-century Mongol tribe dialect), Millard seemed unhappy with his assignment right from the start. The writer knew someone like John Wayne was the top choice in Hughes's mind to play the part, an idea he scoffed at, fearing his words were doomed to come out completely wrong. Millard chose to ignore the impending casting catastrophe and drafted a treatment focusing heavily on dialogue and evidently flipping through history books for what seems to have been only a brief second.

Focusing on the abduction of Temüjin's wife, Börte, and the ensuing quest to retrieve her, there was more than enough historical background to frame the film. What was fabricated were the details of just about everything in between, from their sappy, more modernly groomed relationship to the structured and orderly lives of the supporting Mongols.

In truth, historians have estimated that the couple was married by arrangement at age nine and ten, with the kidnapping occurring some years later. The script ignores all of that, only incorporating a few rearranged facts including the betrayal of Temüjin's close ally, Jamukha.

The move was seen as somewhat of a protest to Hughes's evident lack of seriousness for authenticity or an interest in anything past making movie-star bait. Others, including Millard, claimed the over-the-top language was a small attempt to give the movie a touch of class, though in doing so, everything factual or plot-related got pushed to the back of the writer's mind.

"I decided to write it in stylized, slightly archaic English, mindful of the fact that my story was nothing more than a tarted-up Western," Millard said. "I thought this would give it a certain cachet, and I left no lily unpainted. It was a mistake I never repeated."

While Millard assembled what would be a 138-page script, Hughes sought the help of another important player in the script's development—Dick Powell. If there ever was a versatile talent to grace the entertainment business, Powell was surely one of the best in the entire industry. With a baby-faced look of youth and American wholesomeness, Powell began as a recording artist in the early 1930s, touring with a band throughout the Midwest.

He soon found himself playing boyish and preppy supporting roles in comedies and musicals throughout the decade, like Will Rogers's *Too Busy to Work*, Ruby Keeler's *42nd Street*, and *Gold Diggers of 1933*, working alongside a strange mixture of collaborators like Preston Sturges, Abbot and Costello, and Lucille Ball. He even starred in musical NBC and CBC radio programs during the early forties and eventually landed the starring role on the regular theater production broadcast *Richard Diamond, Private Detective*.

A complete career turnaround happened for the actor when he was cast as Phillip Marlowe in RKO's adaptation of *Murder, My Sweet*. Powell was the first actor to play the iconic private eye from the Raymond Chandler novels and popularized the role long before Bogart or Mitchum ever got to it.

From that point, he was cast in a slew of tough guy roles (he harbored a deep resentment for being passed over for Fred Mac-Murray's role in *Double Indemnity*) and occasionally a romantic song-and-dance story, but now at least he was typically the lead. Powell bounced over to television early, launching his own production company–Four Star Television–with an overwhelming desire to create his own material.

RKO had treated Powell well, providing him with the Marlowe role in 1944 and the occasional acting job throughout that decade. When Hughes took control of the studio, the two were familiar with each other, and Powell was open to offers. Powell was spending most of his time making films with MGM and Columbia, but he wanted to shake up his career by trying his hand at directing, which neither studio would allow him to do.

He had been prepping a theater production of the *Caine Mutiny Court-Martial* when RKO invited him to talk about a potential costarring role in a Debbie Reynolds musical called *Susan Slept Here*. At their meeting, Hughes and Powell ended up chatting about the actor's new television venture and his interest in stepping behind the camera. Hughes, accustomed to tossing out empty promises to anyone he wanted for a role, invited Powell to help develop some pictures, mainly a new starring vehicle for John Wayne.

Powell turned down *Susan Slept Here* but jumped at the chance of drumming up work for the Duke, eagerly pouring through all the scripts RKO had on file. Hoping this was his shot at directing, Powell was puzzled when Millard's *Genghis Khan* treatment landed on his desk with Hughes's endorsement.

After reading the story, Dick wasn't quite sold and was uncomfortable with the notion of Wayne playing the Mongolian lead. Powell suggested to Hughes that someone like Marlon Brando might be more appropriate, pointing to the fact that the actor had just played Mexican revolutionary Emiliano Zapata in *Viva Zapata!* and was currently prepping to play Mark Antony in *Julius Caesar*. Turning a blind eye to his deal with Wayne, Hughes jumped at the Brando idea and encouraged Powell to pursue the actor.

The *Genghis Khan* treatment was altered with Brando in mind and rushed off to the actor, who surprisingly took interest in the role. Powell hunted for other scripts that he could offer to Wayne while he waited for Brando–who at this point had only starred in four films–to say yes.

Weighing his options and stringing RKO along for months, the acclaimed method actor chose to follow through with Joseph L. Mankiewicz's musical *Guys and Dolls* instead. A longstanding rumor is that Brando hated the script, in particular Millard's dialogue, and never intended to do the film in the first place. Yul Brynner, a relative cinematic unknown, was next in line to turn down the role, and Robert Mitchum was completely out of the question.

With their Mongol well running dry, Powell and Hughes filed the document under a possible "maybe" for John Wayne as they continued to search for projects. Recognizing that the idea failed to find any legs or gain any early momentum, both figured the whole Genghis Khan idea more than likely had no future.

Hughes and the RKO crew handed John Wayne dozens of duds, few of which were actually ever shot with other actors. Proposed as a sequel to Wayne's own 1942 Western *The Spoilers, Silver Horde* was, according to him, unsuitable by any reasonable human's standards. He toyed with the idea of taking the role just so he could complete his deal, hiring his own personal writer to polish the script. Ultimately, nothing happened with it, nor did anything happen with Dick Powell's banal project about the invention of the telegraph, *The Long Wire*.

Among the most amusing ideas floated Wayne's way was a romantic adventure called *African Intrigue*, a WWII drama set in Burma called *Pagota*, a political drama with Jane Russell called *The Senator*, and something titled *Man's Story*. Wayne proposed John Ford's true story, *The Long Gray Line*, in which he would play an Irish immigrant who rises through the military ranks. Yet, not even Ford's involvement and a project ready to shoot grabbed Hughes's attention. Because of Wayne's RKO commitments, he lost that role to Tyrone Power.

Wayne still had high hopes for *The Alamo* but was beginning to see that he would have to take matters into his own hands and stop operating on the wishful hope that RKO might one day take it, or anything he wanted to do, seriously.

In the midst of shopping the idea around to a few unenthusiastic contacts, Wayne had an opportunity to speak with Robert

Fellows, a producer with whom he had struck a friendship when filming *Back to Bataan* during his earlier days lent to RKO. Fellows encouraged Wayne to forget the self-serving bigwigs, forget Howard Hughes's flimsy promises, and start his own production company to create his own roles.

Hesitant at first, Wayne looked to the state of Ford's Argosy Pictures. The burden of debt and a lukewarm response to *Wagon Master* began to tumble the very business venture that led Wayne to partner with Hughes in the first place. Argosy's silver lining was that it managed to go out with *The Quiet Man*, the Ireland-set romantic boxing comedy that Ford and Wayne had been gunning to make for several years.

Ultimately, it won Ford his fourth Best Director Academy Award, while the relatively unusual and more sensitive entry in the Duke's filmography held strong at the box office and earned him rave reviews. Faulty bookkeeping during production led Ford to enter into a legal dispute with Republic Pictures. Partner Merian C. Cooper departed to head Cinerama Corporation.

Argosy collected dust for several years until officially dissolving in 1956. Evidently, the talents of Hollywood's most celebrated filmmaker couldn't keep a production company going, leaving Wayne to wonder if his mentor couldn't do it, how in the world would he?

Wayne-Fellows ultimately did get itself ignited in 1952 with their first release, *Big Jim McLain*. In it, Wayne struts around as a modern-day lawman working for the House Un-American Activities Committee and thwarting Hawaiian Communist plots. Critics were unamused, but audiences came running. *Big Jim McLain* was enough of a success to launch three back-to-back projects–*Plunder of the Sun, Island in the Sky*, and *Hondo*–into development with Warner Bros. coproducing and distributing.

On occasion, Duke expressed dismay at not having earned an Academy Award. Content portraying cowboys and marines, he seemed at a loss on how to go about it, prompting his contemporaries to wonder if the company was all a bid to cinch Oscar gold.

"I wonder what they think acting is?" he fumed at the academy. "I don't go in for chichi or the dirty shirt school of acting. Perhaps nobody but another actor knows how difficult it is to play a straight character part."

Wayne not only surpassed Argosy's success right out of the gate but was getting projects before cameras at triple the rate Hughes could. Wayne-Fellows froze whenever RKO flirted with a new idea, proposing shoot dates that the actor would block off only to see nothing actually go through. Fearing juicy roles were being lost, Wayne was growing impatient while Hughes was getting bored.

Amid his sparse amount of free time, the billionaire had begun palling around with Ralph Stolkin, a Chicago-based businessman described in the newspapers as one of the country's "top promotional wizards." Stolkin had just formed a syndicate with an array of money-hungry partners like his father-in-law, Abraham Koolish; Texas oilmen Ray Ryan and Edward G. Burke; and movie theater chain owner Sherrill Corwin.

After a few casual get-togethers, the Stolkin syndicate announced, for reasons unknown other than a misguided hunger for financial gain, that they were potentially interested in acquiring Hughes's controlling ownership in RKO.

Looking around at the exhaustive mess he was in—made up of flops, fiscal losses, obligations to big-name actors, and legal sagas—Hughes breathed a sigh of giddy relief and agreed to hear them out.

# 5: Treasures from the Trash

Howard Hughes had headed RKO for more than four years by the middle of 1952, and if any remaining staff member figured that management at the studio couldn't possibly get any worse, they were dead wrong. The output had decreased by nearly half since Hughes took over, averaging around twelve in-house productions each year and relying on distribution deals to bring in virtually all their earnings. The RKO of the early 1940s had nearly fifty RKO films released each year, with well over half of them being original in-house works.

In 1950, no motion picture from RKO earned more than $100,000 at the box office, resulting in the first and largest net loss for the studio—$5.8 million. Without the mega-success of Walt Disney's

*Cinderella* and the distribution of Akira Kurosawa's *Rashomon* to cover the tab, RKO may have fallen at that very moment. From the thirty-eight films released in 1951, the studio barely squeaked out a marginal profit, thanks to a string of headaches, bad breaks, and, yes, more awful decisions.

Onscreen, there was too much time between quality or financial successes. Robert Mitchum's star status was utilized as often as possible. He and Jane Russell were paired again in the Nicolas Ray noir *Macao*, a dark and exotic romance that managed to fare better than most releases at the time. Mitchum's presence certainly enabled duds like *Angel Face* and *One Minute to Zero* to at least gain an audience, unlike many of the releases that found far too few viewers.

Mitchum was ready to move on; his celebrity had far outgrown Hughes's RKO, and many opportunities were waiting outside the studio gates. He parted ways with Hughes, leaving after completing the romantic flop *She Couldn't Say No* to work with Marilyn Monroe in *River of No Return* at 20th Century Fox.

Left with little to work with, Hughes was now entering a brand-new phase of studio ownership where wronged and angered employees were starting to fight back. *The Las Vegas Story*, a run-of-the-mill noir about an affair-turned-murder-plot, became a source of major trouble when Hughes ordered that writer Paul Jarrico be fired and have his credit removed for possessing Communist connections.

Jarrico, who claimed to have worn his beliefs on his sleeve, sued RKO for unfairly removing his name from the film. Called into court, the Screen Writers Guild attempted to force Hughes into arbitration, with the mogul citing Jarrico's political stances were in violation of the House Un-American Activities Committee's morals clause.

Jarrico's rebuttal came with a laugh, intimating that Hughes was guilty of breaking morals clauses more than anyone. "[RKO] well knows that Howard Hughes, its chief executive, is a person who in the motion picture industry generally, and in Hollywood in particular, is reputed to be an individual whose personal acts and conduct are in constant violation of generally accepted public 'conventions' and 'morals in the ordinary sense.'"

Piggybacking on Jarrico's claim, actress Jean Simmons had also grown frustrated with the billionaire's actions, insisting that he purposely cost her work and mistreated her throughout her contract with RKO. Simmons's attorney, Martin Gang, additionally filed his own suit against Hughes during court proceedings, citing damaging instances of libel and slander against him.

Bouncing from courtroom to courtroom, Hughes found himself once again losing his luster for motion picture making, just as he had done decades prior. With the United States embroiled in the Korean War, the other side of the entrepreneur made up of TWA stock and aircraft manufacturing ideas wished to run wild and take to the sky. Hughes sat on the Transcontinental and Western Air board of directors and also held a majority share.

Hughes Aircraft Company simultaneously initiated an electronics division, constructing a missile plant in Tucson, Arizona, while the billionaire launched the Howard Hughes Medical Institute in Miami, Florida. He stated the organization was to appease his desire to enter philanthropy and explore "the genesis of life itself." Others accused the charity of being solely founded as a tax dodge and took him to court for that, too.

With Hughes Aircraft's facility covering 1,200 acres in Culver City, California, and then the 4,480-acre factory in Tucson, Hughes had eighty thousand employees working for him in the aircraft and weaponry industries alone. On the motion picture side of things, RKO losses were shaping up to be $4 million ($38 million today)—and that was only at the halfway mark of 1952. The future was not looking bright with a discouraging slate of bland releases to come.

So, when the rare and unexpected opportunity of interested buyers—the Stolkin syndicate—came along and actually put in an offer for Hughes's shareholdings, he pounced on his ticket out. Hughes cited the studio as a "headache" and claimed, "I need RKO like I need to come down with the black plague."

The deal Hughes and Ralph Stolkin struck inside a Beverly Hills bungalow on September 23, 1952, was for $7.35 million (roughly $71 million in modern day), plus a down payment of $1.25 million. The bulk of the cash was to be delivered through installments over a two-year period. Hughes lent RKO upward of $8 million of his own dough just to keep the company alive through the transition.

Stolkin was appointed president on October 2, and the most insecure of the Big Five studios wobbled into a brand-new era, delaying Wayne's final commitment into the unforeseeable future.

When Ralph Stolkin and his cronies entered the studio lot, they must have observed RKO like a family of homeowners walking into a newly purchased house previously belonging to negligent party animals. Green as can be, none of the syndicate members was particularly well versed on how an actual motion picture studio operated, and finding anyone left who was knowledgeable seemed like a lost cause.

Hughes's right-hand man, corporate president Ned E. Depinet, got in on the deal when Hughes announced he was selling, leaving virtually no one in charge of production. The *Genghis Khan* treatment wasn't touched as Stolkin seemed to be woefully unaware of what kind of contracts and scripts he was inheriting. In fact, the only production that was remotely ready to go before cameras when the new owner showed up was a low-level B thriller called *Split Second*. Executives had assigned Dick Powell the task of shepherding the project along with the tease of getting to sit in the director's chair.

The story centered around a gang of escaped convicts holed up with hostages in a Nevada ghost town—nothing fancy—but Powell was grateful to flex the leadership talents he was certain he possessed. With relative unknowns Stephen McNally, Alexis Smith, Jan Sterling, and Keith Andes confined to mostly one interior set, the chances for Powell to muck up the movie to a worse state than other RKO releases at the time were slim.

"The best thing about switching from being an actor to being a director is that you don't have to shave or hold your stomach in anymore," Powell joked.

It would be the blind leading the blind, however, as the only film experience Stolkin or his syndicate really had was investing in the Dean Martin and Jerry Lewis comedy *At War with the Army* in 1950. Every producer scratched his head, trying to solve the puzzle on how a virtual nobody, even less experienced than Hughes, nabbed one of the industry's most prized positions.

The confusion turned almost instantly to a mass outrage; within two weeks of the takeover, a series of articles in the *Wall Street Journal* exposed the shady dealings Stolkin had been associated with during his previous career. RKO's new head honcho had apparently etched out a comfy fortune for himself through punchboard gambling schemes, while his father-in-law did jail time for orchestrating a mail-order insurance racket. Oilman Ray Ryan was a former business associate of notorious mob boss Frank Costello, leader of the Luciano crime family and known by the nickname "Prime Minister of the Underworld."

Newly appointed chairman Arnold Grant had an association with Hollywood "fixer" Sidney Korshak, notorious for business relationships with other powerful gangsters like Bugsy Siegel. Not one of the new members had a clean record, and now the world was hearing all about RKO's burgeoning load of dirty laundry.

Hollywood was stunned. Many believed rumors that the iconic studio had just been acquired outright by the mafia. Fingers pointed to Hughes, scrutinizing his ill-informed sales blunder. Marred by these unwholesome revelations, Hughes attempted to keep his head low as the syndicate looked at each other, wide-eyed and at a loss for answers on how to move past the public tarring-and-feathering.

Shaken by the claims, Stolkin ultimately stepped down from his board position, with the other members following one by one through the month of November. Grant vacated his position as chairman, leaving RKO in absolute limbo with nobody in control.

Minority shareholders were left with no choice but to step into action and file a suit so a receiver could be named and the Stolkin syndicate could be forced to sell off their shares and exit the company. The disgraced bunch agreed to go quietly and release their interests; no receiver or buyer would touch RKO at this point. Hughes couldn't just turn a blind eye, either; Stolkin begged him to undo their deal. He was "gifted" the syndicate's down payment as they returned his controlling interest and ran for cover.

He could have easily said no, yet Hughes figured the best way for his own reputation to rise above the controversy and save his investment was to rejoin the board of directors. Only this time, he assumed more responsibility by scooping up the roles of chairman and managing director of production–positions he had been nosing around with and influencing right from the start. In other words, Hughes did not get even one full month away from RKO; he was back in charge of a studio now in far worse condition, and he had more responsibility than before.

The year ended with RKO doubling its losses with a staggering total of $10,178,004 ($96 million). Hughes officially took control in March 1953, and Stolkin's regime completely removed themselves from their involvement.

During that five-month period, just one production went before the cameras–just one! Dick Powell's *Split Second*. Of all the possible plots of all the possible movies ever made, this one, which failed to succeed at the box office and do anything of merit for RKO, this movie, Powell's directorial debut at RKO, told the high-stakes story of escaped convicts hiding out in a ghost town in the wake of a looming threat. That threat, no word of a lie, is that they're all about to get nuked by a nearby atomic bomb test.

Since Hughes had taken charge, $22,324,583 ($212 million adjusted for inflation) had been lost. People associated with gangsters had been handed the keys. Everyone who was anyone knew to keep driving past Melrose Avenue and Gower Street. RKO's future under Hughes's leadership was publicly being questioned for the first time in his producing career.

John Wayne vowed to be a man of his word and finish the infernal contract made with Hughes nearly half a decade prior. The ownership shakeup happened so rapidly, it's hard to know what Duke made of the situation. The leading man certainly had every right to be angry and walk away from the whole public relations mess, but he didn't. Wayne stuck by Hughes with nothing but good faith that the final script would get the go-ahead–something Hughes still seemingly had no interest in doing.

During the new phase of absolute turmoil, ties were severed suddenly and unwillingly. Goldwyn ended his eleven-year distribution deal with RKO and semiretiring from making movies altogether.

The absence of his high-quality work would leave an unfillable hole while Hughes was left having to relocate his office.

Next up, the Encino Ranch, RKO's sprawling eighty-nine-acre backlot where everything from *Cimarron*'s Oklahoman plains to *It's a Wonderful Life*'s beloved Bedford Falls once stood became bludgeoned by an army of bulldozers. Countless pictures that built the studio into a celebrated success—*King Kong, Hunchback of Notre Dame,* and *Cat People*—were but distant memories.

Hughes closed the location permanently in 1953, selling off the hallowed ground to the Encino Park housing development just so the studio could stay in operation for a little longer, though without an extensive home in which to shoot.

Another detrimental blow came when Walt Disney saw the dim light of hope fading into darkness. With the declining quality tarnishing his quality family entertainment name, not to mention Hughes's risqué plotlines and own lothario image, Disney sought to leave and start his own distribution company, Buena Vista Pictures. *Peter Pan* was the studio's highest-grossing project under the Hughes era, but the nearly two-decades-long partnership had reached a bitter end with one completely outgrowing the other. Hughes actually offered to sell the studio outright to Walt Disney, but the animation giant wisely walked away in the aftermath of the poor, mishandled release of *Rob Roy: The Highland Rogue*.

The RKO owner finally managed to get one looming weight off his loaded to-do list: RKO divested its theater chains into a separate business as per the antitrust laws' request in 1948. Hughes had put RKO Theatre Corporation into trust for two years, biding his time for the perfect buyer.

Former majority holder Floyd Odlum had actually been promised the stock but was livid to learn Hughes struck a deal with New England industrialist Albert A. List for $3.27 million. That sole deal may have been the reason why RKO survived past 1953, but Odlum would not forget about their broken agreement and hungered for the opportune moment to strike back.

The billionaire was spread ludicrously thin, having no time to mourn any of the losses; not only did he refuse to set up shop on the RKO lot—still deeming it unclean—he was missing production meetings because of an exorbitant amount of court dates, time he deemed nothing more than wasteful distractions since nothing at RKO could get off the ground without him.

Lengthy troubles with writer Paul Jarrico and actress Jean Simmons were silenced, with Hughes actually emerging victorious over the blacklisted scribe and settling out of court with the starlet.

Minority shareholders picked up where those two left off, nipping at his heals following the Stolkin incident by filing five separate lawsuits, each one claiming mismanagement, misappropriation, and financial misconduct.

Hughes's only source of backup was newly appointed president James R. Grainger (father of former producer Edmund Grainger). Optimistic, Grainger chose to spoonfeed quips of comfort, relaying to the world that RKO was "the Showmanship Company" and plenty of gold would soon hit theaters in the coming year.

Dick Powell deprecatingly snapped that "RKO's contract list is down to three actors and 127 lawyers." Few had the blind faith and positivity Grainger did, given the record amount of court dates; he opted to stay on board through the thick, thin, and completely intangible.

Production choices got far stranger than anyone figured possible. Grasping for straws and swinging for the fences, Hughes recognized that the only card he held at this point was the ability to craft the most bizarre spectacles ever seen on film.

Under the encouragement of Grainger, RKO's three-dimensional golden era took hold to capture on the popular novelty that swept cinema in the early fifties. The Africa-set hit *Bwana Devil*, a film regarded as the first full-length color 3-D production, made movie makers frantic to cash in on the fad.

*Second Chance* was Hughes's first 3-D movie–shot entirely on location in Mexico–where a climactic scuffle on a dangling cable car utilized the new sensory-tingling technology. Much to everyone's surprise, the film earned money.

The same can't be said for a Western called *Devil's Canyon*, a picture that benefited little from the addition of 3-D. Hughes's problematic picture, *The French Line*, was given the 3-D treatment to amplify Jane Russell's physical assets, unsurprisingly evoking shock, anger, and censorship demands. By the time he got to *Son of Sinbad*, 3-D had worn out its welcome, and Hughes felt its only use was to amplify objectification by going all out with his own sexual fantasies.

The Baghdad-set period piece featuring Vincent Price joyfully objectified more than 127 women, including celebrity stripteaser Lili St. Cyr. Its thin plot was merely an excuse to set titillating dance routines inside flesh-filled harems. The Catholic Legion of Decency forced Hughes to shelve the film, an action he complied with, leaving any screenings of the film 100 percent private.

Hughes's last wild experiment was *Underwater!* The self-explanatory Jane Russell picture spent more than half its runtime deep below the ocean surface, where two scuba divers find treasure—a daring Hollywood first if pulled off correctly. It was RKO's first SuperScope project, a fifties' trend involving an expensive anamorphic lens that allowed the film to be projected on a theater screen almost twice the typical size.

Director John Sturgess never met Hughes; they merely chatted over the phone as the dangerous and expensive production commenced off the coast of Hawaii. Several months in, the crew lost a barge full of cameras, and a large portion of the film had to be reshot. Since it was storm season, production moved to Jamaica, where hundreds of thousands of dollars' worth of equipment was again lost to water damage.

With a disturbingly bare slate of RKO pictures ahead—ones with titles like *Killers from Space*—there was absolutely nothing Hughes could do. That was it. He was licked this time: out of ideas, out of motivation, and out of luck. Without a single asset backing RKO, no gimmick flashy enough to dazzle an audience, and streams of cash leaking from its bank account every day, it made sense to sell. It was either that or continue as the biggest laughingstock in the motion picture industry. Hughes, for all his faults, felt he had more self-respect than to piddle his life away sparring with shareholders and celebrities over garbage.

And just like that, the light bulb over his head shone brightly, and the solution to every studio problem was right in front of him: money and power. "What," Hughes asked himself, "if there wasn't anyone to spar with at all?"

On February 8, 1954, Hughes silenced the "distracting" stock-holders taking him to court by offering to buy them out at $6 per share–a price higher than market value. Relieved to step away from the decaying operation and consuming lawsuits, they happily obliged. Hughes hastily paid an unimaginable total of $23,489,478 ($225 million today) for the rest of the studio and passed along the task of dealing with everything to Noah Dietrich to juggle.

Hughes was set to become the sole and outright owner on March 18, 1954, an action that had not been done since the very creation of the film industry. Business insiders indicated that the buyout would allow Hughes to write off the studio's losses against his own earnings from another one of his companies like Tool Co. and completely dissolve the subsidiary. If it had not been for Floyd Odlum's revenge, RKO would have died right then and there.

The industrialist reemerged out of sheer spite to stop the complete takeover from happening. Childishly sour over the theater chain betrayal, Odlum purchased the remaining studio stock–slightly more than 5 percent of company shares–so Hughes would not have absolute ownership and the ability to do what he wished with RKO.

Stuck with the debt load, Hughes could still go forward with production on anything he chose–the man did have a larger stake in a major studio than anyone else in Hollywood; it was just that Odlum made it trickier for him to dispose of the studio through the fastest method.

RKO was saved by the transaction for the time being; the only two actions Hughes was left with were to try to sell the studio again or actually try to turn a profit by producing a quality motion picture.

By actually managing to make a successful motion picture at RKO, Dick Powell was seen as a shining star. Not only was he asked to completely take over Wayne's projects, but he was appointed to direct them. He ultimately took his final onscreen role in the listless musical *Susan Slept Here* as a last-minute favor to the studio. Still, Dick was moving up the Hollywood food chain, even if foreclosure loomed and his boss was in the midst of gaining total control.

Wayne was called in to finally discuss some options and what direction the two of them might like to take for his final RKO picture. At this point, it had been well over two years since *Flying Leathernecks* was released.

The next portion of John Wayne's developmental journey with RKO is where it gets a little hazy. What transpired has become legend muddled with myth and sprinkled with fact. What is known for sure is that when Wayne came down to RKO, the star grew annoyed when Powell had nothing of merit to offer.

Powell had dusted off a few idle selections, including *Genghis Khan*. Powell still had little faith in the idea and set it aside . . . far aside. This is where the facts begin to compete with one another. It is true that Dick Powell had Oscar Millard's treatment in his possession and was hesitant to give it to Wayne. It is also true that Powell had that document physically in the room. Some historians and film history buffs have claimed that Wayne spied the half-written script during that very meeting and picked it up off Powell's desk, but many others have preferred to believe it was discovered by Wayne inside a trash receptacle.

This secret has gone to the grave with these two men, meaning it's far too easy to debunk yet far too pleasing to ignore. Powell didn't want much more to do with Millard's script and could have easily chucked it into the garbage. Perhaps Wayne recognized the script format sticking out from the bin and inquisitively went to retrieve it. Perhaps Powell had a particular filing system on his desk—a tray of some kind—where unwanted screenplays went to die. Maybe it was sitting on his desk among crumpled papers and scribbled notes. Some have claimed Powell had frustratingly thrown it on the floor and Wayne had recovered it from there. Given the rejection from the other actors who read Millard's treatment, it's far too satisfying to think that Wayne fished it out of a heap of rubbish. He was growing impatient; and at that point in time, he would have accepted anything put in front of him to get the RKO deal done and out of the way.

One way or another, John Wayne picked up a document in Dick Powell's RKO office during that meeting, a story devised for him about Mongol emperor Genghis Khan, and flipped through the pages. After haphazardly ingesting Millard's words shaping distant lands, scantily clad Tatar women, and a mighty conqueror, Wayne looked up at the actor-turned-director with enthusiasm and said, "Well, how about this?"

# PART TWO

DURING

# 6: America Goes Atomic

Some three hundred miles northeast of Hollywood's bright lights, a war was underway; a silent skirmish that tipped the entire worldly population toward the very brink. The desert between Los Angeles and Las Vegas had stood silent for centuries, but a mixture of scientific advancement and paranoia had led the Nevadan sand to become the most perilous place on the planet, even more so than any theater screening a "Howard Hughes presents" movie.

Operation Upshot-Knothole, a proof-test continuation of emerging combat weapons and radiation implosion effects, was underway. Sponsored by the US Atomic Energy Commission (AEC), Upshot-Knothole was America's tenth nuclear testing series in only eight short years. Altogether, eleven atomic detonations took place between March 17 and June 4, 1953.

Seven tower tests, three free air drops, and one gun-deployed shot made up the varying experiments of Upshot-Knothole, mainly done to advance both land and sky military weaponry. The operation involved more than twenty-one thousand Department of Defense personnel participating in observer programs, tactical maneuvers, scientific studies, and plenty of shock and awe moments.

An analysis of the bomb's chemical materials was conducted, and ultra-high-speed photographs were taken to capture and record fireball growth—components necessary to understand the yield of radioactive particles, also known as *fissile*, that are produced during detonation. As complicated and harmful as that all sounds, cutesy names like Badger, Dixie, and Ruth were slapped on each project in an attempt to ease the tension attached to the controversial research.

The first Upshot-Knothole blast, Operation Annie, was nationally televised to the American public and consisted of a grainy white flash followed by a plume of smoke. Two wooden frame homes, fifty automobiles, and eight bomb shelters were involved in that particular test to study the effects of nuclear survival safety. It was determined that if a car's windows were left open to minimize exploding glass and a total collapse, vehicles were deemed safe if they were parked at least ten blocks away from the bomb's hypocenter.

Operation Encore saw 145 Ponderosa pine trees cemented into the desert by the US Forest Service in order to test nuclear effects on plant life; many caught fire from the thermal radiation, while the blast knocked only 20 percent of them to the ground.

Operation Grable proved to be a weapon of mass power, becoming the second of four gun warhead tests, shooting the first and only artillery-fired atomic projectile more than eleven thousand yards over the dry lakebed of Frenchman Flat.

With so many staff members working on weapons of destruction—capable of destroying every single employee there not to mention the very ground underneath them—it is a small miracle that the methodology of these tests actually went according to plan. Operation Nancy underperformed, but no notable injuries were ever recorded, and the AEC felt they achieved what the agency sought to understand. The immediate atomic experiments conducted through Upshot-Knothole were therefore deemed a success.

Outside the proving grounds, far away from soulless data and mindless record books, citizens begged to differ. Issues unaccounted for did arise amid operations, particularly two shots known as Harry and Simon.

Simon, the April 25 shot, mushroomed as to be expected, but the radioactive matter did not disperse as other tests suggested it would. The excess matter, known as *fallout*, apparently hung in the air and traveled eastward for days, passing over settlements like Glendale and prompting radiation examinations by the way of vehicle roadblocks.

At least forty people met the criteria to undergo decontamination procedures, which at that point was a good shakedown and a shower. Rensselaer Polytechnic students in New York claimed two days later to have found overwhelming radiation readings on Geiger counters linked to Simon.

And then there was Harry.

The Mark 13 warhead design, known by crew members as codename Hamlet, was test number nine in Operation Upshot-Knothole.

Designed by Mexican-born physicist Ted Taylor at the Los Alamos National Laboratory, Harry possessed what researchers felt was the most efficient pure fission model–a hollow-core concept intended to yield far less unwanted radioactive byproducts than its atomic predecessors. In far simpler terms, the weapon itself was designed to do far more damage while giving off less harmful side effects by using less fissionable material; a "cleaner bomb," if you will. It was lauded for these advancements and stood out as one of the more highly anticipated shots of the eleven.

Following Operation Encore, Harry would stand out for two monumentally overlooked snags: One, the bomb itself negatively defied radioactive expectations, and two, there was a change in wind.

The decision by the United States to participate in the ill-fated Upshot-Knothole and even to capitalize on Nevada's deserts was done with intense haste fueled not only by nuclear elements but by a driving fear that caused corners to be cut and long-term effects overlooked in favor of productivity.

The reality of the bomb being used as a potential option for defense came to the forefront after chemists Otto Hahn and Fritz Strassmann discovered the possibility of nuclear fission in 1938. A sobering fact for many, the chemists were German and feared Adolf Hitler would attempt to develop such a weapon capable of deadly destruction when the Second World War began.

Quickly gathering physicists, engineers, and a collection of great minds and thinkers from a multitude of countries including Great Britain and Canada, President Roosevelt approved a secret atomic program in October 1941 to beat Axis powers and unofficially kick-start the nuclear arms race; it was called the Manhattan Project.

Research facilities were built in Oak Ridge, Tennessee, and Richland, Washington, throughout 1942 to 1943 due to their plentiful space and readily available workforce. The nucleus of the Manhattan Project was erected north of Albuquerque, New Mexico, near a boys' ranching school called Los Alamos. Initially known as Project Y, the Los Alamos Laboratory was apparently supported by chief physicist and "Coordinator of Rapid Rupture" Robert Oppenheimer for its secretive location and natural beauty, which he hoped would inspire his team.

Three and a half years of toil and two billion dollars later, the possibilities of fission, a process of splitting the atom, were explored—particularly with ultra-rare uranium-235 and pluto-nium-240. The unstable isotope was found to carry out the desired explosive effect when hit by a separate neutron, therefore setting off a chain reaction by multiplying and releasing high amounts of energy. Once the amount of fissionable material, otherwise known as the *critical mass*, could be properly calculated, far larger and more specific chain reactions could occur.

The world was forever changed on July 16, 1945, when a vessel that could contain the fission process, dubbed by the Manhattan Project committee as "the Gadget," became the very first nuclear bomb.

The plutonium-based Trinity test was carried out at the White Sands missile range in the Alamogordo desert—eighty-eight miles north of the Mexican border. Residents of the southern state said the blast from the implosion device was visible for up to ten miles, with many noting it was far brighter than the sun.

On the success of his operation, Oppenheimer later was quoted as saying, "I remembered the line from the Hindu scripture, the Bhagavad Gita; Vishnu is trying to persuade the Prince that he should do his duty and, to impress him, takes on his multi-armed form and says, 'Now I am become Death, the destroyer of worlds.' "

US Senator Brien McMahon, on the other hand, called it "the most important thing in history since the birth of Jesus Christ."

The Second World War ultimately came to a horrific and sudden close with the deployment of Fat Man and Little Boy (names inspired by the Dashiell Hammett novel *The Thin Man* to identify their shape) over Japan in August 1945. Though an estimated 150,000 lives were lost in the nuclear attack, atomic testing experienced a far more challenging conclusion, even with inaugurated President Harry Truman, Albert Einstein, and Oppenheimer calling for more control and an end to nuclear advancements.

On the tail of the Hiroshima and Nagasaki bombings, the next atomic measure was taken through an isolated plutonium implosion called Operation Crossroads, which was carried out at a remote military base on the Marshall Islands.

The South Pacific coral reef known as Bikini Atoll had been taken from the Japanese, who had occupied it since World War I. The Battle of Kwajalein saw the United States gain the ground in February 1944, where they established a naval epicenter including several bars plus a ship graveyard for expired or damaged destroyers and submarines to decay. With ample land and sea space, plus no one to interfere, researchers felt they had struck testing ground gold.

Relocating 167 Micronesian inhabitants from Bikini Atoll to Rongerik, the next and less-inhabitable atoll over, ABLE (a bomb affectionately nicknamed Gilda after the Rita Hayworth movie) was dropped from an aircraft. BAKER (dubbed "Helen of Bikini") was detonated ninety feet underwater, sinking a multitude of target ships and creating a two-million-ton geyser of water. Made public by the press, opinions were mixed, certainly on an international level, whether or not the operations were necessary.

The Atomic Energy Act was signed into effect August 1, 1946, by President Truman; this gave the newly formed and civilian-operated Atomic Energy Commission control of what would essentially be guardians of nuclear advancements, thus removing the military and, for the most part, the government from the equation.

It was in September 1949 when fears far beyond what they already were became realized. The Air Force Office of Atomic Energy had a WB-29 fly from Misawa Air Base in Japan to Eielson Air Force Base in Alaska. The plane allegedly collected debris passing Siberia. Through test samples, it was determined that the USSR was also conducting nuclear experiments of their own.

RDS-1 (codenamed "Joe-1" by the United States in reference to Joseph Stalin) was in fact a successful plutonium detonation held at the Semipalatinsk test site in Soviet Kazakhstan on August 29, 1949.

The United States had entered a moratorium for nearly two years to grapple with their newfound power, but with pressure silently mounting between the two superpowers, all chances at postwar peace were lost. The AEC ultimately chose to continue nuclear advancements, turning to hydrogen bombs at Los Alamos and further design tests in the South Pacific. This truly ushered in what would be one of the most highly tensioned geopolitical battles in the twentieth century: the Cold War.

With three Marshall Island campaigns, nine device tests, and hundreds of thousands of people dispatched to the blink-and-you-miss-them atolls, the atomic advancements were a weighty expense to America's wallet. The reefs may have been remote and undisturbed, perfectly chosen for the public's safety, but those very positive attributes also added to the frivolous costs of research thousands of miles from the country's mainland.

President Truman looked elsewhere for testing possibilities, apparently eyeing an island or two in the Galápagos archipelago of Ecuador.

Los Alamos could have continued tests near their research facility and the White Sands missile range (the spot where Trinity was detonated), but the rocky terrain to the north and west seemed far too unstable, while the growing communities of Albuquerque and Santa Fe to the east and south were too close to unleash a continuous barrage of unpredictable explosions.

Desert stretched across much of America's Southwest, but little of it was flat and sprawling–just an empty portion seven hundred miles east of the New Mexico laboratory in Nevada. A former silver mining capital, the unpopulated land had formally been used as a wildlife reservation until the War Department heavily restricted public access in 1942 and used much of the space as a gunnery school. The Las Vegas Army Airfield operated there during the war until it was expanded and renamed Nellis Air Force Base in 1950.

Nevada's longtime senator Pat McCarran knew the location was sublime and pushed for the site to begin operation in his state; the swelling training ground, now recognized as the Nevada Test and Training Range, made it the obvious solution.

The dry lake bed of Frenchman Lake, surrounded by the 123-square-mile basin was used as an airstrip just north of the air force base. Ten miles north, the sandy stretch of Yucca Flat sat empty. On December 18, 1950, President Truman designated the entire 680-square-mile section, also including the more valley-like

Pahute Mesa and Rainier Mesa, to be used for nuclear research and officially commissioned the Nevada Proving Grounds (renamed the Nevada Test Site in 1955).

Covering a total of 1,350 square miles over Nye County, the site became one of the most sizable and secured government research facilities of the US mainland. The initial hope was that the southeasterly winds would blow "radiological hazards" toward uninhabited stretches of desert west of the site.

Because of the isolated and relatively unsettled geography, a closed village called Mercury was built from the ground up by the Atomic Energy Commission just south of the proving grounds on what was known as Jackass Flats. Constructed to house staff, Mercury came with a $6.7 million price tag and actually used a village concept with a post office among other amenities. By the end of the 1950s, a full shopping mall, movie theater, bowling alley, and nondenominational chapel served more than ten thousand staff members.

Inner workings and layout of the actual site were kept tightly under wraps, with specific areas being designated and segregated for various tests and operations. Each was acknowledged as Area 1, Area 2, Area 3, and so forth—all the way up to 30.

Six years after Trinity, the first official test would be conducted on the mainland on January 27, 1951; Operation Ranger saw five B-50D bombers drop four MK-4 and one MK-6 devices over Frenchman Flat's Area 5.

Subsequent Operations Buster-Jangle and Tumbler-Snapper ensued at the Nevada Proving Grounds, yet tests were still routinely being conducted at the Pacific Proving Grounds in the Marshall Islands; the Mike shot, part of Operation Ivy in late 1952, was the first successful hydrogen bomb.

With the real paramount blasts saved for the South Pacific, the apparent upside to having such accessible and close proving grounds was that any old half-baked idea could get the thumbs up. An increase in audacity as time went on led to experiments such as the one where more than one thousand pigs were placed in cages, some wrapped with protective coverings, and moved various distances from the nuclear hypocenter to test skin reactions.

Humans weren't treated much better; thousands of soldiers were brought in for specialized exercises under the Desert Rock training program, which saw them hiding in trenches dug just one mile from the test site and carrying out tactical maneuvers while detonations were occurring.

Coated with what was known and referred to as radioactive material, troops stood in meandering lineups at the end of the day so they could be professionally decontaminated by personnel; their method consisted of dusting soldiers off with run-of-the-mill hardware store brooms.

The use of nuclear fission also ventured into more constructive territory, with tests carried out on the proving grounds aimed at figuring out whether bombs could safely and productively be put to more peaceful use. Massive craters were formed through a sudden soil displacement method. Rails and I-beams were put to the test to see what would melt or bend. Different types of brick and concrete walls were erected to see how they'd withstand the heat. Bank vaults were hauled out to the middle of the desert to test their resistance; a Mosler safe—albeit empty—is still apparently sitting unopened on the test site to this day.

The initial lesson, particularly from Upshot-Knothole, lent itself to a nice piece of propaganda. The American people were told that a home littered with garbage and negligence had a far greater chance of catching fire and collapsing from a nuclear blast than one with a tidy, well-cared-for yard. A large portion of the population lapped up every word, seeing as how the atomic industry was infiltrating all things recreation and pop culture.

The threat of the bomb—Soviet-made of course—had folks nervous, but the revelation that mankind could actually cook up such an intelligent device was cause to celebrate. There was fear for an impending nuclear skirmish, yet side effects and hazards beyond the "big boom" weren't quite in the public eye. Curiosity and a sweltering pride were far too distracting to dwell on the harms of fallout for long; the public didn't possess the information to begin to understand what could happen.

"You are, in a very real sense, active participants in the nation's atomic test program," wrote James E. Reeves, the proving grounds test manager, in a 1955 report. "I want you to know that each shot is justified by national or international security and that none will be fired unless there is adequate assurance of public safety. We are grateful for your continued cooperation and your understanding."

A glassy green mineral called trinitite, left behind from the Trinity test, was spattered across New Mexico's desert. It was sold as jewelry before concerned minds pulled it off the market since no one was quite sure what it was. That didn't stop picnickers from flocking to the inaugural test area to collect it as a treasured souvenir.

Tourists were heading to Las Vegas in droves not because Bugsy Siegel's sinful paradise was burgeoning with casinos and night club shows but because the proving grounds were only eighty-some-odd miles away. Every time a test went off, hotels on the strip would rumble. People were eager to experience the patriotic thrill ride, attending parties that caught their guests' interests and stopped the music every time there was a shake.

"Atomic cocktails" were mixed. Women competed for the title of "Miss Atomic Bomb," a beauty contest aimed at finding a winner that "radiated loveliness instead of deadly atomic particles."

Locals got their kicks by getting closer to the action, driving to makeshift lookouts near the proving grounds to get a closer glimpse of the mushroom clouds. People who resided in those desert states were issued a copy of an AEC booklet of facts and messages of comfort: "Your best action is not to be worried about fallout," it instructed.

Children happily frolicked in dusty pinkish clouds. Their parents read upbeat news in local papers, cheering the progress being made in combatting the Russians.

The unknown side effects left creative minds dreaming up wild tales of superpowers and fantastical defects. Atomic Man made his debut in *Headline* comic books in 1945; he was a physicist who gained the powers of strength, flight, and "atomic blasts" with uranium-235 experiments. The bomb found its way into the music industry with Lyle Griffin establishing his Atomic Records label and the Five Stars releasing the sexually charged song "Atom Bomb Baby."

Hollywood had caught on to the curiosity, starting with the 1945 spy flick *The House on 92nd Street,* the first to make mention of bomb development. The 1951 science fiction classic *The Day the Earth Stood Still* was first to take it seriously, having the alien Klaatu warn the human race of the dangers nuclear weapons could have on other civilizations.

Yes, "atomic this" and "nuclear that" were everywhere. General Mills plunked "Atomic Bomb Rings" inside cereal boxes, advising purchasers to look in the "sealed atom chamber in the gleaming aluminum warhead and see genuine atoms split to smithereens!"

Even the bikini itself took its name from the whole nuclear craze. Upon inventing the scandalous bathing suit in 1946, Louis Réard called it the bikini because of the testing over on Bikini Atoll. He hoped to capitalize on the atomic stories filling newspapers and suggested the look was absolutely explosive. Other sources have suggested it was a rebuttal to Parisian fashion designer Jacques Heim's design, which he called the Atome.

Nuclear was new! It was exciting! Dangerous! Scandalous! Incomprehensible! Evidently marketable! What started as a secret defense mechanism soon involved the whole country in a strange cocktail of every possible emotion. The atomic craze only began to lose its innocence and fantastical glow just as movie studios came poking around for production space.

Upshot-Knothole's Mark 13 Hamlet shot, Harry, took place at 4:00 a.m., May 19, 1953. Detonated over Yucca Flat at the proving grounds—specifically Area 3—Harry was fifty-six inches wide and sixty-six inches long, held high over the ground by a three-hundred-foot tower; it weighed four tonnes.

Nothing too out of the ordinary occurred that morning, except for the fact that Harry was designed for efficiency and byproduct reduction; when the bomb was detonated, a yield of thirty-two kilotonnes was produced—almost double what scientists were anticipating. For reference, the bomb dropped on Hiroshima was only thirteen kilotonnes, not even half of Harry.

A handful of unpronounceable chemicals such as niobium-95m, praseodymium-144, and yttrium-90, to name a few, shot to the sky as per usual. The findings were an alarming twenty kilotonnes over the AEC chief medical officer's yield level recommendation, a standard advised to help limit radiation exposure. But what could they do other than record their findings?

The testing tower itself had been vaporized, and a mushroom cloud formed high across the sky. Researchers dusted their hands and retreated to the water cooler, thinking that the whole efficiency thing didn't pan out this time around. The only thing that could or should be done was to go back to the drawing board. The winds picked up, changing from the southeast to the southwest for the remainder of the morning.

Wafting in those winds was heavy fallout from the test in an amount more than usual. Because Harry was so massive, it had managed to kick up more dirt; the majority of radioactive isotopes failed to break down and clung to other debris. Because of this extra weight, the aftermath from Harry didn't travel far—more than half of the radioactive isotopes settled in ditches and pastures, streets and low spots, intertwined with desert sand within twenty-four hours.

In the days that followed, residents of small southern Nevada and Utah settlements, fresh up-and-coming Main Street USA towns to the east of the proving grounds, apparently reported a metallic taste in their mouths. A few folks maxed out their Geiger counters (acquired years prior for private uranium prospecting) after getting curious. A sudden uptick in headaches, diarrhea, nausea, and vomiting was also cause for local alarm.

No one was given instruction or comment by the AEC in the immediate aftermath of Harry. Only after questions began to pour in from concerned community members did the message go out that individuals should probably stay indoors until the fallout passed. Nothing was issued to recommend washing thoroughly or throwing away garden-grown vegetables. Nothing was issued about how to properly go about decontaminating one's self. As the skies dropped a flaky gray ash that children reportedly mistook as snow—rolling around and actively eating it—the AEC deployed medical staff and screened an emergency educational film to illustrate to the public that they were perfectly safe. The response repeated by the AEC to calm jangled nerves was that radiation was "about one-twentieth of that experienced in an X-ray."

AEC chairman Lewis L. Strauss insisted to the Congressional Joint Committee on Atomic Energy that the Soviet threat left them "no alternative but to maintain our scientific and technical progress and maintain our strength at peak levels."

Newspapers in distant epicenters like Salt Lake City, published patriotic touts, alarmed letters to the editor, and AEC penned assurances, which supplied little clarity.

Harry Ferguson, a syndicated columnist, poked holes in the atomic testing process, noting "it's a long way from Las Vegas to Moscow," in the *Deseret News*. Columnist Clint Mosher, on the other hand, praised the work that was being done: "I never saw a prettier sight; it was like a letter from home or the firm handshake of someone you admire and trust."

A documentary soon produced by the US Department of Energy's Albuquerque Operations Office contained a snippet of sweet, wholesome life in St. George, a docile desert settlement tucked away in the southwest corner of Utah with forty-eight hundred residents.

Actors hung clothing out to dry, took a stroll down Main Street, and fed their baby a bottle of milk as typical human beings do. "It's old stuff to St. George—routine," says a narrator as a nuclear bomb detonates. "They've seen a lot of them ever since 1951; nothing to get excited about anymore."

A radio alert announces a change in winds, warning that atomic residue is blowing toward the town. In the same breath, the radio announcer advises that people take cover and stay indoors but that there is no danger and that everything is routine.

As the real panic and fear dissipated and the piles of ash mixed with the desert sand, thousands of sheep being raised on nearby farms began to suddenly die. Farmers reported that entire flocks were suddenly discovered dead, while lambs were being born with deformities, particularly unsightly potbellies, or in some cases without wool.

From the day the Harry blast took place to July of that year, an estimated forty-three hundred animals, or 25 percent of sheep herds, in southern Utah and Nevada expired.

Phones began to ring. People began to talk. A case was brought before the Federal District Court in Salt Lake City in 1956, but the government emerged victorious over the farmers, arguing a stretch of unusually cold weather and malnutrition were to blame.

Once all the dust settled both literally and figuratively, Operation Upshot-Knothole continued testing a week later with two more shots, Grable and Climax, while the people of the American Southwest continued with their lives.

Immediate and obvious effects on human beings were nil, prompting most to shrug off and forget the panic that Harry caused. It would be nearly two years until the next series of tests, Operation Teapot, would commence, giving some a chance to forgive and forget in between.

Senator Wallace F. B. Bennett took national security very seriously and assured the people of Utah this was the right step for their country. The delay was seen as an attempt to slow down and get it right, even if testing was part of a fast-paced international do-or-die nuclear arms race.

Behind closed doors at an AEC meeting, commissioners gathered to hash out the concerns of the people, to reflect on the string on mainland tests, and to plan for the unpredictable future that lay ahead. Commissioner Thomas E. Murray stated firmly, "We must not let anything interfere with this series of tests–nothing."

Commissioner Willard Libby was a little less brazen at the table chat but perfectly clear on where he, the AEC, and human beings should stand on atomic testing. "People have got to learn to live with the facts of life," Libby insisted, "and part of the facts of life are fallout."

# 7: Yearning to Be Yellow

Howard Hughes showed up unannounced to John Wayne's Palm Avenue offices with a fleet of seven Chevrolets one afternoon in the spring of 1954. The billionaire got out of the third car and demanded that every single employee exit the building so he and Wayne could deliberate. Wayne protested, so Hughes permitted only the secretary to stay inside and answer the phones. The rest would have to stand in the parking lot and chat among themselves until the two temperamental icons could have it out and reach an agreement over Wayne's interest in a new project. When he caught wind that Marlon Brando was considering the role, Duke knew he had to act fast.

The Wayne-Fellows company had altered direction after Wayne and Robert Fellows parted ways; friction mounted when the actor objected to Fellows's affair with one of their secretaries. Instead of folding while producing *Ring of Fear* and *Track of the Cat*, Wayne took control and lined up more back-to-back shoots than he could count on his fingers.

In the midst of waiting on Hughes, he managed to shoot *The High and the Mighty,* which would go on to earn six Oscar nominations, and *Blood Alley*, costarring Hughes's former rebellious protégé, Robert Mitchum. After Fellows's departure, the production company was quickly renamed Batjak in reference to a trading company from the 1948 movie *Wake of the Witch.* The secretary misspelled the word as Batjac on early documents, but Wayne let the little blunder stick and set up his own little haven for creative control off of Sunset Boulevard.

Wayne and Hughes had been communicating through messages sent over wire service before their face-to-face showdown to get the conditions just right. A four-page letter from Wayne officially inaugurated development in February 1954 to iron out a few beefs the actor had with RKO and vouch for a particular script he felt "enthused" about that Dick Powell had asked him to read.

"If my quarter of a century experience in this business means anything," Wayne writes in the letter, "I am positive this can be a very important, powerful picture. This is the first script–and it is only a first draft–I have read from your studio that really excites me. I have the honest feelings for this that I had when I approached pictures like *Stagecoach, Red River, The Quiet Man,* and *Hondo.*"

Duke goes on to ask for "the green light on it" to get the last commitment of his RKO agreement wrapped. He assured Hughes the picture would be no more costly than anything he had been pitched before by the studio. By Wayne's estimates, he had lost out on one million dollars because of his RKO commitments while waiting for a green light that never came. Wayne landed himself in hot water with Warner Bros., who were subsequently delayed with their production of *The Sea Chase* and demanded extra charges from the holdup be paid back by the star.

On top of the $250,000 acting fee, Hughes agreed to pay Wayne an extra $100,000 for his patience once their contract wrapped, but the actor responded with temperamental retaliation. A wire from Wayne was sent to RKO stating, "$100,000 does not even start to make the necessary adjustment. I insist it be done right now."

Wayne and Hughes left the Batjac building within twenty minutes of going inside, but the Duke didn't stay with his team for very long. He got in the third Chevy and drove off with the caravan of cars to traverse a maze of Los Angeles backstreets. He didn't return to Batjac until the next day, claiming to his curious staff that he was taken to an abandoned laundry business where he and Hughes finished negotiating their deal in a private back room.

On paper, the actor received $250,000 plus the extra $100,000 Hughes owed for the delaying damages upfront. Longstanding rumors speculate Duke did get his million-dollar wish quietly fulfilled, which could explain why he entered into the agreement so quickly.

All anyone got out of Wayne concerning details from the laundry room dealing was one juicy tidbit more exciting to the actor than his paycheck: Duke was going to star in the RKO production of *The Conqueror*, officially playing the role of Temüjin, otherwise known as Genghis Khan.

Dick Powell had been skeptical of the whole project right from the start. He was the one pegged to lead the monster-sized Mongol epic, but something didn't sit right with him concerning John Wayne playing Genghis Khan. Their races were different . . . physique completely askew . . . speech patterns and languages and facial features . . . the list of why Wayne was unsuitable for the part was endless. He had held off showing Wayne the script and was absent when the actor negotiated the deal with RKO for the part; he worried the production, and end result, would be absolute pandemonium.

Powell couldn't quite put his finger on exactly why the Western icon lobbied for this specific role and wouldn't take no for an answer, but the actor-turned-director figured the world's biggest star was in need of work, just as he was. And if that work was for Powell to direct Hollywood's biggest star in a high-paying and wildly ambitious project, so be it.

"Who am I to turn down John Wayne?" Powell humbly shrugged to the press. Acting was nothing more than dressing up in funny outfits and creating characters. As far as casting went, Powell figured there was no harm done.

The first order of business was to bring Wayne over to RKO and do a few fittings and makeup tests. The historically accepted image of Khan taken from a fourteenth-century silk tapestry became their model; it was one of the only traceable images of the warrior taken from the Yuan Dynasty. Thin strands of lengthy beard hair trickled down to his chest as an elongated mustache dipped down each cheek. Khan wore earrings and, like in most other depictions, a traditional garment around his head—all of which would play into Wayne's character design.

Wayne was comfortable dawning thick clothing thanks to the countless times he had played soldiers and cowboys covered in Stetson hats and ammo belts. Here, designed by Yvonne Wood, he'd have flowing silk clinging to carefully cut rubber. Cloth draped around his head with an array of hats that would make Audrey Hepburn jealous—they ranged from fluffy Mongolian loovuuz caps with faux fur wrapped in a rim to foam battle helmets made to look metallic. Red fabric spun across what looked like a black bowl with a horn would become the character's signature—and most marketable—style.

In order for his rippling masculine physique to be properly amplified—he was to spend a fairly sizable portion of the film either shirtless or in a sleeveless outfit—Wayne took to shaping his body. Rigorously hitting the gym to trim his belly and make his muscles bulge, Duke also apparently put himself on a crash diet to lose weight, though he was never officially instructed to do so. When starving himself seemed to be more of a challenge than he first thought, the seasoned star turned to medication to do the trick.

Dexedrine, an earlier over-the-counter amphetamine cousin to Adderall, was merely viewed as a helpful stimulant in Wayne's day; it was used as an athletic performance enhancer and thought to be a cure for attention deficit hyperactivity.

It wasn't uncommon for soldiers sent out on lengthy missions during the war or movie stars attached to a demanding role to pop a couple for focus. The popular pill was also known to decrease appetite and facilitate sudden weight loss. Wayne began to swallow as many as four every day to be able to squeeze into armor and achieve his trim Temüjin look. Never before had he been so dedicated to the actor's transformative process, but then again, up until that day, he had really only played versions of himself.

The elephant in the room was that Wayne's Caucasian features would have to drastically change to an Asian aesthetic without completely losing the star's recognizable crowd-drawing qualities. The solution, hardly considered taboo at that point in time, was to apply yellowface makeup. Hollywood had been rather successful at switching skin tones, and *The Conqueror* was far from being the first feature film to ever grapple with the practice of whitewashing.

From the 1915 silent adaptation of *Madame Butterfly* starring Mary Pickford to Katharine Hepburn playing the Japanese role of Jade in 1944's *Dragon Seed*, yellowface was not only common but accepted by Hollywood's heavyweights. Asian actors were rarely invited onscreen in American pictures, and when they were, it was to play an Eastern novelty to boast exotic flare; that or a no-line cook, laundry owner, or servant.

As a result of unequal prosperity and acts of segregation when it came to movie house admittance, Asian audiences were not recorded as making up a significant enough audience, and white audiences were rumored to avoid any with a more diverse cast. So, the snake would continue to feed itself its own tail, with producers unwilling to hire entertainers or craft stories for the specific ethnic group—people who avoided the movies as they saw nothing of themselves onscreen to watch.

Voltaire's play *Orphan in China,* which opened in 1767, is often noted as the American origin of yellowface, perpetuating stereotypes with white actors in a time when many had not met a person of Asian ethnicity. Skip ahead to the days of the Hollywood Golden Age, and you'll find the two most outrageous and infamous portrayals, Fu Manchu and Charlie Chan.

The former was introduced in literature by British novelist Sax Rohmer, portrayed in early UK silent cinema, and popularized through an American film series, starting with *The Mysterious Dr. Fu Manchu* in 1929. The character was portrayed by yellowed-up Caucasian actor Warner Oland then Dracula himself, Boris Karloff. The character of Fu Manchu was almost always a maniacal and over-the-top power-hungry villain (in Karloff's installment, ironically hunting for the tomb of Genghis Khan), and yes, popularized the droopy mustache fashion of the same name.

Charlie Chan was another book-to-screen adaptation of a Chinese stereotype (also originally portrayed by Warner Oland), but this time a mild-mannered detective type (with a troubled grasp of the English language). The character appeared in well over fifty films throughout the 1930s and '40s, with a revolving door of white actors taking over the role. Produced with slightly more reality behind them, the films actually fared well in the Asian movie market. Due to a severe lack of diversity, these characters were what audiences grew to believe was reality, as they were two of the only "Asian" protagonists.

Much can be said about the state of Hollywood with *The Good Earth* in 1937, one of the most notorious instances of yellowface in film history. The film outraged members of the Asian community but actually garnered a Best Actress win for Luise Rainer at the Academy Awards and did strong business at the box office. The beloved Pearl S. Buck novel, and later an Owen Davis play, detailed the lives of Chinese farmers; it would be completely whitewashed with American actors including Rainer, Paul Muni, and Charley Grapewin.

Buck and producer Irving Thalberg both planned the film with Chinese actors but changed their minds when they figured audiences would not be ready for that diverse of a picture. Almost the entire cast was Caucasian since anti-miscegenation laws brought on by the Hays Code forbid most mixed-race relationships from appearing onscreen.

Jack Dawn, a celebrated makeup artist known for lending his talents to help bring the world of *The Wizard of Oz* to life, worked on this film; he developed vinylite resin, a plastic application first used for *The Good Earth*'s yellowface portrayals. In a more favorable remembrance, Dawn's methods were revolutionary and helped make character faces, whether cowardly lions or whitewashed humans, look more elasticized. The techniques would again come into play when Wayne came galloping over to RKO.

Yes, Powell may have batted an eye about that history, but he moved on. No way could *The Conqueror* catch hell for its whitewashing portrayal. Marlon Brando may have passed on that script, but he was simultaneously prepping his own makeup-heavy role, Sakini, a peppy Japanese interpreter in *The Teahouse of the August Moon* over at MGM. Yul Brynner, with his cornucopia of ancestry, having Swiss, German, Russian, and, yes, even some Buryat (Mongol) flowing in his DNA, was readying for his top two race-bending career makers, *The King and I* and *The Ten Commandments*.

Powell figured the RKO crew was in good company; they weren't doing anything wrong. Wayne was beloved, knew what he was capable of, and that was that. It was common practice, facilitated by two headstrong individuals with a lot of cash and time invested in the project. For Dick to do anything other than his job would be ill-advised–this shining opportunity was certainly not the time for him to make waves and question whether anything being done could be deemed as insensitive.

Longtime RKO makeup artist Mel Berns took to the challenge; name an RKO movie, and he'd have been involved with it, having started with the company right from the beginning. Every classic from *Kong* to *Kane* was his doing, having risen through the ranks to be head of makeup. Hairstylist Larry Germain came aboard just before the Hughes era began–together the duo had formed a reliable system. Wayne brought along his own trusted makeup artist, Web Overlander, just to be sure they got the look just right.

They started with the actor's skin; any part of Wayne's white flesh that was showing got painted over with varying shades of yellow, white, and brown theatrical foundation makeup to strike the right tone. His eyes would have to give off the illusion of having an epicanthic fold, so the actor's sockets were surrounded by specially sized jelly eye molds taken from Asian models. Rubber bands were hooked to small hidden tabs by Wayne's temples to pull his own skin in whichever direction was needed. Then, using Dawn's patented product, the false lids were blended with his own, making the facial region puffier and giving off the desired race-bending effect. His natural brown eye color was about the only facial feature left untouched.

Next came false whiskers in the shape of a Fu Manchu mustache, albeit a very small one, glued to the edges of his upper lip and hanging wispily over his chin. Dark eyebrows were added for good measure before a shaggy black wig was placed on top of John Wayne's head.

Berns and Germain wiped their hands and deemed him passable. Powell gulped and worked with what was made available. Whether it was ill will left over from World War II and the propaganda that characterized the Axis Japanese as subhuman, the lack of diversity in film itself, or the sheer panic to hastily get something, anything, out the door and in front of the camera, the makeup tests to transform Caucasian John Wayne into Mongolian warlord Genghis Khan were figured to be a success.

Pill-filled and makeup heavy, John Wayne began his duties as an actor to construct a character and bring back to life the spirit of Genghis Khan; evidently more committed and determined than ever, no matter what was done, he'd give his audience a performance that no one would soon forget.

Pedro Armendáriz was an obvious choice to play Wayne's onscreen sidekick Jamuga, a character inspired by Genghis Khan's real-life rival (spelling altered from Jamukha), who allied with the conqueror to search for his stolen wife.

Armendáriz was born and raised in Mexico City and had held a series of odd jobs like tour guide and magazine editor until turning his attention to the Latin American film industry, then in its heyday. Clad almost always with a thick mustache or forest of facial hair, he made a living playing manly men, peasants, and Mexican revolutionaries.

He broke into Hollywood in the late forties with several roles in John Ford Westerns, pairing him with Wayne on multiple occasions, which instigated a close friendship. With dozens of Spanish language roles and several Ariel Film Awards (handed out by the Mexican Academy of Film) under his belt, the sidekick character in *The Conqueror* would be a cake walk for him, a no-brainer role taken to gain further American exposure.

Armendáriz quickly received the same eye treatment as Wayne, but his own dark hair and brown skin tone were an ethnic enough color for the crew to pass him off as a Mongol with hardly any makeup at all.

Not such obvious casting was that of Agnes Moorehead, who accepted the role of Hunlun (historically spelled Hoelun), Khan's mother. Only seven years older than Wayne, a trait of Moorehead's was her stern, often cold expression and mature demeanor, which made her seem older than she was. What made her take on the relatively small and unrewarding role is beyond anyone's guess.

Moorehead had gotten her start by joining Orson Welles's Mercury Players theater group, which landed her an immortal film role as the title character's mother in *Citizen Kane*. After success in radio, she was nominated in the 1940s three times for Best Supporting Actress Oscars: one for Welles's *Magnificent Ambersons* then another two for the social dramas *Mrs. Parkington* and *Johnny Belinda*.

Her sexuality became a subject of controversy, with many speculating due to her androgynous style that Moorehead was gay—even when married to John Griffith Lee and Robert Gist. The rumors may have cost her a role or two, but the seasoned actress seemed to tackle just about any genre out of curiosity.

Moorehead hadn't worked with RKO in well over a decade and didn't have evident connections with Wayne, Hughes, or Powell; still, she accepted the role and soon underwent the Mongol makeup ritual.

Rounding out the principal cast was a peculiar bunch of character actors from a varying background of genres. With a homely mug and a body built for brute roles, Thomas Gomez was frequently cast as henchmen until his roles as Curly in John Huston's *Key Largo* and his Oscar-nominated performance in *Ride the Pink Horse* increased his range. Gomez would become the first actor of Spanish descent to be up for an acting Academy Award. Later found lumbering in the background of Hughes's RKO productions like *I Married a Communist* and *Macao*, Gomez's chubby, intimidating features made him a top candidate for the antagonistic Wang Khan.

Newbie Lee Van Cleef had only just nabbed his first significant role in the Western *High Noon* before landing his small part in *The Conqueror* as Chepei. Gruff, tough, and full of grit, Van Cleef followed in Wayne's footsteps, climbing the Hollywood ladder with a string of B cowboy roles until he'd hit his niche in Sergio Leone spaghetti Westerns. Most would remember him in the iconic Mexican standoff with Clint Eastwood and Eli Wallach in *The Good, the Bad and the Ugly*.

Long-faced character actor John Hoyt would play a shaman, coming off of hits like *The Lawless, Julius Caesar*, and *Blackboard Jungle*. Gangster film staple Ted de Corsia came aboard, taking on the role of Kumlek, the father of the bride.

Serving five years in prison for armed robbery, Leo Gordon was released and turned to acting and screenwriting, penning Jack Nicholson's first feature *The Cry Baby Killer* and playing bank robber John Dillinger in *Baby Face Nelson* at the same time he landed his *Conqueror* role—that of a Tatar capitan. Having just appeared with Wayne in the Western *Hondo* surely aided his selection process.

William Conrad might be the most fascinating addition; before accepting his supportive ally role of Kasar, his famous voice echoed across every speaker in the country as Marshal Matt Dillon, a role he created and popularized in the *Gunsmoke* radio series before the iconic show ever aired on television. His unmistakable dulcet tone would later be heard narrating everything from *The Fugitive* to *The Rocky and Bullwinkle Show*. Conrad's only connection to the RKO project was a role in Hughes's remake of *The Racket* several years prior. His interest in accepting such a pea-sized involvement with the troubled production, like most of the film's cast and crew, remains a mystery.

*The Conqueror* was a sizable epic, a story packed with Mongol tribesmen and nomadic campers. Battlers and warriors and prison guards were needed to populate every scene, therefore every buff background performer in the book was enlisted to perform in the production. You had seasoned Western extras like Lane Bradford,

Gregg Barton, Phil Arnold, stuntman Ken Terrell, and Fred Aldrich, all pals with Wayne who popped up in split-second roles as saloon patrons and horse riders—even air force recruits in *Jet Pilot*, a project that did nothing more than decay on the shelf.

You had folks of every dark-skinned ethnicity to ease the makeup work: Syrian actor John George and Greek descendant Peter Mamakos, both with hundreds of credits and a knack for playing any nationality thrown their way. You had the period piece experts like Leslie Bradley and Torben Meyer, the latter best known for sitting at a card table in *Casablanca*.

There were bit-part careerists like Max Wagner and George E. Stone to fill the screen, even Fred Graham, another actor who appeared in countless projects, most famously the falling police officer at the beginning of Alfred Hitchcock's *Vertigo*.

*The Conqueror* credits twenty-three different stuntmen, a notably high number of men, who served as the rough-and-tumble stand-ins for the more dangerous aspects of production, such as the battle sequences. Wayne's frequent thrill-seeker Cliff Lyons and "best in the business" stuntman Charles Horvath were a couple who stood out, not to mention Ken Terrell, Ray Spiker, Chuck Roberson, Boyd "Red" Morgan, and Gil Perkins, who each had several hundred credits to their names.

Sons of the top dogs, Michael and Patrick Wayne and Norman Powell, all in their teens, were shoved into frame in blink-and-you-miss-it Mongol guard roles.

Chinese character actor Richard Loo, a frequent staple of 1940s and '50s World War II movies, was cast to add "Asian authenticity" in a hardly existent role, captain of Wang's guard. Loo was actually one of two actors of Asian descent in the film and the only one with a credited role—though most of his time was spent standing motionless.

Lacking in this story were any sort of diverse roles for women. Any lady cast beyond Moorehead, such as period piece background actor extraordinaire Jeanne Gerson, was either given the role of a slave or a dancer. One actress is simply credited as "girl in bath."

Professional dancer and choreographer Sylvia Lewis, fresh off of *Singin' in the Rain* and an impressive amount of musical appearances, was brought in to lead a dance sequence. Barrie Chase, best known for being one of Fred Astaire's dancing partners and the one-night-stand battered by Robert Mitchum in *Cape Fear*, was one of the backup dancer standouts, though the exploitative role had about as much depth as the paper the script was written on. It was a male-oriented film, designed by males for males with a story about masculinity.

True, a promising opportunity was that the sizable part next to Wayne's was for a female, an important role that sets the whole story in motion by providing the motivations for Khan's actions and conquests. Bortai, the Tatar princess and object of Temüjin's desires, required an actress to pull off a certain glamour and style of a distant time. But that would be her only attribute; that specific character was to be shapely and stunning, existing only for eye candy and not for emotion during the one-sided romance.

His working relationship with longtime muse Ava Gardner remained rocky as usual, probably because Howard Hughes was still hungry to exploit his dwindling collection of starlets. Sally Forrest was coerced into doing a near-nude dance in his period piece, *Son of Sinbad*, but it ultimately led her to end her contract with the studio.

Linda Darnell had become too big of a star to piddle around in Hughes's low-grade projects, so she, too, ended her working relationship with the mogul. Hughes had only *Devil's Canyon* blonde Virginia Mayo stashed around by the time *The Conqueror* entered production, so the mogul searched elsewhere, hoping to borrow whatever body they could manage to borrow.

Hughes had kept his nose relatively out of the casting process until the allure of festering over decisions regarding the female form was too strong to stay away. With every desirable actress's name thrown around as a suggestion, only one would truly do in Hughes's mind; he was sure to save the female lead for old flame Susan Hayward.

With hair flaming red and an equally fiery tempestuous Irish-Brooklyn ancestry running through her veins, Hayward was just about the hottest thing going in Hollywood at the time. She had clawed her way past a childhood full of poverty and abuse, landing modeling gigs before test screening for the role of Scarlett O'Hara in *Gone with the Wind*. She lost the coveted role to Vivien Leigh, ironically because of her look.

It would be her illuminating hair color that made her popular with producers, as the arrival to Technicolor film drummed up a demand for bright stars, both physically and emotionally. The actress bounced around dim B pictures and restrictive contracts with Warner Bros. and Paramount, landing her only significant gig at the time in *Reap the Wild Wind* in 1942, a swashbuckling Florida-set adventure costarring John Wayne.

"I learned at a very early age that life is a battle. My family was poor, my neighborhood was poor," Hayward said of her early life. "The only way that I could get away from the awfulness of life, at that time, was at the movies. There I decided that my big aim was to make money. And it was there that I became a very determined woman."

Hayward had become known as a feisty flirt on and off the screen, with a lust for fame and fortune driving her career, and her staggering looks awarding her with strings of opportunities in both fields. When the price wasn't high enough or a role not right, she had a habit of refusing work, even when contracted and therefore obligated—an act that also punished her with studios doling out no-pay suspensions. At the end of a long string of romances, she eventually settled, marrying actor Jess Barker in 1944 and giving birth to twin boys Gregory and Timothy.

Their relationship was volatile, ripe with competition and jealousy stemming from their drifting film careers. Barker was struggling to land anything of note, dumped into the role of stay-at-home father, while Hayward's stature rose throughout the end of the decade. Moving past sugary comedies like *I Married a Witch* and war stories like *The Fighting Seabees* (yet another project where she was paired with John Wayne), the red-headed queen of the silver screen signed a seven-year contract ($100,000 paid annually) with producer Walter Wagner and began appearing in Oscar-nominated productions.

Life should have been splendid for the family; instead, the stress of stardom and loneliness of her marriage prompted Hayward to start drinking and taking sleeping pills. A climactic fight between her and Barker led to him bruising her eye and Hayward pushing him into their swimming pool.

The turn of the decade saw tumultuous contrasts in her personal and public life. Hayward had scored three Academy Award nominations for her performances in *Smash-Up: The Story of a Woman*, *My Foolish Heart*, and *With a Song in My Heart*. Her talents brought a certain gritty realism to stories such as *I'd Climb the Highest Mountain*, while her chiseled aesthetic suited period piece *David and Bathsheba*; creative projects like *The Snows of Kilimanjaro* demonstrated her vast range.

With an increasing alcohol and medication intake clouding her judgment, Hayward's troubles escalated when she and Barker filed for divorce in February 1954. Naturally, at her weakest point, Howard Hughes slithered his way over to talk business.

Hayward had worked with RKO quite frequently during the time of the Hughes takeover but appeared only in *The Lusty Men*—a film the billionaire had little to do with. He had been keeping tabs on her ever since their failed rendezvous decades back, but the 1952 release costarring Robert Mitchum put the two back in contact with each other.

As Hayward battled her way through divorce court, juggled custody of her boys, and awaited plum film roles, thousands of dollars in legal fees and reprimands began to pile up. Always one to save and scrimp in fear of once again ending up penniless, Hayward was desperate to keep herself upright.

The character of Bortai was to be carried about and slung over shoulders. She was to stare daggers and ooze sex appeal from chariots venturing across the sand. She was to dance for her Mongol captors, shimmying her belly and twirling her wrists to rhythmic Mediterranean drums and bells. Hayward would have little to do physically and far less to say.

The rumor attached to RKO's epic is that Hughes had all along recognized the script's lack in quality and knew that any actress who played Bortai would suffer embarrassment beyond belief. Some have speculated Hughes was willing to destroy RKO and lose millions, all just to stick Hayward in a terrible flop. Vengeance, albeit many years later for their lackluster date, would therefore be his.

As *The Conqueror* stretched ever closer to becoming an actual, physical, in-production reality, Hughes endorsed Hayward as the movie's female lead and secured a deal with Fox to have her lent out. She declined the part at first but was told by Fox that she would be put on suspension if she didn't say yes. Lonely, watching her marriage dissipate and bank account dwindle, inflicting pain on herself with pills and cocktails, and at thirty-six, aging out of leading lady status, Susan Hayward accepted the role.

Absolutely no effort was put into altering Hayward's look as she arrived at RKO; her skin remained milky white and hair blazing red throughout the shoot. Hughes knew her image was a selling feature, even if she was playing an ancient Tatar princess from East Asia.

The actress had worked with Wayne multiple times in the past, so it's reasonable to believe that she took the role to be comforted by a familiar face. In 1953, the two of them had been awarded the distinction of being the two most popular stars on the planet by the Foreign Press Association. The prize was based on popularity, box office numbers, and award success; and the year this specific pair won was only the third installment. The award was an oversized novelty statuette called the Henrietta Award (aka World Film Favorites) and was presented to them at the Tenth Golden Globes.

In other words, Hughes had bagged the two most bankable and beloved stars possible. If he was swinging for the fences with such an expensive endeavor to save RKO, he had just struck the greatest assurance that people would actually see whatever was made. Whether he was just making the epic to get revenge or was simply, as per usual, hell bent on lust, Hughes had to have noticed that with the two biggest stars on the planet attached to *The Conqueror*, there'd be no way the film could fail.

# 8: Deciding on a Desert

*The Conqueror* was planned to be what Wayne and crew referred to as a "Chinese Western." Readers may be racking their brain, trying to come up with a proper image of what exactly that could be, and arriving at something along the lines of Jackie Chan and Owen Wilson in *Shanghai Noon*.

Oscar Millard had more of an adventurous Middle Eastern throwback in mind when he started assembling the script, channeling old black-and-white swashbuckling adventures like *Arabian Nights* to shape the right aesthetic. But there were just too many troublesome factors to keep the genre focused. With the principal cast locked down, the production designers drove themselves crazy with too little time and too much inspiration on their hands.

The rise of their biggest influence, the biblical epic, was cemented by Cecil B. DeMille's *Samson and Delilah* in 1949. Realistic stone walls were imitated by cheap foams and lumber. Tattered clothes covered each actor–the extras looked like they were plucked from the Old Testament. Historical period pieces had been a Hollywood staple since day one, but technological restraints and present-day distractions were no longer an issue.

With the invention of CinemaScope, an anamorphic lens that sped the aspect ratio, and the peak of Technicolor, a process of dyeing film strips to brighten scenes, the sword and sandal epidemic begun.

What DeMille did so skillfully was pay ten thousand dollars to historian Harold Lamb in 1935 so he could draft an accurate film treatment. It took more than ten years for the film to be released, with the famed director ditching production several times; but the wait was worth it as the detailed production value became incomparably immaculate. It earned almost ten times its budget, and producers rushed to follow in *Samson and Delilah*'s successful footsteps as new showy cinematic bells and whistles became readily available. They did not, however, have the luxury of time or the interest to conduct proper research.

No, John Wayne's Mongol movie was not the first to skewer history. Howard Hawks ripped ancient Egypt apart in 1955's *Land of the Pharaohs*; its unknown cast and lack of historic focus failed to make a dent in the box office. Talented thespians like Richard Burton were lambasted for their performance; his role in *Alexander the Great* was criticized when some felt the thirty-year-old was miscast as a teenager. As we know, real-life events don't usually unfold in the most cinematic of ways.

History was rearranged in favor of adding a completely fictional plot for audiences to relate to–usually a romance with a familiar lead.

Not just *The Conqueror*, but all of Hollywood productions at the time ended up with very distant representations of places and time. Yet, it is these cheesy 1950s' tropes that still surface in our minds when we think of Roman gladiators or Moses parting the Red Sea.

Think about those sprawling afternoon reruns that play around Easter on TCM. Clunky dialogue pontificated in an overdone delivery. A drowning trumpet score kicking off the credits to let the audience know what's to follow is indeed a film of biblical proportions. Overwhelming amounts of prop-waving extras making the environment look lived in. It's exhaustingly rare for the runtime to be under three hours. Many of these methods have not aged well as they are now viewed as tedious, corny, and obviously staged. This was not quite the intention.

Escapist stories were created for pure enjoyment and marketed to every soul that had a buck to spare. Factor in the clenching grip of the censorship board, who barked at any instance of realistic conflict, and the Catholic Church, which halted the release of anything immoral. Moviemakers had a lot of folks to answer to, and epic films aimed to please all but the historian.

Mervin LeRoy's *Quo Vadis* and Henry Koster's *The Robe* only furthered this style, raking in a profit comparable to a superhero movie in present day. That reason alone was surely why the formula didn't deviate and quickly became a financial tent pole for the studios. The spectacle of this type of film proved to be an insurmountable road block in television's runaway success as postwar people sought to have fun and escape; dark detective noirs of the 1940s no longer fit the mood.

Film ticket sales had taken a nosedive since 1949 due to a mixture of television's seemingly limitless popularity and dwindling cinema quality. Big-screen biblical escapism began to lure audiences back by the middle of the decade. This type of film came at a high cost, but producers like Howard Hughes were willing to take that risk in pursuit of such an enormous return.

RKO board president James R. Grainger was now busy touting to the eye-rolling press that *The Conqueror* would be the biggest adventure of the decade, despite his company providing nothing of merit for far too many years. Joyous that an actual production was on the table, few entrenched behind the scenes believed it would actually pass preproduction.

*The Conqueror* actually took shape at lightning speed once all of the big names signed on. Grainger's words, the talk-of-the-town cast, and the sheer grandiosity of a period piece seemed to get the studio head hopeful, a feeling Hughes surely never had since taking over the production company more than six years prior.

Early on, Hughes toyed with the idea of personally buying out everyone single crew and cast member's contracts just so he could have some peace and quiet to restructure the company. On other days, the aviator apparently expressed that *The Conqueror* could quite possibly end up being his masterpiece.

Even with a lonely Susan Hayward pining over her divorce, showing up at Hughes's office drunk and demanding his company, the man refused to part from the task at hand. Via the "eggs in one basket" method with every resource RKO had left, the whole company ran the risk of collapsing into a penniless laughingstock (more so than it already was) if every detail wasn't carefully accounted for and *The Conqueror* wasn't a success. With an unrestricted budget that blew past any comparable RKO project ever made, initial estimates of Hughes's frivolous spending pointed to a total of $2.8 million ($25 million adjusted for inflation).

The mogul officially gave *The Conqueror* the green light to go ahead with production in the spring of 1954 and hoped that the box office success would reverse the damage he had done over the past six years and give cinemagoers the greatest adventure the big screen had ever seen.

Morale had hit an all-time low at RKO, but the promise of such a large-scale production actually going through glistened as a beacon of hope that the company certainly wasn't licked yet. After all, they had the Duke! John Wayne! The king of the Old West! Up until that point, the star had not appeared in a period piece other than an old Western, *Allegheny Uprising*, which took place in Colonial America of the 1760s (and he was an extra in 1928's *Noah's Ark*).

That's why *The Conqueror* was special: It was a theatrical flex that ruffled his image. Standing in front of the camera and just doing whatever it was he was told wasn't going to cut it this time around. He was playing a real figure from another era, which required research and dedication to present authenticity.

For such a stable star who didn't seem to mind typecasting to forgo all that was familiar to him pointed to the fact that he was interested in shaking up the monotony of his career. But for an actor who never cared to tinker with the more high-falutin' methods of performing arts to jump into such a vastly different role . . . could the actor really have taken on such a stretch just for the sake of work?

Sure, Wayne was bound to RKO by contract and wanted to wrap up the deal so he could move on; but one would hope he was at least a smidge excited about branching out. Most critics had been particularly rough on his acting style, expressing that his typecast image came across as flat and emotionless. There was also his quiet desire for recognition from the academy; he had yet to earn an award at this point in his career. "The Academy Awards are important," Wayne said. "They've given size to our industry. They hand us back a little of the dignity I feel we deserve."

He did repeat that he thoroughly loved the script, a fact that could have blinded him to the fact he was not right for any part in that story. Friends and family members have said he was immediately attracted to Khan's confident characteristics. And to be fair, he did try to pull together a character different from his gunslinger image during rehearsals.

"You're beautiful in your wrath," Wayne uttered to himself over and over in attempts to properly recite his dialogue out loud. Lines like "While I live . . . while my blood burns hot . . . your daughter is not safe in her tent," or "She is a woman . . . much woman! Should her perfidy be less than that of other women?" unsurprisingly did not role off the actor's tongue.

With most of Millard's words separated by ellipsis for dramatic effect, the delivery came out especially flat and drawn out. Every second sentence seemed to end with the words "Tatar woman." We'll never know if anyone got to hear Wayne attempt a Mongolian accent—no publicized account of that trial-and-error moment seems to exist. The dialogue in his own drawl was causing him enough grief to call up the writer days before production began. "You've got to do something about these lines," Wayne begged Millard over the phone. "I can't read 'em."

The screenwriter insisted that he had already written the script specifically for Wayne and tailored each dramatic syllable for the time period—a style he referred to as "archaic flourish." He replied by saying he'd have to rewrite the entire script for the actor, something that was way too late in the game to do. Wayne gulped, knowing full well no amount of practice and mouth exercises in the world would help him sound like Genghis Khan.

The movie star began to fear that he was about to risk alienating his loyal audience with the role and quietly doubted his abilities to portray the great ruler. And that was just how Wayne saw him—great. The acts of rape and slaughter and cannibalism were either dismissed or the facts just generally were unknown to Wayne. Either way, the actor felt some admiration for Khan and deemed him to be a mighty conqueror indeed.

Duke explained his project selection process by saying, "I want to play a real man in all my films, and I define manhood simply; men should be tough, fair, and courageous, never petty, never looking for a fight, but never backing down from one, either."

In the postwar era, it wouldn't be a stretch to say America had the general feeling that they were just that. So, the character had to reflect strength in as much a positive light as possible. Unlike the pained private eyes of the 1940s and the seismic cinematic shift to come in the 1960s, the films of the 1950s featured few flawed protagonists in order to provide more wholesome family entertainment. Recognizing his own limits, even the limits of good and bad taste, Wayne reexamined his Mongol approach and looked to his manly mantra for an answer.

"The way the screenplay read, it is a cowboy picture, and that is how I am going to play Genghis Khan," Wayne announced to Dick Powell. "I see him as a gunfighter."

The director must have winced, wondering how in the world they could possibly pull that one off. People would expect an actor to adhere to some minimal line of accuracy. But again, in the postwar era, the hero was all the rage; and no one better than John Wayne could play your true blue American hero. He had fans after all–loyal deep-pocketed fans who adored his Westerns.

Susan Hayward was already bringing her tried-and-true physicality to the screen. She demanded her natural glamorous essence– even in dry and dusty desert sands–was not to be tampered with. The Duke, therefore, was able to throw all attempts to speak with an accent out the window, which probably in the end for Powell and the team was a blessing in disguise.

Once again, a cowboy he would be, albeit a gun swapped for a sword and in a picture that had several competing genres. The concoction that became the "Chinese Western" was therefore born– despite the film having nothing to do with China or the West.

On the technical side, production was far from a cake walk. Determining that CinemaScope lenses were the only devices fit to capture such an epic image, the overcrowded production quickly became a "too many cooks in the kitchen" scenario.

Joseph LaShelle was a nine-time Oscar-nominated director of photography noted for his work with comedic director Billy Wilder. He had already earned himself an Oscar for his cinematography work on *Laura* before entering the production via Howard Hughes's insistence.

William E. Snyder was a resident DP at RKO who was used to capturing B movies like *Creature from the Black Lagoon*. Leo Tover had the longest career of the bunch, starting out in silent pictures like the original *Great Gatsby*, while Harry J. Wild came with a background of *Tarzan* sequels.

With such varied views of film production, it was evident early on that their ideas were not going to gel–even if comingling meant creating something brand spanking new. The majority of movies have one director of photography to oversee lenses and lighting; because of his high hopes for such a colossal picture and some crew versus cast clashes along the way, Howard Hughes ended up appointing four.

Perplexing decisions were coming from art decoration, where films receive their distinctive aesthetic. Carroll Clark was RKO's long-term art director, having joined the studio in the early 1930s.

He did uncredited work on *King Kong*, later turning to otherworldly Disney live-action features like *Mary Poppins*. Albert S. D'Agostino had a hand in more than three hundred RKO films–many noted for his gritty style.

By the time Hughes came along, these two had been paired together for a decade and had developed a solid working relationship with a track record of professional experience behind them. Both were applauded for their hand in the art deco RKO look under Van Ness Polglase's decorative movement.

The sleekness radiating from Rogers-Astaire ballrooms to the futuristic RKO logo itself was the studio's image and a staple in the work of these men. Something as massive or ethnic as *The Conqueror* had rarely come their way before. Their domed tents for the Mongol camp and frivolous golden interiors were partly based on history; the cylindrical nomadic tent structures known as *yurts* were represented to a degree. But the general atmosphere and extravagance of the camps catered more to a general ethnic appeal as the golden production rule clearly demanded them to be exotic and engaging at any cost necessary.

Dick Powell was saddled with the toughest task of all–cohesively bringing these elements together. For a second-time director to be commanding such a big-budget behemoth required help to push the project successfully onward.

Powell and Hughes were both producers on the picture, but the eccentric studio head was hardly involved after logistics were finalized. Masterpiece or not, Hughes still had an avalanche of lawsuits to fight against and airline operations to attend to. "Dick, this one's all yours," Hughes advised. "Just make the biggest spectacular ever. Don't worry about the money." He was still battling Floyd Odlum for the remaining 5 percent of RKO stock, offering himself up on the other end of the telephone line when Powell needed help.

Friend and writer Richard Sokolove served as an associate producer on *The Conqueror* to help with the day-to-day preparations, but he had no other credits to his name. He would only go on to produce Powell's next picture, making him severely inexperienced and essentially pointless.

Powell's own side projects may have slowed preproduction from time to time. Through his company, Powell launched a television program called *Four Star Playhouse,* which starred himself and David Niven in different anthological episodes from 1952 to 1956. Serving as the creator and producer to boot, he reveled in the creative medium, spending more of his knowledge and energy on television than he did his own movie.

Wife June Allyson remembered her husband contending with phone calls all night long when he trudged home from work. "Day after grueling day, Richard interviewed and screened an army of actors and extras, and when he was through, he had seen 2,000 people," Allyson wrote. "He would come in and say, 'Let me sit here in silence,' or 'Just let me eat without talking.'"

The director struggled with round-the-clock meetings that ranged from script notes to legal roadblocks. Lawfully, if there were going to be horses—and a panther—there had to be a wrangler. Mel Koontz was the absolute best in the business, having famously directed Jackie, MGM's most remembered lion mascot used for their logo from 1928 to 1956. He could do the job all right, but the question then became *Where are all the critters and their riders going to come from?*

Linwood Dunn, a pioneer in RKO special effects, had been part of the *King Kong* team. He safely paired Katharine Hepburn with a leopard in *Bringing Up Baby* and participated in the mammary debacle in Hughes's own film, *The Outlaw*; Dunn was the one who blurred the definition on close-ups of Jane Russell's cleavage by softening the lens with fabric.

He, along with RKO effects artist Daniel Hays, carefully staged these looming Mongol battles using Dunn's own renowned travelling matte method. Using a blue screen, actors could be paired with a background—or animal—they themselves were not present with. The photography trick had been used for decades and would allow for close-up shots of actors galloping on fake or single horses in near-seamless shots. Unfortunately, a cumbersome trend that came with these colossal costume dramas was that everything was to be shot on location for grandiose style and excitement.

*The Conqueror* was no exception and would forgo trickery for prestigious glory, all at the expense of a pretty penny. Dunn's brilliant cost-effective technology was rendered useless for the sake of authenticity.

The American studio system had only just recently begun venturing outside of the country, with John Huston's *Treasure of the Sierra Madre* in 1948 being one of the first completely shot on location in Mexico. Movies like *Secret of the Incas* in 1954 starring Charlton Heston were later green lit all because they had an exotic location to market. Mongolia was a little too far and costly to shoot for RKO as was their second choice of North Africa, so a local substitute was chosen in its place.

The heftiest task was to find a barren American location that could emulate the Gobi Desert: red sand and chiseled peaks with no signs of life. It needed to be somewhere that could host a small army and make it seem the actors were pillaging prime territory eight hundred years back.

The Mojave Desert had been home to hundreds of movie productions beforehand, including the majority of Wayne's own Westerns. Its vibrant sand and rock covered southeast California, western Arizona, and southern Nevada, including the bright lights of Las Vegas. To the north were the sizzling slopes of Death Valley, and west was the gold-gifting Sierra Nevada range. You'd be hard-pressed to find a more diverse and exciting landscape around the world let alone in the United States.

Harold Lewis, *The Conqueror*'s location manager, began his hunt in that terrain. The lonesome butte hills beckoned to Lewis; he searched in the country's sparse corner. The desert dunes and rock spires were unimaginable to a Hollywood suit tucked away in his office. Surely moviegoers would be fooled by the natural wonders hiding in their own country. Harold Lewis and Dick Powell toured a total of eight states until they found what they were looking for.

"By chance," Lewis described when speaking about local resident W. Brown Hail, "I talked to a Chamber of Commerce man in St. George, who said he had flown the hump in World War II. He was familiar with the Gobi and advised us to look at the canyons around St. George. We looked and settled immediately."

The Anasazi and Paiute Native American tribes called the rocky terrain home before the arrival of Europeans and settlement for cotton farming by Lorenzo and Erastus Snow in 1861. Pioneers of the Jesus Christ of Latter-Day Saints faith came in during the mid-nineteenth-century movement, when life in southern Utah began to thrive under Mormon irrigation technology. The town took its name from George A. Smith, a Latter-Day Saints apostle and became home to the oldest operating LDS temple in the world.

What Harold Lewis wanted was a patch of land known as Dixie State Park. Later nicknamed for the area's founders, it officially adopted Snow Canyon as its title in 1962. The seventy-four hundred acres of concentrated dunes and wrinkled orange Navajo sandstone became the remnants of a meeting between a volcanic eruption and an ancient sea. Not a single road led to this little oasis at that point. Horseback or foot were the only options to get there. Used for cattle grazing and recreation, the untouched and generally unknown gem was their Mongolian ticket. Situated just ten miles north of St. George, for once *The Conqueror* was blessed with fortune and good luck.

Film-wise, the town was inexperienced. Wayne's first production, *The Big Trail,* briefly filmed nearby back in 1928. Ray Milland's *A Man Alone* was shooting a quick scene when Harold and Dick came by to look. Their arrival would forever alter the shape and feel of little St. George if production was okayed; housing hundreds of people would potentially jog business but no doubt leave behind a footprint. One hundred twenty miles northeast of Las Vegas, it was the only major community around and in need of some positive publicity.

A Chamber of Commerce meeting held near the end of March was where W. Brown Hail mentioned the arrival of eight Hollywood scouts among mundane agenda items like the potential construction of a shirt and duffel bag factory. Little was known about the production as far as its content, stars, or the involvement of Howard Hughes. Only Dick Powell's name was recognized, and this group consisted of starstruck fans. Local development was kicked into high gear immediately, and local crews began constructing proper roads to Snow Canyon. The town was tipped off, and the consensus was that this was one of the biggest opportunities the community ever had to come their way.

One of the many mythic stories surrounding Howard Hughes concerns a time when he was chatting with a business associate on New Year's Eve. Realizing the date and time, Hughes was surprised to learn that the man was stone-cold sober. The man's defense was that he was Mormon and did not drink or smoke. He was abruptly hired as an aide and suddenly set a strict precedent for all employees to follow. Howard liked Mormons because he could trust that lust and liquor vices would not hinder business.

Throughout the 1940s and 1950s, Hughes's personal staff grew and grew until there were only Mormons left on the payroll—the very same people who would care for him later in his life. Their apparent cleanliness appealed to his obsessive-compulsive side, plus he identified with their sobriety as Howard himself did not drink.

When he learned that a potential shooting location was a Mormon town and hypocritically near his precious party spot, Sin City, Hughes signed off immediately. He could trust everything would go smoothly; therefore, production could finally begin in April 1954.

Carroll Clark and Albert S. D'Agostino's Mongol camp exteriors were at last erected in Snow Canyon. Mel Koontz wrangled hundreds of horses shipped from LA training facilities, but later went door knocking around local farms when it became clear there wouldn't be enough. Linwood Dunn and Daniel Hays hoped to high heaven no one would get themselves hurt during these giant battle sequences, which bordered on special effects and real-life combat. With such a remote shoot location, the budget skyrocketed to $4 million ($40 million adjusted for inflation), putting it on track to be one of the most expensive movies of the decade.

Four chartered planes carried John Wayne, Pedro Armendáriz, Susan Hayward, and the principal cast; semi-trucks with costumes and props convoyed up the road to Utah. June Allyson recalled a fifty-five-mile-per-hour wind that threatened to botch their landing; it had already destroyed their production tent, serving as what she felt was a bad omen. The plane landed, and what became clear was that St. George would be overrun and primitive living was the only option for the Hollywood elite.

All nine local school buses doubled as a transport to and from the bumpy road-in-progress to Snow Canyon. The high school became the costume storage shed for over twelve hundred outfits and the space where Wayne put on his armor every morning. An estimated twenty-two motels opened their doors to house the 220 cast and crew members. The Boy Scouts donated tables and chairs so everyone had a spot to sit.

Wendell Motter happened to be headed away on National Guard duty, so he happily rented out his house to John Wayne and his third wife-to-be, Pilar Pallete; his own wife, Betty, lived with the neighbors next door.

Susan Hayward brought along her twin sons and rented Howard Schmutz's house. The lineups for autographs outside her home got to be so long, they were limited to two and a half hours per day. An article in the local paper prepped the residents for the arrival of Hollywood folk with a specific line urging parents to talk to their teenagers about how to "cooperate in Miss Hayward's midst."

Trust began to develop between the stars and the residents as *The Conqueror* crew made themselves comfortable. Dick Hammer's diner became a consistent hangout for folks of every ilk to come unwind after a day on the set or a day on the farm. They swapped RKO woes with the locals, who nonchalantly informed them nuclear tests had been recently conducted nearby—you know, bonding banter among newfound pals.

"Hold everything!" demanded Dick Powell. As sets were going up and cast members were flying out, Harold Lewis discovered through run-of-the-mill conversation that Yucca Flat and Frenchman Flat in Nevada had been used for atomic bomb research about 137 miles west. Unshaken, many locals claimed they saw mushrooms clouds and flashes of light in the distance; they had been encouraged by the US government to watch "history unfold." When word got out and spread through *The Conqueror* crew, there was no hiding "history." Lewis and Powell convened—production was put on hold. Alarmed that no one had mentioned the nuclear news, proper research was to be done in order to deem St. George safe.

Maybe they learned about the site when scouting and kept it to themselves or never read much into the potential hazards to begin with. It is damning to say no one bothered to share this with the crew, but it is highly unlikely location scouts wouldn't have looked into the matter in the first place; it was well beyond national news.

Whatever the case—rumors spread like wildfire. Though terms like *radiation* and *fallout* were not widely understood, people had concluded weapons of this nature were dangerous on some level ever since they wreaked havoc on Japan.

Three months before shooting, the thermonuclear Castle Bravo test held at Bikini Atoll in the Marshall Islands unexpectedly contaminated nearby locals and a nearby Japanese fishing boat that sailed too close to the proving ground. Many were evacuated and quarantined as signs of radiation sickness began to surface on their bodies. Vomiting, diarrhea, and nausea took hold as burns and open soars covered the Pacific Islanders' skin. Because of such a gross miscalculation, Bravo was by far the worst nuclear accident to date. It was widely publicized and marked somewhat of a turning point in public opinion on atomic testing.

Howard Hughes was notified about the problem. He assured the frantic director they'd solve it by any means necessary. He vowed to look into the issue and immediately contacted the Atomic Energy Commission to explain the situation. Their response? No worries. Shooting in St. George is completely safe. And that was that.

Whatever was driving Howard Hughes began to dwindle. Six long years of squabbling left him drained. Deeper yet, the man still despised the Reds and wanted Communism eliminated by all costs. This may have instilled a grander unabashed faith in his government while the allure of atomic weaponry gave him a patriotic blinder that saw only Soviets as potential targets.

Hughes gave the okay to Dick Powell, who exhaustedly agreed. Production would go ahead as long as the AEC said it was okay to do so. It didn't matter much to the head honcho anyway—Hughes never stepped foot in St. George or Snow Canyon. He corresponded through telephone calls and mailed photographs.

Now, you just don't overcome something as big as the threat of nuclear testing fallout. People on *The Conqueror* crew were talking, some considering this the end of the line for them. The budding consensus was that Hughes was crazy and Powell inexperienced– their assurances helped some, but there still was collective panic that their lives were going to be put in danger. And for most of the grunt workers, a picture didn't seem like a solid enough reason to put their life on the line.

In full Genghis Khan regalia, their star stepped up to address the troops. Clad in his Fu Manchu mustache and blackened hair; skin slathered into a darkened tone; and strapped together in golden breast plates, satin shoulder pads, and a furry loovuuz hat, John Wayne spoke to the people. Hands shaking, not from nerves but from a consistent dose of Dexedrine pills, he was a rippling version of himself fans and coworkers had not seen before.

"It would be un-American," he argued, "to step away from production now." He insisted that everyone ought to show a little faith in their government and in their superiors. Neither Hughes nor Powell nor the AEC was trying to wrong them. If they said it was okay, Wayne said, he believed them.

Filming began in May 1954; hardly three months of preproduction had ensued to piece the picture together. From the day Wayne and Hughes struck a deal, makeup, costume design, sets, and location scouting were miraculously and evidently far too hastily prepared. The general mood lifted once Wayne comforted the crew and denounced swirling fears.

The actor was no stranger to Utah; Wayne had shot scenes for the film *Hondo*, a 3-D Western with Geraldine Page a couple of years back. Nothing had happened to him, so the general consensus was that all was fine.

To illustrate his point further, Duke brought a Geiger counter to set before shooting was to begin. This nifty portable box could read ionizing radiation by the wave of a connected wand. Depending on the degree found, the universally recognizable crackle of static starts to hiss. Sure enough, Duke got the contraption working atop a nearby bluff, where he waved the wand in all directions. The counter hissed and clicked out of control. Confused, Wayne resituated himself and waved the Geiger wand to overwhelming results. Apparently, he just scowled at the machine and let the wand drop as Dick Powell watched the demonstration from nearby. "Thing must be broken," he concluded before readying himself for a long month's worth of work in the Utah desert.

# 9: Stories from the Sand

When the cast and crew woke each morning, the sky was still dark and the desert cool. It would likely have been everyone's favorite part of the day, seeing as how that would be the only time there'd be shade and a tolerable temperature. Of course, it would have simultaneously been the absolute worst moment for them, too; the fear and dread of having to endure another round of shooting *The Conqueror* surely robbed everyone of a rational mood.

The trip out to Snow Canyon was crowded and tedious; hundreds climbed into school busses, some carrying swords and makeup, others dressed for fourteenth-century war. The several hundred actors, extras, camera operators, and others didn't cut it, though, when it came to bringing together such a large-scale production; townspeople from St. George were roped into the mess to help run cables or hold reflectors and booms. Folks were needed to tend to the lonely, overheated livestock and be there as an extra pair of hands or a stand-in. An estimated seven hundred residents were hired to come aboard and work in some capacity during the production—a move that no doubt contributed to risky logistics and an exploding budget.

Then there were the "Mongol" tribesman and warriors who populated faux villages to give *The Conqueror* as much production value as the RKO team could muster. The salt-of-the-earth St. George townsfolk were ill-prepared and unsuitable to supply the desired gruff-and-tough combatant image . . . or maybe there just wasn't enough yellow makeup to go around.

Dick Powell got wind of the nearby Shivwits band of Paiutes, a tribe indigenous to the southern Utah area. To him, they looked authentic in a primitive sort of way. From afar, with all of the horseback action and sword swinging blurring people's view, the crew figured no viewer would stop to question if the extras were really Mongolian; their skin was darker, and that's all that mattered.

More than three hundred were hired to suit up in furs and armor to do battle for the director. The tribe was fed, but not much more hospitality came their way. Left off the books, they were paid in pocket change—two or three dollars per day, ten if they could ride a horse. The Shivwits' presence during the more spectacular shooting days brought the total number of people standing out in the desert on set to above one thousand.

Additionally shot in Warner Valley, fifteen miles south of St. George, and in Harrisburg, twelve miles north, caravans of stampeding horse riders certainly illuminated the desert scenes, but the strenuous demands took a toll on each body. The heat in southern Utah, particularly in the months of June, July, and August—exactly when *The Conqueror* shot—was expected to hover around the 120 degrees Fahrenheit mark each day. There were rarely any clouds to provide a glimpse of shade. No plant life other than low-lying shrubs provided something to stand under.

In the rocky, uninhabited desert of Snow Canyon, major players like John Wayne and Susan Hayward had personal trailers, a few others had tents, but most of the one thousand had to stand out in the open, running behind bluffs when shade was made available. Keeping in mind this was the 1950s, sunscreen was unavailable. Protection wasn't even thought of.

For those onscreen, skin care didn't matter much; the wooly hats, cloaks, and tight body-hugging armor made of all sorts of absorbent foams, cloths, and rubbers sealed in every drop of perspiration.

The sun was treacherous, and overexposure was making the team sick. On numerous occasions, people working on the film fainted or began vomiting from heat stroke. A medic was there to help, but the cases of overheated employees became so frequent, they could hardly keep up. If people had to be trucked back to the small town hospital, which up until two years prior had been operated out of a two-story family home, a journey ten miles down the bumpy make-shift dirt road made sure they were in complete agony before treatment.

Wayne shuffled his way over to the high school in the cool mornings to pick up his costume and get suited up by the team. The eye molds and yellow makeup were applied at that time, too; but even Duke was no match for the blistering rays. For any outdoor scene, the whole yellowing process would have to be reapplied take after take; all of the dust and dirt and grime floating around and coating his face with another layer made everything take that much longer. Multiply that time and effort by every other actor who had to endure the warmth while remaining yellow, and you can understand why the makeup crew faced certain defeat.

For all of Hayward's problems with the shoot—remaining glamorous being one of them—the heat wasn't as big of a worry as it was for the others. Her revealing dresses helped her skin to breathe while for most of her outdoor scenes, she was hauled around in a shaded chariot. She had a more vicious enemy to contend with . . . and no, it wasn't Howard Hughes. A live panther was requested for a scene to give perhaps authenticity and a grander sense of realism to the film. Whatever the case, the "tamed" wildcat was delivered and placed by the actress's side.

Two accounts of the same incident have been shared over the years; in one, Hayward waved her arm in front of the panther, which decided to nip at her limb. It narrowly missed taking a chunk out of her, thanks to Hayward's quick reaction. The second account had Hayward waiting around for the cameras to roll beside her feline costar; the panther apparently grew infatuated with a waggling feather in her costume and actually pounced. The cat was quickly wrestled off of her, and Hayward was quickly pulled to safety. Either way, it was replaced by a hand-painted statue.

Pedro Armendáriz didn't have it any better; he was galloping along on a horse for one scene when it stumbled over some rocky, unleveled terrain. Armendáriz was thrown off suddenly, landing face-first on the hard ground. The actor broke his jaw, lost three teeth, and had to be rushed to the hospital for twenty-six stitches. Production shot around him for eight days until he came back, in pain, but determined to carry on with his performance.

When it wasn't the heat or misbehaving mammals at fault, it was the sand. A constant wind seemed to whip through the canyon, stirring up dust in all sorts of hazy directions, a problem that stopped production on several occasions. Being a film set and all, control was preferred; so, to strike up the right dramatic effect and keep with consistency on the odd day the wind kept still, giant fans were brought in to blow the sand around in bigger clouds.

On days requiring stampeding horses–a logistical headache unto itself while the dust got so unbearably kicked up–Dick Powell's directions were often muffled through a surgical mask to keep the particles at bay.

All that grit and grime stuck around, too. It was in actors' costumes. Woven into their hair. Taken into their lungs after every breath. Local restaurateur Dick Hammer came to the catering rescue with a crew of fifty-five and his "stainless steel kitchen on wheels" to serve hundreds of hot lunches. What he and everyone else failed to account for was the healthy topping of sand that coated each of their outdoor-ingested meals; June Allyson said it was referred to on set as "Utah chili powder." Everyone, the actors especially, had to be hosed down at the end of the day to get the sand out, and working showers were even set up to help keep the crew clean.

Internally, well, that was a different story.

Nothing much could be done about the amounts being inherently eaten except a good swig of water to wash out the taste. That, in itself, became a major pain; a makeshift well was dug in the dirt to ensure enough aqua was onsite to quench the *Conqueror* community's thirst. Hayward, Wayne, Agnes Moorehead, and a few crew members were allegedly crowded around the watering hole when storm clouds rolled in and rain poured over their heads.

A few tents were standing, but the canvases did not provide enough shelter to go around. Jeeps, buses, and any vehicle that could come save the day started hauling soaked extras and waterlogged equipment. The well proved to be a problem and contributed to rising waters, turning everything into a muddy swampland; it delayed production for days. When cameras finally started rolling again, everyone's drinking glass was half water and half earth.

The physical elements took a toll, but by far the mental warfare and internal battles happening on the *Conqueror* shoot burned the principal players far deeper than the sun ever could. For starters, many felt that Dick Powell just wasn't up to snuff. To be fair, a director of any experience level tasked with babysitting a crew of one thousand would absolutely have high blood pressure. To break the tension, Powell clung to humor and apparently crooned crackly renditions of old tunes through a bullhorn. Critics later figured that the picture's period piece style failed to suit his skill set or, worse yet, his interest.

Film cans were routinely shipped back to Culver City, where Hughes chewed his nails at the sight. He'd frequently call Powell's hotel in St. George–almost always in the middle of the night–frantic over the money being dished out and the dailies he'd been sent. The budget blew past the four million dollar mark, with no end in sight, as technological and environmental complications delayed production. The St. George residents taking part, who were initially unplanned for but desperately needed, pushed the spending sum upward as did the number of meals needed to feed the growing roster.

Mother Nature's apparent objection to *The Conqueror* should have been a fairly acceptable excuse for delays, but more often than not, ridiculous motives were behind the standstills. A segment requiring Wayne to hold a pet falcon somehow halted the whole show; when the bird got sick and needed care, everything stood silent for multiple days until it was able to perform its one scene.

Hughes fretted over RKO's emptying bank accounts but was seemingly capable of only working amid brewing trouble. He worried alright but offered up few solutions to Powell, instead suggesting unscripted add-ons like Lee Van Cleef giving a barbaric shirtless dance and the addition of a pet black bear for the Mongols, which was also made to do a little dance.

At the same time, Hughes had one foot out the door, having absolutely nothing else in the works for further film projects. His eyes were drifted away from *The Conqueror*, though no one who knew the busy man would have expected anything else. He was off developing aircrafts with manufacturing business Convair, an effort to rival the Boeing 707 for TWA while simultaneously attempting to transfer control of his own aircraft company to his medical foundation.

On top of that, the battle raged on with Floyd Odlum for the remaining 5 percent of RKO–the industrialist still wouldn't budge. Odlum's insatiable resentment made him toy with the billionaire, and he figured the leverage could earn him a couple more pie pieces out of Hughes's other companies. Hughes was equally as stubborn, desperate not to lose the proverbial chess game by being ready to pounce on any options that presented themselves first: dissolve RKO, sell again, or continue to operate at a reckless snail's pace.

Duke could hardly get through the days on set. With the scorching heat weighing down on the physicality of the Genghis Khan role, Wayne was exhausted having to run, ride, and do battle with prop blades. At his most docile, he tripped and stumbled over every line, fearful of giving the words any hint of inflection by spitting them past his lips as quickly as possible to be over and done with them.

"When he complained about something, and he never did it belligerently, he was always right," Lee Van Cleef recalled. "He knew as much about making movies as anyone. He was in trouble because of the part and because of the director."

Glimpses in the mirror of himself as Khan began to make him shudder. In the middle of the shoot it was becoming clear that he was not right for the role, but Duke also apparently saw that the whole film was destined to be a turkey he should never have endorsed from day one. Costars picked up on his disinterest and emotional withdrawal; the world's most popular actor was publicly counting down the days until his job was complete and he could move on to a better part.

The daily perk that kept him going was his increasing intake of Dexedrine pills, just enough of an adrenaline boost to give him the pep to keep appearing as Genghis Khan. Wayne relied on the substance so heavily, he had to wrap his hand in a towel at breakfast in the morning because the limb shook so uncontrollably.

Hayward's substance of choice for coping was alcohol, no small feat to find in a desert Mormon town. Availability didn't seem to slow her from showing up to set drunk, apparently entering into disruptive laughing fits. Some have attributed the erratic behavior to her frustration with the awkward dialogue. She held up production to review each take in search of physical flaws that would call for a reshoot. Sunlight sparkling off her nose led her to get director of photography Joe LaShelle sacked and replaced.

Petrified of her apparent lack of dancing skills, Hayward spent her time with choreographer Bob Sidney to practice the film's out-of-place dance number, a hip-shimmying and sword-swinging sequence in a transparent negligée. Self-conscious of her legs, which she deemed to be far too thin, she almost demanded the whole idea be thrown out. Instead, she negotiated that specified shots of her own body would be inserted with shots of a dancing double.

Sons Timothy and Gregory ran about, keeping their mother company and having the time of their lives with other celebrity progenies like Pedro Armendáriz Jr. and Patrick and Mary Wayne. When she wasn't busy with autograph signings, Hayward was alone and prone to isolate herself for the evening to imbibe nonstop. If she did, by chance, stick her head out the window for air, she would have been subjected to the gushy sights of her costar and his wife-to-be smooching in the neighboring home.

Wayne's marriage to second wife Chata Baur was apparently a stormy coupling full of jealousy and one he described "like shaking two volatile chemicals in a jar." After separating in 1952, Wayne fell for Peruvian actress Pilar Pallete while out on a location scout. One year of courtship later, he proposed and brought her out to St. George to spend more time together; it was Pallete's first movie set experience alongside her new beau.

Bored and lonely, it had been rumored that Hayward developed some soft feeling for her onscreen love interest, having grown accustomed to driving her leading men wild. When Wayne showed no interest in her flirtations, a piece of gossip floating around the set claimed that she had drunkenly stormed over to the house, ordered Pallete to take her shoes off, and challenged her to a physical fight over the actor. The tale ended mildly, however, with Wayne intervening and politely escorting Hayward back to her house.

Sometime later, the pair did share a short onscreen kiss that Hayward used as another play for the Duke. She mustered all the passion and lust possible during a particular take, running her hand up the actor's thigh while opening her mouth. Wayne finished the scene but apparently ranted to his secretary on his break. "That goddamn bitch just stuck her tongue halfway down my throat," he roared. Wayne kept his distance from Hayward, but her admiration never ceased.

She told her biographer sometime later, "He was tough and strong just like his screen image. But there was a tremendous gentleness about him. Of all my leading men, he was my favorite."

The townspeople of St. George were the most, if not the only, delighted and awestruck folks involved with the production. Many had grown accustomed to heading off to work in the mornings while passing Mongol warriors walking in one direction and oxen pulling chariots going in the other; iconic movie stars stopped to chat in between. Not only had *The Conqueror* provided jobs, but it brought in tourists from miles away, too; all were journeying to the desert community to get a glimpse of a real-live movie set.

Journalists looking to cover the shoot for tabloid magazines hung around town, waiting for a photo opportunity to arise. With hotel rooms booked solid, restaurant tables never empty, and a functional road to Snow Canyon, an estimated $750,000 was brought into the town's economy after production in southwest Utah was all said and done.

If there was a downside to the sudden flash of prosperity, it was that the residents of St. George could hardly keep up with demand; an influx of guests meant overcrowding and considerable disruption to daily life. To smooth over their relationship with the Chamber of Commerce, a charity baseball game was organized on July 6, where local players from the Elks Lodge got a chance to play against the Hollywood heavyweights.

According to town records, Hayward stole first base and enlisted her boys to bat for the team. Wayne and Powell doubled as players and the evening's officials as fifteen hundred spectators crowded the Dixie Sun Bowl for fifty cents apiece.

When the game wrapped, Duke delivered a gushing kudos to the people. "This is the way we like to think of America—people cheerfully helping people simply because that's a good way to live," he praised.

Others, throughout their stay, gave their own regards to the community. Powell singled out the crops as well as the well-mannered children. Armendáriz called St. George "a wonderful community of very considerate people." Location manager Harold Lewis was a tad regretful in his choice of rocky desert but noted that it would have been a lot tougher if the people hadn't been so helpful.

As the cast and crew departed, Nora Lyman, columnist for *Washington Country* newspaper, bid them all a publicized farewell on behalf of St. George. "There's a sort of lonesome feeling around the streets like your home is for a time after a houseguest has said the last goodbye and departed. This was our first visit by a major motion picture company, and I'm sure we are unintentionally guilty of many sins of omission and commission. But, as a whole community, it was our greatest desire to be helpful when needed and out of the way at all other times . . . We sincerely hope they will come back to mingle with us."

Trucks full of Mongol apparel and swords and fuzzy hats and yurts rolled out on August 5, 1954, with the stars flying off overhead in a small passenger plane. The hundreds of horses were brought back to their stables (and a few to nearby farms from which they had been borrowed). God only knows where the oxen and panther ended up.

Owners filtered back into their rightful homes, still smelling of movie star. Buckets of yellow makeup and eye molds ended up with the weekly trash. What remained were scrapes, bruises, sunburns, a broken jaw, quivering appendages, and sand accidentally smuggled in the most unmentionable of places—all of it battle scars to prove the shoot was a beastly battle but a battle that was, on the surface, won.

With thirteen weeks of production—more than two months of making what very well seemed to be the middle of nowhere their home—everyone survived the brunt of *The Conqueror* and headed back to Hollywood to finish the long, hot journey they had begun.

**John Wayne in full Genghis Kahn costume and makeup, equipped with Fu Manchu moustache, epicanthic eye folds, and yellowed skin.** (RKO Radio Pictures/Photofest)

In the sizzling 120-degree heat, John Wayne cooled down costar Pedro Armendáriz on-set in Snow Canyon. Because of dry conditions, water had to be trucked to a makeshift well, though crew members recall the supply consisting of mostly mud, dust, and dirt.

(RKO Radio Pictures/Photofest)

**Temüjin (John Wayne) and Kumlek (Ted de Corsia) in the heat of a climactic desert-set battle over control of the Tatar princess, Bortai.** (RKO Radio Pictures/Photofest)

**In one of *The Conqueror*'s more stellar scenes, hundreds of "Mongol" extras ride on horseback while Temüjin (John Wayne) and Bortai (Susan Hayward) hide from captors and killers in search of the exiled pair.** (RKO Radio Pictures/Photofest)

A 1956 poster boasts *The Conqueror*'s $6,000,000 price tag while overzealously touting the film's sexuality. Hollywood legend Saul Bass was commissioned to design original posters, but his more artistic work was dropped in favor of more appealing imagery from RKO staffers. (RKO Radio Pictures/Photofest)

**Amid the chaotic *Conqueror* production, John Wayne and Susan Hayward still found the time to put differences aside, smile together, and share a cigarette between takes. Both would contract cancer in their later lives.** (RKO Radio Pictures/Photofest)

**Director Dick Powell mulls over a late-night shoot on *The Conqueror*'s desert set with actors John Wayne and Pedro Armendáriz, script supervisor Bill Hole, and numerous unnamed crew members.** (RKO Radio Pictures/Photofest)

**Location manager Hal Lewis (left), director Dick Powell, and John Wayne watch Susan Hayward cut a sizable cake with a sword that looks to be taken straight from the set. Hayward stands between twin sons Gregory and Timothy Barker.** (RKO Radio Pictures/Photofest)

One of the best-known and widely used promotional posters for *The Conqueror*, which made no effort in altering John Wayne or Susan Hayward's familiar Caucasian likenesses, despite the pair playing Mongol characters. (Wikimedia Commons)

**In 1953, more than 21,000 soldiers took part in ground exercises for Operation Upshot-Knothole; a series of eleven nuclear test shots were conducted at the Nevada Test Site.** (Library of Congress)

# 10: Sand and the Studio

Several interior scenes were shot on the remaining sliver of the RKO backlot, a space quickly flipped into lavish imitations of fortress dens and golden harems blanketed with bright rugs and intricate vases. The décor, right down to the molding on the background pillars, was actually quite admirably executed, but that was supposed to be the end of it. The grand finale! The highly anticipated wrap!

The final shots were meant to round out production in a more secure and stable environment, free of sun and sand, to give the *Conqueror* crew a stretch of ease. After nearing the end of principal photography of his masterpiece, Howard Hughes soon realized this was how the whole production should have been done in the first place.

The billionaire demanded reshoots and summoned Powell and Wayne and Hayward and all the cast and crew back for another attempt–a budgetary nightmare just to appease the man's obsessive-compulsive side. The battles were fine, but Mongol village footage came back from St. George far too unsuitable to appease Hughes's tastes.

Yurts were again erected so that *The Conqueror* team could redo a significant portion of the story in a more controlled space. All of it came at the cost of a pretty penny, pushing expenses far past any imaginable movie shoot figure. Hughes didn't care. He was willing to spend whatever it took to achieve . . . well . . . whatever it was Hughes wanted to achieve with *The Conqueror*.

Hughes might have been acting from the point of view of a concerned producer, and re-dos were necessary to get his picture right. But Hughes's idea of continuity (and overall grasp on logistics) went quite far off the map. The scenes required sand, not much of a problem for a major Hollywood motion picture studio that was only a stone's throw away from the beach.

If that idea failed, why not take a trip out to California's own mountains of sand dunes in Death Valley? Down south to Baja? Mix up a big batch of flour and oil? No, none of those ideas would do for Hughes–the sands of southern Utah just possessed such a distinct red tinge that only imported dust straight from the source, Snow Canyon, would pass.

A fleet of semi-trucks was ordered to drive the four-hundred-mile trek out to Utah and bring back nothing but the good stuff from *The Conqueror*'s exact shooting locations—sixty tons of it. It was dumped on the floor and professionally scattered across RKO soundstages by a team of Mexican gardeners so the floor unmistakably resembled a desert.

No audience member would ever in a million years have raised a fuss by standing up in the middle of the theater and screaming at the screen that the sand was not the same. Hughes covered his bases and ensured that something as small as a grain of sand remained indistinguishable.

The cast had to have grumbled, not only because they were brought in for longer than expected but because they were reunited with the pesky particles that were still probably filling their pockets and suitcases. Hughes, on the other hand, still refused to step foot on his studio's grounds; he never actually personally checked if the sand's red tinge matched what he had seen onscreen. Hughes gave the order from another office and assumed the costly sixty-ton shipment did the trick.

Hughes also left much of this production time and the added employees off the books, wrapping in late 1954, though the exact date is unclear. Reshoots were not without troubles, either, as a tipped lantern one day set a tent interior ablaze. The sets were disassembled for the final time, but the fate of the imported dirt remains a mystery. No recollection seems to have survived on the sand's fate, leaving minds to wonder just exactly where the Utah earth ended up.

Hughes may have had it trucked back to Snow Canyon or dumped in the nearest desert outside city limits. He could have had it flushed down the sewer or locked away in storage, only to be reused for subsequent desert adventures. No one can ever be sure where it all went.

Sand being sand—no matter the efforts to get it cleared away—a particle or two would have likely been left behind, wafting around the airy soundstage or clinging to someone's shoe to catch a ride home. Perhaps it could even be found spilling onto the streets and inching forth to the craft services table, the costume department, or washed into LA's gutters.

John Wayne was at the end of his rope with RKO. Having finished his commitments, though rumors have speculated Wayne had agreed to do an even four films instead of only three, Duke wanted nothing more to do with Howard Hughes. The actor never went nosing around for another script to bring to Dick Powell's attention. No more talk of *The Alamo* getting a green light, no more honoring a studio that launched his career, and no more loyalty to old pals. When *The Conqueror* wrapped, Wayne called it quits and brought his and Howard's partnership, and even longer friendship, to an end.

Maybe Wayne figured he needed a breather and would come back in a couple years when he cooled off. Either way, he sought comfort from the familiar—a good old-fashioned Western made with older and trusted friends. After marrying Pilar Pallete in November 1954 and kicking the Dexedrine pills, he went looking for something, anything that could get his mind off Mongols and Howard Hughes. He jumped at the first film he was offered: John Ford's *The Searchers*.

Powell lined up his next few projects, still confined to RKO's editing room. Giving up movie roles altogether, he focused solely on directing and occasionally appearing in episodes of *Four Star Playhouse*. His first non-RKO picture would be a loose remake of the 1934 Frank Capra classic *It Happened One Night* called *You Can't Run Away from It*. The significantly smaller-scale job was over at Columbia Pictures and starred his wife, June Allyson, and a relatively unknown Jack Lemmon.

Pedro Armendáriz nabbed a steady stream of leading roles in Spanish language productions and began playing second fiddle to action stars like Errol Flynn and Roger Moore in American and British B movies.

Agnes Moorehead almost immediately returned to the desert to shoot *Meet Me in Las Vegas* as several of the smaller players moved on to astoundingly more prestigious work.

Ted de Corsia earned a plum role in Stanley Kubrick's first big hit, *The Killing*, while Leo Gordon appeared in Alfred Hitchcock's *The Man Who Knew Too Much*.

Most of the actors had no trouble whatsoever moving on with other projects; it was Hayward who floundered following *The Conqueror* wrap. A double dose of duds, *Untamed* and *Soldier of Fortune*, did nothing to help her dampened spirits after Utah, nor did any of the cozying done by her boss. Hughes ultimately did rub shoulders with her once the film was safely in the can, lurking in the background of her private life as an occasional lover.

Hayward's ex-husband, Jess Barker, was not amused by Hughes's presence, fearing his influence mixed with Hayward's own erratic behavior would bring harm to their young boys. A court battle for custody rocked Hayward's mental state for the final months of 1954, though she did emerge victorious in the end.

A script based on Broadway star Lilian Roth's autobiography, *I'll Cry Tomorrow*, found its way into Hayward's hands; the story was a stark and rare look at alcoholism from the female perspective. Connecting with the conflicted main character, Hayward immediately launched herself into the juicy role. In the midst of production in the spring of 1955, she gulped down a handful of sleeping pills and a chaser of bourbon, frantically calling her mother for help moments later. Police ended up kicking down her door and carting the unconscious star to the hospital. Papers simultaneously peddled pictures of the actress wearing an oxygen mask and the words "attempted suicide" to every newsstand in the country. Hayward recovered quickly and headed back to work on *I'll Cry Tomorrow* within weeks, but Hughes wasn't keen on the actress's own real-life drama and left the picture for good.

Away in a dark, unglamorous editing suite, his own picture dragged along the cutting room floor. Robert Ford and Kennie Marstella repeatedly snipped together rough cuts of *The Conqueror*, only to find themselves waiting tirelessly for Hughes's word. At this point, Hughes was more of an invisible figurehead than a producer; he gave few constructive suggestions and let weeks–months–pass by before he viewed the film in his own private screening room. The Mongol epic could have debuted at the end of 1954, but his sudden disinterest kept the picture from coming together at a reasonable pace.

The budget for *The Conqueror* had risen to such unimaginable figures; totals had escalated toward the $5 million ($48 million today) mark with still no definite end in sight. Alongside big-budget epics like *The Robe* and *Quo Vadis*, it was about to "earn" the distinction of being one of the most expensive cinematic ventures of all time; and if Hughes didn't send it out soon, *The Conqueror* would thus go down as one of the biggest financial disasters, too.

The studio was down to the lowest number of employees in its history—mainly because there was nothing for anyone to do. No original production had been lined up, nor did any lucrative distribution deals come their way; the remaining few twiddled their thumbs and waited. A few micro-budget productions rented out the facilities to film in exchange for distribution, but it was all lower than B-grade work.

When you compare Warner Bros.' twenty-two picture slate of originals for 1955 and twenty-eight from 20th Century Fox, RKO, formerly a contemporary force to be reckoned with, was nothing more than an empty shack waiting for its electricity to be cut.

In a final bid for normalcy, Hughes did release a few of his other opuses in the spring; *Son of Sinbad* raised eyebrows and the waving fists of the Catholic Church. *Underwater!* opened in Silver Springs, Florida, to an audience of stars, models, and journalists made to wear bathing suits for over-the-top publicity. To push the stunt further, they drank in the picture twenty feet below the surface from specially constructed pools and submarine portholes. It drowned at the box office.

With *The Conqueror* still not ready to follow in their pitiful paths, Hughes reached the end of time he had bought himself. Floyd Odlum reemerged with another collection of demands in exchange for his 5 percent stock, still hopelessly eyeing the RKO's theater corporation. Unwilling to reach an agreement in the midst of 1955 and unable to focus on his film, Hughes grew tired of the stalemate and the whole motion picture business entirely.

Having no further ideas to bring to the table and with some early glimpses of John Wayne's performance in the desert, Hughes knew there was only one surefire way to turn the tables on Odlum: sell RKO . . . again.

Leery from the lessons learned from the whole Stolkin scandal, Hughes made sure RKO would be placed in the hands of someone more reputable and experienced. Hoping to up his Batjac real estate, John Wayne expressed interest but was quickly talked out of the move by financial advisors.

Relying on his persuasive talents, Hughes unexpectedly took a meeting with Tom O'Neil, president of General Teleradio—a media subsidiary of the General Tire and Rubber Company, which owned six television stations and a major stake in the American radio market. O'Neil had noticed that airing classic films on television was a profitable endeavor, having acquired a collection of decaying film strips that he aired on one of his TV stations as *Million Dollar Movie* features.

He wondered if Hughes might be interested in lending him RKO's cinema library. The billionaire insisted that Teleradio take the whole studio if they wanted access to RKO's catalogue—for an upped price.

O'Neil surprisingly jumped at the chance to acquire a production company and swiftly agreed to fork over a cool $25 million ($250 million) on July 19, 1955, through three $8 million installments, a contract allegedly signed inside a Beverly Hills Hotel men's room.

O'Neil was instantly elected chairman of the board and replaced president of production James R. Grainger with Daniel T. O'Shea, a senior vice president of Columbia Broadcasting. William Dozier, a former assistant to former RKO executive Charles Koerner, was subsequently named vice president.

Excitement glistened across Tinseltown; the fact that radio was going to be brought back into the equation of Radio-Keith-Orpheum was cause for nostalgic cheer. O'Neil proudly announced that RKO would continue with original in-house productions and began hiring new crew members to make it so. Mostly, celebrations stemmed from the departure of Hollywood's most reviled mogul.

For a second and final time, Hughes exited RKO in sudden silence and abandoned his Mongol masterpiece mid-edit. As part of the deal, he would still retain his "Howard Hughes Presents" credit, but the film's producer would have no further say on how it or any other production was cut or released. Genghis Khan was their problem now, no matter the blood and toil he had conjured to bring it to that point. Historian Betty Lasky famously summed up Hughes's reign in her book *RKO: The Biggest Little Major of Them All* as a "systematic seven-year rape."

Hughes more than likely looked at his involvement in a different light. Because of the theater chain divestment, the syndicate forfeiture, and the smoking-good deal from the Teleradio sale, he left RKO pocketing a $6.5 million ($62 million today) profit.

No expense was spared to get the word out about the picture; newspaper advertisements were placed, often taking up entire pages to let readers know that *The Conqueror* was coming—for most, the lengthy delay in production was embellished to create hype.

"Two years in the making," they'd say, popping up on the walls of more artistic urban centers and inside the pages of papers from the *Los Angeles Times* to the New York's *Daily News*. A comic book adaptation, designed by pulp publisher Dell Comics, was drawn into circulation to attract younger viewers.

A three-minute-long preview strung together all of the picture's action sequences and overzealously touted to moviegoers that *The Conqueror* was "Titanic in scope! Titanic in action! Never has a picture breathed such . . . Fire! Drama! Power! Scene after scene of unimaginable splendor, barbaric passions, and savage conquests. For sheer might and magnetism, it surpasses anything filmed before!" Print advertisements went so far as to quote Wayne as saying, "This is one of the best pictures I have ever seen, certainly the best I've ever been in."

Saul Bass, the highly regarded graphic designer, had been originally brought on by Hughes to do advertisement and title work on *The Conqueror* in the early part of his career. Bass would be responsible for dozens of company logos like AT&T and Bell System, innovative movie title sequences like the fractured kinetic typography for Hitchcock's *Anatomy of a Murder*, and countless posters for films like *Vertigo*, *Love in the Afternoon*, and *It's a Mad, Mad, Mad,*

*Mad World.* Three poster designs, two of which contained a John Wayne–styled Genghis Khan riding a horse and leading an army to battle, were designed by Bass and drawn by Al Kallis. "He'd blood drench the earth . . . for one more kingdom . . . or one more woman!" read one of the taglines printed above Khan's face. "He's coming to seize your city!" claimed another.

European influenced with minimal detail, none of them explicitly showed the film's stars and were apparently not what Hughes was looking for.

"A man of myopic obsessive temperament, his notion of a good film ad was to use pretty hard-boiled photographic kind of illustration," Bass recalled of Hughes in *Saul Bass: A Life in Film and Design.* "I was naive and really believed I could sway people by doing what I thought were wonderful designs. But I didn't understand how rigid he was."

Bass's sleek images were scrapped for more traditional posters, most of them featuring an unclothed Susan Hayward sprawled next to a rippling John Wayne—no hint of Mongol makeup at all. The simpler designs were passed down from the Hughes realm and kept because RKO couldn't afford to gamble with artsy ambiguity quite yet; pure adrenaline and sex appeal were pumped so people knew exactly what they were getting into.

For the first time since 1948, the road ahead was looking up for the studio, and no one behind the scenes wanted to add any curves. Former employees were welcomed back in droves; Tom O'Neil proudly announced that the production side of the company was back in business and hired hundreds to get new feature films to camera. RKO also had a stroke of luck by distributing a hefty hit at the end of 1955–the Rodgers and Hammerstein musical *Oklahoma.*

Merged with the new company, RKO Radio Pictures became known as RKO Teleradio Pictures Inc., ushering in a brand-new era of possibilities for the thirty-year-old studio. O'Neil began signing new talent, offering companies like C & C Corporations television rights to 740 RKO films, and pushing new entities such as commercials, short films, even industrial documentaries into production.

He struck a deal with former production chief and RKO legend David O. Selznick to rerelease the producer's classics and, after decades apart, brought Selznick himself back to the lot, offering to back his adaptation of Ernest Hemingway's *A Farewell to Arms.*

With a crew that swelled from hardly one hundred to several thousand, the new owner graced the cover of *Newsweek* and called his studio "one of the fastest and most super colossal comebacks in Hollywood history." The press seemed to agree, dubbing RKO "the busiest lot in Hollywood."

*The Conqueror* meanwhile waited in the vault at RKO for half a year, viewed by a multitude of fresh eyes and wide perspectives; new mouths, however, gave no notes. Business insiders at the time claimed Hughes held both *The Conqueror* and *Jet Pilot* as collateral until Teleradio made their payments, forcing them into a bind where they'd have no choice but to push out his works first.

Hughes actually came knocking the January following the sale, agreeing to essentially knock eight million dollars off RKO's bill in exchange for the rights to *The Conqueror* and his old, disheveled print of shelf-warmer *Jet Pilot.* It was seen as a helpful gesture to help revive RKO's production, but more than likely the mogul just couldn't stand to be left out of the loop.

While Hughes now personally owned the picture, RKO was still tasked with the release and saddled with all costs associated with it, including $1.4 million for advertising. He did apparently sweeten the deal by promising $4 million of *The Conqueror*'s profits.

The picture was more or less cut when Hughes handed it off to the new owners—aspects like Victor Young's thunderous drum-heavy score needed to be included for greater dramatic effect. It received an A classification from the Board of Film Censors, who asked for several cuts to be made in order to obtain the rating.

O'Neil was smart to start with the Mongol movie no matter what bind Hughes put them in—that film was really all Teleradio inherited that was in releasable shape. Settling into Culver City with dreams of turning a profit and breaking out of the B-picture rut, the new RKO would see that Genghis Khan finally got his day in Hollywood at the dawn of 1956.

# 11: Debut of a Disaster

Out came the red carpet as the bright lights of Tinseltown beamed high across the sky. The long overdue promise made by former president James R. Grainger that *The Conqueror* would be one of the biggest adventures of the decade was about to be made good. Few in Hollywood could say that they didn't know the mighty Mongol epic was arriving on the big screen, nor could the movie-going public both in America and across the world ignore its arrival–it was poised to take every possible theater by storm.

The world premieres in which *The Conqueror* debuted were unprecedented. Movies began their life in Hollywood and only occasionally journeyed overseas and never with their stars in tow. Throughout January and February, the Mongol epic played like a travelling road show, first appearing at a series of benefit screenings in exotic corners of the earth–all done to heighten anticipation and illustrate just how "important" the movie apparently was.

Manila, Paris, London, Berlin; *The Conqueror* absolutely lived up to its title by conquering the movie-going public in a span that the real Genghis Khan never dreamed of claiming. A story in a January edition of the *Hollywood Reporter* said that a near-riot was caused in Berlin; residents from the east side of the wall attempted to storm past border police to get a glimpse of John Wayne at the premiere. The actor suggested that they take *The Conqueror* to Moscow for a showing in a bid to make peace amid the Cold War, an idea that never did come to fruition.

Beginning with a special showing in Washington, DC, Los Angeles finally got its turn to meet the Mongols. RKO's two-years-in-the-making so-called masterpiece was privately screened for all the critics and aristocratic patrons on February 22 in its official premiere. Reaction from critics and the rest of the cinema-going world had not been given much publicity, only that foreign audiences had merely witnessed the film.

No one quite knew what they were getting into when the lights dimmed and the curtain rose. It was assumed that the marketing must have cost a fortune, and that it must have been worthwhile if it was being carted all around the globe and that all involved with the picture had been waiting for this very moment for a long, long time.

The Radio-Keith-Orpheum globe glistened proudly with its horn-like antenna, boasting simultaneously that the following picture was filmed in Cinemascope. "Howard Hughes Presents" spanned the screen next and was imposed over the top of jagged mountains and a blue sky. And then desert. A sudden camera pan ushered in a sword-waving John Wayne as Temüjin, leading the Mongol army on horseback across a desert plain to the sound of a blaring trumpet score.

Like any sweeping epic of the era, *The Conqueror*'s title and credits were followed by scrolling text setting the scene for what was to come. "This story, though fiction, is based on fact," read the prologue.

> In the twelfth century the Gobi Desert stretched with unrest. Mongols, Merkits, Tatars, and Karkaits struggled for survival in a harsh and arid land. Petty chieftains pursued their small ambitions with cunning and wanton cruelty. Plunder and rapine were a way of life and no man trusted his brother. Out of this welter of treachery and violence, there arose one of the greatest warriors the world has ever known–a conqueror whose coming changed the face of the world.

Within the very first frames, Temüjin traverses down the same steep hill on his steed twice in a row. From that point onward, almost anything goes for the remainder of the one hour and fifty minute runtime (a fairly short time compared to other films it was to emulate). The actor's unmistakably charming, almost bashful, grin stretches across his face as he lays eyes on a feisty and evidently bored Hayward as Bortai.

The story's second minute already has him meeting the Tatar princess, who he unwaveringly knows from the start is destined for him. The pair does not converse or interact in any way; the Mongol ruler merely lays eyes on the woman in the middle of a convoy and plots to steal her.

The premiere audience was quickly whisked off to the exotic Mongol camp, where extras took part in overly exaggerated iron-bending exercises, roasting fake meat over a flame, and drinking from otherworldly props that were supposed to resemble the carcass of a dead animal; instrumental music interludes attempted to get the party started. Blink and you'd miss the panther.

A bug-eyed Agnes Moorehead waddles in and out of her scenes early in the film, constantly glaring as she channels her best pirate wench impression, nagging Temüjin over his relations whenever she appears. *The Conqueror*, when chiseled down beyond its many plotlines that have few resolutions, seems to exist merely to be a voyeuristic glimpse of muddled history.

Temüjin, who successfully claims Bortai from the gluttonous Wang Khan, is driven by lust and the minor backstory that her father killed his. Most of what follows from kidnapping onward is bartering battle back and forth for their feminine prize. When *The Conqueror* holds attention, it does so in grand fashion with its sweeping horseback wars.

The desolate orange beauty of Snow Canyon does pay off in production value, particularly when scores of men stampeding through the land with spears, swords, and bows. A mix of busy wide shots and close-up inserts of stabs and jabs elevate it immediately. Unfortunately, the desert-set battles are not as plentiful as one would hope, merely leading into a parade of pining, plotting, and problems exuding the proper degree of emotion.

*The Conqueror* is certainly tame by any standard when it comes to depicting Mongol violence. But for the mid-1950s, there was certainly an alarming number of stabs that the inaugural audiences would have been both thrilled and frightened by. There is no drop of blood anywhere in the movie; many get pierced by objects straight through the chest, most notably a shoddy effect where Wayne throws a spear at a soldier who's already holding one in place. Another character unexpectedly gets bludgeoned in the back of the head by a wooden restraint–yet nobody bleeds.

That gaff is hardly the production's fault, having to follow with strict Breen production codes on what could be shown; but it certainly adds to the wild universe unto itself that the actors were operating in.

The crew seems to lose all sense of self-control when the temptations of naked, dancing women are made available at the halfway mark. Anytime a woman is present onscreen, no male character knows quite what to do but to ogle them or abuse them.

"Are you women that you tremble before a force half your number?" Wayne barks to belittle his hesitant army. More alarming is his rebuttal to Bortai's own father, Kumlek, who manages to steal her back. "While I have fingers to grasp a sword and eyes to see, your treacherous head is not safe on your shoulders . . . nor your daughter in her bed," he warns; however, at this point in the picture, audiences were supposed to want nothing more than the leads to be together and cheer with passion at such romantic claims.

Some could argue Hayward took the role as a Mongol trophy more literal than she was meant to—her lifeless performance is never elevated in the slim moments of passion between her and Wayne. A fondness is supposed to gradually grow between her and her captor, but Bortai's change of heart seems to happen more suddenly than Howard Hughes selling RKO, and mostly off-screen, too.

Then again, her mere presence was all that was really wanted from her. Whatever scene she was forced to be in, Hayward is pulled, thrown, and slapped like a ragdoll or swept into the arms of men twice her size to emphasize that she's utterly helpless.

"For good or ill, she is my destiny," Temüjin pines when it seems his love is out of reach—an attempt at giving reason for domineering behavior. Wayne apparently shook Hayward so violently on set, she complained to choreographer Bob Sidney that he was actually hurting her; she found bruises all over her body at the end of the day. According to Sidney, when he went to speak to the actor, Wayne told him, "She's stronger than I am. I don't want to come across as though she's putting me down."

Sidney's concern for any woman's well-being is immediately washed away by his tedious and bizarre parade of performers. Shimmying sexpots wearing pink see-through skirts and curly snake-inspired hats kick off a four-part dance-a-thon that stretches over a ten-minute segment. Sylvia Lewis comes out wearing only thinly cut ribbons wrapped around her limbs and genitals, performing something influenced by a heavy mixture of Middle Eastern, Indian, and pure striptease entertainment.

Hayward, full of apprehension, went through with her number, performing all of the movements herself evidently without an aforementioned body double for close-ups. Writhing around with a sword, which she pretends frequently to stab at herself, Hayward's moves bring about more sympathy than sex appeal and could be mistaken for involuntary convulsions. To her credit, she does get to fling the sword at her audience for the grand finale.

Wayne's makeup appears in some scenes to have been forgotten; his eyebrows are lifted and angled rather than his actual skin. John Hoyt's shaman character, who speaks in meandering riddles and made-up gibberish to evoke mysticism, doesn't get the eye treatment at all; the Caucasian actor instead squints every time he appears on camera.

The only actor who turns in a somewhat believable performance is Pedro Armendáriz as the friend and essential sidekick Jamuga; he at least seems comfortable in the period setting and capable of exuding emotion through some of the words he's given.

By the time the third act is reached, it almost feels as though the screenwriter realized there was no confrontation or goal in place, so he quickly scrambled to construct a little bit of makeshift action. Before audiences can properly settle in for a decent skirmish, every character drops their plotline like a ball at the recess bell and rushes toward the fadeout so they can finally finish. A plump William Conrad getting himself stuck in a window during a daring escape does provide one of the larger climactic thrills.

As for any meaning that's supposed to linger in viewers' minds, there are a lot of mentions of the phrase "blood brothers," though the trouble that stealing a woman can get a person in seems to be more appropriate. Temüjin does take back Bortai through force and in doing so earns his title Genghis Khan.

When "The End" eclipses the screen, that's all there is to it. Two years of fighting and filming are abruptly brought to a close. *The Conqueror* was officially released on March 28, 1956, with a special East Coast debut at the Criterion Theatre in Manhattan two days later.

The *New York Times* review of *The Conqueror* stated that "the facts appeared to have been lost in a Technicolored cloud of charging horsemen, childish dialogue and rudimentary romance. Although it purports to detail the early career of the twelfth-century Mongol leader whose world conquests earned him the august title Genghis Khan, it is simply an Oriental Western. An illusion persists that this Genghis Khan is merely Hopalong Cassidy in Cathay."

*Time* magazine said, "Wayne portrays the great conqueror as a sort of cross between a square-shootin' sheriff and a Mongolian idiot. The idea is good for a couple of snickers, but after that it never Waynes but it bores."

The *Monthly Film Bulletin* dubbed the film "a rambling and rather ordinary Western-type spectacle . . . the weakly contrived narrative is singularly lacking in dramatic tension, and it is difficult to see this Temüjin, for all his high-flown cries to heaven to support his destiny, as a potential world-beater or as even an amiable bandit."

Edwin Schallert of the *Los Angeles Times* felt it was "odd to find Wayne and Miss Hayward depicting Asiatic characters," but did praise some of Powell's direction when it came to the "sensational battle scenes." "It has a storming quality about it overall," Schallert went on to write, "which unfortunately makes some of the love scenes all but laughable."

*Variety* took a kinder approach, suggesting with the film's opening note that it is technically a work of fiction: "The viewer can sit back and thoroughly enjoy a huge, brawling, sex-and-sand actioner purporting to show how a 12th century Mongol leader became known as Genghis Khan."

While many, still to this day, decide whether to see a picture by how the critics receive it, *The Conqueror* was unscathed by all the mud slung at it. RKO's Mongol epic was a popular cinema rental, filling movie houses to full capacity throughout the entire spring and selling an estimated eighteen million tickets by the end of its run; problematic production and bad reviews be damned, *The Conqueror* was actually a hit.

"All I ever cared about was that the public liked my pictures," Wayne assured when the reviews came out.

On the surface, Howard Hughes's gamble looked like it would pay off; and though he was no longer in charge, the studio would be basking in profit and therefore saved. Audiences marveled in seeing their most cherished movie stars, Wayne and Hayward, while the exotic locale proved to be more than enough to lure them from their living room chairs for the better part of that year.

What Hughes, RKO's new owners, and all of Hollywood failed to consider, however, was the fact that 1956 would be one of the biggest years ever for the movies.

Unlike 1949, a rough cinematic year when the eccentric billionaire's reign over production was only just beginning, the industry had grown by leaps and bounds–pulling itself out of a rut carved out by both dwindling audiences and quality releases, not to mention stiff competition. Film fought with everything it had to keep up with television amid a bleak and expensive future; the rise of the epic genre thankfully created a new reason to go see stories on the big screen. Spectacle films finally culminated in 1956; that surge started with *The Conqueror*, but very quickly, audiences were unable to keep up with its competition.

*War and Peace*, directed by King Vidor, was a Napoleonic war drama starring Henry Fonda and Audrey Hepburn. It tore up the box office with a three-and-a-half-hour length. There was also the sprawling Texas-set soap opera *Giant*, a mosaic of Rock Hudson's ranching career and James Dean–in his last role–as his farmhand who strikes oil.

The whale-sized adaptation of *Moby Dick* flooded theaters, as did the film version of cherished musical *The King and I*; the life story of *Anastasia*; and *High Society*, a comedy that couldn't fail with a huge cast featuring Bing Crosby, Grace Kelly, and Frank Sinatra.

*The Conqueror*'s own star outdid himself by supplying pure cinematic gold. Duke's pinnacle Western, *The Searchers*, was released mere weeks later and provided a very mature and elevated plot involving the actor as a racist Civil War veteran who tracks the tribe that slaughtered his family and stole his niece. Mixed reviews during its release were replaced by later assessments that dubbed the Western as the very best of the genre and Wayne's most layered and emotional performance–a fine pairing to go along with Genghis Khan.

The year 1956 belonged to two gargantuan pictures in particular: first, the colorful adaptation of Jules Verne's *Around the World in*

*80 Days* in which protagonist Phileas Fogg (David Niven) attempts to do just that . . . travel around the world in eighty days. Clocking in at just over three hours and boasting more than forty celebrity cameos, that year's Academy Award winner for Best Picture earned a heaping fortune of $42 million ($395 million).

The *Ten Commandments*, a three-hour-and-forty-minute Cecil B. DeMille whopper, which charted the life of Moses, became the sole entertainment vessel of that year. The Bible story collected $91 million (more than $1 billion today), making it the second most successful movie of the entire decade behind *Ben-Hur*.

Motion pictures had become so massive when it came to budgets, settings, and lengths, that nothing mediocre or smaller in scale could hold a candle to them, even if they were still massive in their own right. With authentic history, hokey gimmicks, and outright Christianity quaking the box office, *The Conqueror* did not fade away slowly; it was shoved straight into distant memory after theaters stopped bringing it in.

Make no mistake, people still saw the picture; *The Conqueror* actually wound up being the eleventh highest-grossing film of 1956. But that admirable distinction was not enough to recoup what the production costs lost.

Trucked-in sand and movie star fees in check, Snow Canyon shots and everything but the advertising and its international campaign were accounted for–the picture did finally hit an end point. *The Conqueror* racked up a then unheard of $6 million budget ($56 million in modern terms), officially distinguishing it as one of the most expensive productions to date (albeit that budget being half of what *The Ten Commandments* took to produce).

Some sources claimed the studio pulled the same stunt Howard Hughes had with one of his earlier pictures, *Hell's Angels*, where he fibbed to the press about the gargantuan financial toll, letting them erroneously report a sum almost twice the actual number to build buzz. *The Conqueror*'s budget was rumored to be a meager $4.5 million, which would have allowed for only a miniscule amount of financial loss and havoc inside the offices at RKO.

The Mongol movie took in a total of $4.5 million at the domestic box office, which were earnings certainly worth celebrating in the picture business during the 1950s. What basic accounting tells us is that RKO would have broken even if the inflated budget claims were true, shrugging off the release and going ahead with yet another day. But $4.5 million earned on a $6 million budget alludes to the fact that there would have been more than just a few problems headed their way. With no profit to be had, it meant RKO wouldn't receive the $4 million Hughes had promised when he bought the rights.

Owner O'Neil and President O'Shea watched in panic as the studio's 1956 flagship failed to finish its theatrical run with enough dough to cover the tab. What followed *The Conqueror*, thanks to Hughes's eight million dollar investment was a small batch of insignificant releases that don't merit a mention. The "busiest lot in Hollywood" attempted to return to what O'Shea referred to as "the great things that the organization stood for in the past"; nothing past preliminary promise seemed to work.

David O. Selznik broke off his distribution deal with RKO to produce what would end up being his last picture, *A Farewell to Arms*, on his own—working with 20th Century Fox for distribution instead. *Oklahoma*'s distribution overseas turned out to only lose money; apparently beautiful countryside mornings and surreys with fringes on top did not translate with foreign audiences.

The next year, 1957, began with a public statement claiming that RKO was looking for "merger of distribution interests for purposes of economy." By the end of January, the studio announced it would stop producing films altogether. The move was said to have been made in order to reflect on the poor earnings from the previous year and to do some soul searching on where RKO should go. Ideas of limited productions and European distribution services were all thrown out with the garbage as the year progressed.

But an absent production department meant a decline in jobs; the recently rehired employees were again shown the door. While the Teleradio team weighed their options, the handful of ready-to-go releases they did have were sloughed off to Universal-International to deal with.

The distributors started with *Jet Pilot*, finally dusting off the ancient film canisters that had been sitting idle since 1953 and spit-shining the relic so they had a "brand-new" John Wayne picture to flog. With a conception dating back nearly ten years, everything about the goofy Communist love affair seemed horribly dated. Advertisements claimed that the picture showcased the US Air Force's latest jets, but by that point, most of the aircrafts had become obsolete. Critics and audiences were more befuddled by the painfully delayed release and dismissed it entirely.

"The final budget was something like four million dollars. It was just too stupid for words," Wayne said, admitting that the project was nothing more than "silly."

Accompanying *Jet Pilot* was a Red Skelton comedy called *Public Pigeon No. 1*, a Ginger Rogers comedy called *The First Travelling Sales Lady*, and the final films of acclaimed German director Fritz Lang; that was all. The stockpile, which had been shakily built up in the past year, ran empty.

Maybe RKO had been bent by so many handoffs during its final decade; maybe the new bunch was learning that there was something to Howard Hughes's struggles, and it wasn't so easy to keep a major motion picture studio in check. They had other assets to deal with and were savvy enough to recognize that the biggest department of financial loss out of the radio, television programming, and distribution service sectors was film production.

The General Tire and Rubber subsidiary bailed water from their sinking ship by putting the RKO Forty Acres and RKO-Pathé backlots on the market. Hughes had essentially abandoned the Forty Acres ranch, hallowed ground where exterior shots for hundreds of classics had been filmed. Teleradio parting with that particular stretch of land wasn't too terribly unforeseeable given its unkempt condition.

RKO-Pathé (later known as Culver City) housed physical production facilities, which David O. Selznick had rented since 1935. Few RKO productions were physically shot there but had become an attraction due to its involvement in the "burning of Atlanta" scenes in *Gone With the Wind*. That unimaginable combo of real estate was quickly claimed that autumn by yet another owner; for $6.15 million, the king and queen of television, Desi Arnaz and Lucille Ball, purchased RKO's fate for Desilu Productions.

"I just thought it was the coolest thing ever," recalled daughter Lucie Arnaz to the Television Academy; she would have been six years old at the time of the sale. "They actually said they owned this whole place, so if I wanted to go to the prop department and just fool around for an hour and a half, I could. The guy would say, 'Oh yeah, come on in Lucie, come on in little Desi,' and they'd just go and let us play with King Kong and all those amazing things that were in there. It was magical."

Fresh off wrapping their sixth and final season of *I Love Lucy*, the couple wanted to expand their creative opportunities but lacked the means of paying for the entire lot. Teleradio packed their belongings as Desilu quickly turned to renting out the thirty-three movie sound stages to other television productions. RKO's soiled presence no longer weighed down the owners, who used the assets to build themselves a fresh start; every logo was stripped away and items shoved into storage.

The RKO trademark still existed, retaining only its unproduced screenplays and remake rights to its produced films; but for the former titan that had belonged to the exclusive Big Five club of moviemaking, without production facilities, its historic name was all that remained.

*The Conqueror*'s cast was able to move past the criticisms and uncomplimentary reviews without much of a headache. For Agnes Moorehead, Pedro Armendáriz, Thomas Gomez, John Hoyt, and the bit-part players whose images weren't riding on the film's reception, their careers as supporting actors took them from role to role without much baggage to bring along. As eventful as the making of it was, *The Conqueror* had merely been another day's work for most of them, a paycheck that wasn't supposed to have any sort of lasting effect.

Susan Hayward wasn't about to let her personal momentum be stifled by critics; she had managed to kick the pills and alcohol habit and put her rocky divorce behind her. Following *The Conqueror*'s release, timed almost exactly with an Oscar nomination for *I'll Cry Tomorrow*, the actress held her head high in front of the critics and took a break from the movies to marry rancher and entrepreneur Floyd Eaton Chalkley and relocated to Georgia for a more peaceful life.

Hayward's career slowed by choice, but she managed to follow her Tatar princess portrayal with a comedy with Kirk Douglas called *Top Secret Affair* in 1957 and *I Want to Live!*–a film noir directed by Robert Wise–in 1958. Her portrayal of real-life murderer Barbara Graham finally earned Hayward her long-desired Academy Award for Best Actress, effectively muting any comments about Mongols and sexually charged sword dances.

Oscar Millard, the film's penman, managed to nab steady work. Enduring through somewhat of a tarnished reputation, he crammed his resume with writing on television programs like *The F.B.I.* and *The Alfred Hitchcock Hour*, while still delivering the occasional film script, most notably the Nazi crime thriller *The Salzburg Connection* and the Max von Sydow Western *The Reward*. Critics mostly stuck up their noses at Millard's later work, though none of his fare was comparable in subject or style to *The Conqueror*.

It was John Wayne who got the most stuffing torn out of him by the critical naysayers. As the film's lead, he was the most recognizable face, which ironically seemed to be most people's problem with the picture. The race-altering makeup proved to be the glaring error for audiences; all pointed to Duke's unsuitable aesthetic that threw their enjoyment of the film off course. The actor had been dished plenty of bad reviews before, but he had made a habit of looking ahead and shrugging off the stories that didn't quite work.

Whatever enthusiasm Wayne initially had for *The Conqueror's* script was long gone. Though his unflappable Americana image only journeyed further into legendary proportions, he did seem embarrassed about the miscast, visually shuddering when journalists dredged the film up during later interviews. "Don't make an ass of yourself by trying to play parts you're not suited to," he later said when asked about the role. "But I didn't learn that lesson. I still manage to make an ass out of myself now and then."

RKO did distribute a Western the actor produced called *Man in the Vault* at the tail end of 1956, but that marked their very last interaction with each other. Angered by broken promises and *The*

*Conqueror's* end result, Wayne was determined to take matters into his own hands more than ever.

Landing less than nowhere with *The Alamo* at RKO for so many years (or anywhere in Hollywood), Duke decided that he felt so strongly about getting the story on film, he would produce and direct the production himself. He initially refused to act in it so he could give the film the focus needed to stay true to his vision. Coached by mentor John Ford, Wayne had only been behind the camera for a couple of days on the set of *Blood Alley*; and the star had filled in for director William A. Wellman when he was sick with the flu.

The film was going to be another monumental undertaking in a similar vein as *The Conqueror*. The period setting populated with horses, costumes, and thousands of extras in the desert had to have felt familiar. Written by *Flying Leathernecks* scribe James Edward Grant, the behind-the-scenes spectacle of Wayne's *Alamo* was certainly, at times, just as chaotic. He struck a deal with United Artists, who agreed to put up several million if the actor also starred as Davy Crockett. Wayne agreed, piling the third position onto his plate, agreeing to fund the other half of the production through Batjac Productions and $1.5 million of his own money. The set itself, a three-quarter-scale replica of the Alamo mission, took over two years to construct near the hamlet of Brackettville, Texas, and required more than one million handmade adobe bricks for its walls.

Wayne produced the picture with his son Michael and shot on location for four months at the end of 1959. The 202-minute historical army epic finally saw the light of day in October 1960. *The Alamo's* budget totaled twice what *The Conqueror's* was, yet it still earned twenty million dollars worldwide. Mixed reviews questioned its length but praised its authentic replication of the mission. *The Alamo* racked up seven Oscar nominations, winning one for Best Sound while managing to go up for Best Picture (losing to *The Apartment*).

Critics pointed to Wayne's strong and vocal personal beliefs, saying they had gotten in the way of telling an accurate account of history in a thick layering of patriotism. Duke didn't see the result in any other way than as a success. It became Batjac's most profitable picture and stood out as a personal achievement, demonstrating that the actor could do more than ride horses and shoot guns.

"This picture is America," Wayne recounted. "I hope that seeing the battle of the Alamo will remind Americans that liberty and freedom don't come cheap. This picture, well, I guess making it has made me feel useful to my country."

Just about everyone involved with *The Conqueror* went on to work a career highlight in the late 1950s—everyone except Howard Hughes. *Jet Pilot* does technically hold the distinction of being Hughes's last credit; still *The Conqueror* was the last physical production the mogul ever got involved in, capping a thirty-year career.

Right-hand man Noah Dietrich had grown frustrated with juggling the billionaire's finances. Hughes's reckless spending on jet plane orders and constant accusations that Dietrich wanted to have him committed to a psychiatric ward created an irreparable rift between the two. TWA had had enough of him and voted to remove Hughes from management.

Howard Hughes's behavior had swiftly taken a turn for the worse when he left RKO, heightening his bevy of faults and struggles with mental health to dangerous levels. He suddenly and unexpectedly married film star Jean Peters in 1957, a partner many close to him claimed was "the only woman he ever loved."

Hughes continued to contract young starlets; only this time, the women weren't signed to a studio but to Hughes himself. Each one was lured in with a steady paycheck, promised prestigious schooling and a path to stardom; all of it was hot air he never once made good on.

In the spring of 1958, Hughes locked himself in a studio screening room and remained inside for one-third of that year. Eating nothing but chocolate bars and milk, he spent much of his time naked in fear of germs; he urinated in empty bottles and conducted business by memos and conversations through the door. When he finally left the space, his hair had grown down to his shoulders, and his fingernails and toenails curled out to excessive length.

Still, the man did not receive nor did he ask for any help. Everything went ahead like all was business as usual—well, Hughes's usual.

He had the fortune to press on with whatever project (or eccen-
tricity) he chose, none of it harkening back to his previous life as a
movie producer.

Howard's last hurrah in the film world was when RKO officially sung its swan song in the spring of 1959. After the last batch
of releases hit theaters–officially going out on the Samuel Fuller
neo-Nazi drama *Verboten!*–RKO Pictures was dissolved. Desilu
Productions had settled nicely into their new confines, welcoming
new television productions like *The Andy Griffith Show* to establish
their sets of fictional town Mayberry in Culver City.

What was left were the guardians of the thirty-year backlog,
RKO Teleradio, who quickly renamed themselves RKO General–a
title that accurately summed up its purpose. The new incarnation
turned its attention toward General Tire's collection of radio stations and successfully focused on formatting programming for the
airwaves.

Hughes already held the rights to *Jet Pilot* and *The Conqueror*
following RKO's closure, but he went a step further by attempting
to purchase every single print that existed in the entire world of
those two pictures. Speculation in the industry figured Hughes was
ashamed of the negative reception both received or that he agreed
and pulled them from circulation to protect his image. Others saw
it differently, claiming Hughes cherished them so dearly that he
wanted the two movies all to himself.

At the very least, he felt they were too grand to ever grace the
small screen on television reruns. Whatever the reason, the former
studio head began a hunt for every single print, paying top dollar for
every reel stashed away in theater closets and transport trucks to
get them completely out of public existence.

RKO's clout in the filmmaking business was concretely over,
yet the one thing the shut studio still had going for it was television broadcasts. The studio had managed to capitalize on airing
old movies before any other company allowed their catalogues on
the small screen. RKO General additionally owned numerous TV
stations and kept the legacy of the bleeping radio antenna alive by
airing the classics through their flagship program *Million Dollar*

*Movie.* Radio-Keith-Orpheum, in one form or another, lived on, defining itself as a nostalgic producer of yesteryear through those rebroadcasts.

Completely owned by Howard Hughes, *The Conqueror*, on the other hand, was left out of the television rotation. Without availability for secondary theater showings, the picture faded into obscurity, essentially becoming a lost film.

# PART THREE

# AFTER

# 12: Duke's Date with Destiny

If the streets hadn't stood still in such a complete pin-dropping silence, ordinary people just passing through wouldn't have known the difference. Thankfully, no one did.

Main Street USA stretched on through the desert—grocery stores, radio stations, and prosperous-looking little hardware businesses lined either side. Cars and a fire engine were parked along the neighborhood at differing angles. Farther down the road, five different types of homes, varying between one or two stories and made from different concrete blocks, wood, and bricks, stood sturdy.

Inside, the spitting image of your typical middle-class American family home was fashioned together with the latest trends in sofas, area rugs, and cord phones dangling from the wall. Every pantry was stocked full of canned goods and every fridge a home to butter, veggies, and fresh cuts of meat. The people were all positioned in stereotypical fashion, most surrounding a working television set in the living room. Brother and Sister played on the floor, Dad read the newspaper while sitting in the armchair, and Mom busied herself with various household chores. Each one wore outfits available at JCPenney.

On May 5, 1955, this little community erected at the Nevada Test Site was subject to a nuclear blast that melted a large percentage of its residents and blew most of the buildings to smithereens. The Civil Defense Apple-2 shot was part of Operation Teapot, which was specifically unleashed to look at direct effects an atomic bomb might have on the public. The people (seventy altogether) were mannequins, but every other piece of material that went into making the neighborhood, known by some of the AEC staff as "Doom Town," was authentic.

Apple-2 was dropped from fifteen hundred feet above ground, and some of the bungalow and two-story home structures survived, but the overarching theme published in a short film documenting the project was that few possessions (and humans) would actually survive a nuclear attack.

The Atomic Age was a full decade deep, and by the late 1950s, the love affair with nuclear weapons had run its course. Centered more so on safety and preparedness, nuclear had become an all-too-routine and matter-of-fact aspect of daily living. The "duck and cover" method, first introduced in a 1951 semianimated instructional video featuring Bert the Turtle, became a frequent drill in the classroom. Students were made to scramble underneath their desks when their teacher shouted, "Take cover!"

In the event of an atomic attack, tipped off by a newly implemented national emergency siren warning system, the protective shielding of desks and other hollow objects were deemed safe spots to hide. For those who felt tables weren't quite going to do the trick, fallout shelters hit the market at the end of the decade and spiked in sales during the early part of the sixties.

The Eisenhower administration had pushed for a test moratorium in 1957, but it fell short when the launch of the satellite *Sputnik* caused alarm and the Soviet Union failed to comply with test site inspections. The president was successful in halting atmospheric operations in 1959 and 1960, but an outright ban–due to failed Paris summits and shot-down spy planes–remained out of reach. In fear of a total halt, America's proving grounds packed in as many tests as they could in the 1950s and early '60s, each one, particularly Operation Plumbbob, escalating in audacity, radiation, and strength.

The increased output was also the direct result of stiffening competition, with the British becoming the third nation to get their name on the board as a country with nuclear capabilities. Operation Hurricane's plutonium-implosion device had proven successful during a 1952 test in the Monte Bello Islands off the west coast of Australia.

By the end of the decade, six separate series amounted to twenty-one tests, prompting the United States to partner with the United Kingdom through a Mutual Defense Agreement. When 1960 rolled around, France decided to complicate things and throw their hat in the ring, pulling off four successful tests in French Algeria.

The Union of Soviet Socialist Republics couldn't stand to be out-done, so they set off the most powerful atomic weapon ever made—Tsar Bomba—on October 30, 1961. The hydrogen weapon weighed twenty-seven tons and produced a nuclear yield of fifty megatons of TNT after being dropped over Mityushikha Bay in Russia's far north. Windows shattered as far away as Norway and Finland; the mushroom cloud reached the stratosphere at a height of forty miles (seven times taller than Mount Everest). Every structure in a small, isolated village called Severny was obliterated thirty-four miles down the road. The United States had failed to produce a nuclear weapon that was one-third as powerful as Tsar Bomba, a fact that ratcheted Cold War tensions to an all-time high.

The evident climax of it all was the Cuban Missile Crisis in October 1962—a thirteen-day stretch of mass hysteria that exploded when the Kremlin reached an agreement to place nuclear weapons in the Caribbean country. Ultimately, an agreement was reached and weapons retracted by both the Soviets and the United States. It was the closest the world had come to what has often been referred to as "the brink"—a point of no return that threatened to wipe out all human existence. Naturally, a few folks weren't too keen on any sort of escalation like that.

"Ban the Bomb" movements were spreading throughout the United States; protests and countless opposition groups sprang up to voice their qualms—a key ingredient for the popular growth of the counterculture movement. The Women Strike for Peace saw fifty thousand ladies march in sixty American cities in 1961 to demon-strate against atomic testing while the next year saw Linus Paul-ing earn the Nobel Peace Prize for his efforts to stop atmospheric testing (backed by prolific people such as Pope Pius XII and a very elderly Albert Einstein).

Both celebrities and ordinary citizens built a voice through the grassroots formation of the Committee for a SANE Nuclear Policy in 1957. The Hollywood chapter was later founded and cochaired by *Tonight Show* host Steve Allen and John Wayne's *Flying Leathernecks* costar Robert Ryan. A lengthy list of Hollywood's who's who signed up to fight for nuclear regulations and disarmament altogether, including Henry Fonda, Marlon Brando, and Marilyn Monroe.

Wayne and most of his right-wing cohorts were missing from that list, placing their support behind the US government and the AEC to further arms testing and national defense. The political rift apparently didn't stop him from mingling with old screen pals. When Ryan and his family began to receive death threats for his involvement with SANE, Wayne put his differences and that turbulent RKO shoot aside to allegedly stand guard with a rifle outside the actor's home.

One year after the very last atmospheric test detonation at the Nevada Test Site, Little Feller I, of Operation Sunbeam in 1962, the United States, Soviet Union, and Great Britain signed the Limited Nuclear Test Ban Treaty to ban nuclear weapons in outer space, underwater, or in the atmosphere on August 5, 1963 (France and a suddenly nuclear-capable China refused).

Testing on US soil did continue, only not on top of the earth but underneath it. The 1957 Rainier shot proved that underground testing was feasible, with no fission products escaping into the atmosphere. Essentially operating under an unmentioned loophole, testing commenced at a rapid rate throughout the 1960s in caves and shafts dug thousands of feet deep straight through the Nevada desert. Later, three tests, beginning with Long Shot of Operation Flintlock, took place deep inside the island of Amchitka, Alaska.

The silver lining for the Atomic Energy Commission, which did positively play into the motivation behind the ban, was that the agency confided in their leaders that radiological hazards did stem from atomic testing; they had just never been certain to what extent. But now that the looming threats of annihilation dropped off and operations were moved to a safer location, all would be well for the American people. From the AEC's point of view, a few dead Utahan sheep seemed to be a pretty darn good batting average—meaning their explosive efforts were a unanimous triumph on all fronts.

Back in St. George, Utah, a story far quieter than missiles and protest committees was unfolding. With the word *atomic* seeping to the backs of brains and dramatic threats exiting the world stage, it was easy for most to turn their attention elsewhere. In that specific region of the country—Washington County—an alarming number of thyroid issues began appearing in predominantly newborns and young children.

A 1963 report by Charles W. Mays of the University of Utah identified ten different thyroid cancers in 2,253 children (75 cases in one particular St. George school two years later) who were believed to have been exposed as infants with an average dose of 225 rads (absorbed radiation dose in the body); 0.5 rad had been deemed the absolute maximum a person could safely ingest.

At the time, US lifetime thyroid cancer rates were estimated to be 0.97 percent in females and 0.36 percent in males–dubbed extremely rare in ages younger than twenty-five. With limited knowledge about thyroid cancer, symptoms of weight fluctuation, fatigue, fevers, hair loss, and in a few cases, tumors, went undetected or misdiagnosed.

Clusters of childhood leukemia (90 percent fatal at the time) were reported by the Utah Cancer Registry as being one-and-a-half times the national average between 1956 and 1964, with the highest in the state being a particular four-county region surrounding St. George.

Birth defect rates and mental disabilities began to increase. A rising number of lymphoma, breast cancer, melanoma, bone cancer, brain tumor, and gastrointestinal tract cancer cases were being discovered in adults.

AEC chairman Glenn T. Seaborg combated growing concerns by establishing the Technical Analysis Branch in 1961 to study "nuclear weapons' ecological consequences and their implications for human life." The gesture was seen as nothing more than lip service that had no plans of publishing any findings that could damage the commission's image.

It wouldn't be the humans of St. George to receive initial attention on the matter of illness, either. To the press, sheepherder Ken Bulloch recalled his flock inexplicably falling over dead after an atomic blast went off, a common occurrence that led to thousands of carcasses being bulldozed into mass graves. A lawsuit was filed against the federal government in 1955 on behalf of Utah sheepherders, asking for $30 in compensation for every dead ewe and $15 for each lost lamb. The request, totaling $250,000, made headlines and became one of the first instances to bring attention to nuclear side effects, but it was thrown out two years later when a government panel of experts argued radiation could not have been responsible.

Physicist Dr. Harold Knapp, who had worked with the AEC since 1955, later came to investigate the science behind areas of unexplained high radiation called "hot spots." In his findings, Knapp listed high traces of the radioactive iodine-131, particularly in the milk produced and consumed in the St. George area, among others. Low-level exposure to the radioisotope had been linked to thyroid cancer. The AEC had failed to monitor such specific agricultural instances, warning only of imminent nuclear fallout. Knapp began to connect various dots and propose that the thyroid cancers could be linked to the contaminated dairy that people, particularly young children, had been drinking for the past ten years.

The AEC scrutinized the doctor's research and pressured him not to publish anything, with his superior, Dr. Gordon Dunning, fearing repercussions: "Would it look like the Atomic Energy Commission and Public Health Service had not been doing their job?"

The AEC had in fact sponsored university tests on healthy newborns who were exposed to iodine-131 in 1953; findings were positive. Fearful that the report would be discovered and the AEC made to look like liars attempting to cover up damaging facts, Knapp's report was published; his detailed section of how the Upshot-Knothole Harry test was directly responsible for increased I-131 levels was, however, omitted. Knapp immediately left his position with the AEC and published his full report in a 1964 edition of *Nature* magazine; no further discussions were held on the matter, and further claims of similar findings were either dispelled or ignored.

If Dick Powell had caught any flack for his direction—or involvement—with *The Conqueror*, the negativity must have just rolled off the man's busy back. His second feature, *You Can't Run Away from It*, came and went without making a single squeak; again, it was a critical blow that failed to trip up his momentum. The director stampeded straight into back-to-back war pictures with 20th Century Fox: *The Enemy Below* in 1957 and *The Hunters* in 1958, both of which starred Robert Mitchum.

Neither film rose with any sort of prominence or sunk from sour reviews, so Powell unexpectedly pulled another sudden career switcheroo and decided he was done helming feature productions. The choice to quit directing after years spent clawing for the opportunity was far more sensible than him fighting for more chances or throwing in the towel completely; Powell had about a million and one projects begging to be brought to the small screen.

*Four Star Playhouse* had been a revolutionary television success. In anthological form, it treated audiences to a grab bag of original works—everything from slapstick comedies and gritty mysteries with budding bit players like Joanne Woodward stopping by for guest roles. It also gave directors like Blake Edwards a chance to cut their teeth.

Next, Powell launched *Zane Grey Theatre*, a Western anthology program that ran for 149 episodes from 1956 until 1961. Based on the short stories of American author Pearl Zane Grey—Powell occasionally appeared as various outlaws and sheriffs, additionally playing host for the entire series run. It's also worth noting he gave ultra-successful TV series creator Aaron Spelling (*The Love Boat*; *Beverly Hills, 90210*) his first big gig on that show.

Powell subsequently topped his Western buffet with a smorgasbord of genres through his self-titled program *The Dick Powell Theatre* (later named *The Dick Powell Show*) in 1961. It was clear he had finally found his niche after so many years of shedding skins; there had been no more song and dance routines, nor had Powell accepted a film role since *Susan Slept Here*. Instead, he giddily opted for game show appearances, presenting Emmy and Golden Globe Awards, and popping up on schlocky sitcoms like *Car 54, Where Are You?*

On the romantic side of Powell's life, he was married on three separate occasions, two of them starlets including 1930s' musical icon and frequent gold-digger portrayer Joan Blondell. His longest and most talked about relationship was with actress June Allyson, whom he had met in 1945.

Fifteen years, four children (two from his second marriage and two with June), and two jam-packed Hollywood careers going head-to-head meant marriage problems would rear their ugly head. Allyson allegedly had an affair with costar Alan Ladd and soon asked Powell for a divorce. The couple separated but later wished to reconcile. Dick took his wife and family on a lengthy boating trip during the summer of 1962 in an attempt to make peace with their personal problems. On the water, Powell's demeanor looked dim. He was skinnier than usual and paler in color. His family felt he seemed sluggish and tired. Powell himself complained about back pain. Upon their return, Powell paid a visit to the doctor, where he was diagnosed with cancer of the throat in mid-September.

Word leaked to the press, prompting a flurry of rumors around the entertainment industry. Powell pressed forward with his program in the middle of undergoing treatment. He claimed to be seeking treatment for an allergy before stigma of the still relatively unknown disease drove Powell to face the truth with honesty. "I've got this cancer licked. The very name of the disease terrifies people. The unreasoning fear of cancer must be dispelled," Powell said. He meant it, too, later writing actor and friend James Cagney a letter assuring him that he was "a country boy who can handle this sort of thing."

Powell was temporarily hospitalized to receive cobalt radiation therapy, done through a linear acceleration (LINAC) machine. Still a generally new procedure at the time, gamma rays were directed toward the tumor on his lymph glands during six separate sessions. While the hope was to eradicate the cancerous tissues, the disease quickly spread to Powell's chest, forcing him to step away from hosting his television show and his president position with Four Star Productions near the end of October.

When cancer was discovered in his lower back, he was permanently hospitalized and fell into a coma on New Year's Day. Dick Powell died on January 2, 1963, at the age of fifty-eight. He passed away in a penthouse set up to keep him comfortable, where he was surrounded by family, including his wife.

Hollywood was floored by the news. Powell was young, multitalented, and very successful. Hundreds of colleagues and fans attended his funeral at All Saints Episcopal Church in Beverly Hills. "Dick showed tremendous courage. He was convinced until the end he was going to lick it," said Powell's Four Star successor, Tom McDermott.

Writer and employee Aaron Spelling singled out Powell's work ethic, recalling that he would ask that no one left the studio before him. "He never left any earlier than 7 p.m., and even when he did, he'd say, 'I'm leaving now, Skinny. I'll look for your taillights behind me.'"

The *Dick Powell Show* filtered through several months of pre-taped episodes until it was permanently taken off the air, earning an Emmy nomination for "Outstanding Drama Series." Powell himself was posthumously honored with a Television Academy Trustee Award; it was accepted by his partners, Charles Boyer and David Niven.

Left widowed, June Allyson temporarily withdrew from public life, leaving behind film roles and plentiful interview requests. She struggled with an alcohol addiction for much of the sixties, particularly when the tabloids had a field day with the news that Allyson decided to marry Powell's barber, Alfred Glenn Maxwell. Dick lived on not only in her life but through a dedicated fan base and television rebroadcasts of old pictures; many often remained curious as to why the celebrity was taken away so quickly.

Allyson did publicly address her husband's death on a few occasions, pointing toward a splashy 1954 Camel cigarette advertisement Powell appeared in as evidence. In her autobiography, she felt differently. "It was a movie, *The Conqueror*, that started us sliding down the side of a mountain. Slowly at first like debris in an avalanche. Richard didn't recognize the danger signals."

Pedro Armendáriz was another *Conqueror* alumnus whose schedule was chock-full of working days. A familiar face that appeared in handfuls of productions each year, Armendáriz was, and continues to be, cited as one of the best and brightest stars in the Latin American film industry. The actor possessed multiple portrayals of revolutionary general Pancho Villa on his resume not to mention a plethora of Mexican melodramas and period pieces.

It was said to have been his exceptional bright green eyes that carried him to stardom. Armendáriz's desire to give layered performances helped him dip his toe in the experimental worlds of Italian and French cinema.

Armendáriz was married to actress Carmelita Pardo Bohr since 1938 and was father to son Pedro Jr. and daughter Carmen. It was the Hollywood films in the latter 1950s that kept the Armendáriz family afloat. As illustrious and cherished as Latin films were at the time, they did not match the paycheck from a motion picture produced at one of the Big Five studios.

By the turn of the decade, he was costarring alongside Robert Mitchum in the Mexican-set Western *The Wonderful Country* and with Guy Williams in the fantastical family adventure *Captain Sindbad*. Unfortunately, his name proved tough for American audiences to remember while his talents as a character actor kept his global celebrity image low.

Under the endorsement of John Ford, he was recommended to director Terence Young for a role in the second James Bond film, *From Russia with Love*. The United Artists production had been rushed before cameras since the inaugural Bond adventure, the campy *Dr. No*, was a runaway hit in 1962. Adapted from the Ian Fleming novel, the mood of the sequel shifted toward a more mature, dreary Cold War atmosphere. Pitting the Sean Connery incarnation of 007 against a colorful array of S.P.E.C.T.R.E. agents, assassination plots, and exotic European locales, the suave British spy needed some help navigating the Balkins in the midst of his mission. Armendáriz was thus cast in the key supporting role of Ali Kerim Bey, the helpful head of MI6 Station T in Istanbul, Turkey.

With such a prominent role in his hands, Armendáriz should have had a massive international breakthrough because of *From Russia with Love*. But before filming began, the actor decided to investigate the growing pain that had been ailing his hips. An inoperable cancerous tumor was found on the actor's lymph nodes, and he was told by UCLA Medical Center that the disease would be terminal. Left with the option to withdraw from the role and undergo radiation treatments, Armendáriz passed on hospital care and pressed on with the James Bond production. He not only took the role to distract himself but to ensure his family would have enough financial security after his inevitable passing.

In order to accommodate the actor's wishes, most scenes featuring Armendáriz's character were moved up to the beginning of production and shot on location in the Turkish capital. His physical appearance had changed significantly in mere months–the man's body was thinner and skin far paler. He sported a gray hairpiece in an attempt to cover his balding head and pull his frail look together. The actor experienced such intense physical pain on the set of *From Russia with Love,* he had to move more slowly and walked with a limp–visible throughout the final cut of the film.

When Armendáriz could no longer bear shooting in Istanbul, the Bond production moved to Britain to focus solely on anything pertaining to the character of Ali Kerim Bey. The pain became too much for Armendáriz, and he had to be taken off the film completely before his role was finished. The last of his scenes were performed by a stunt double with director Terence Young serving as an occasional stand-in.

Confined to an LA hospital, the actor knew the road ahead was to be dim and agonizing. He had seen Dick Powell and friend Ernest Hemingway on the losing end of cancer. He wanted no part of the ugly battle to come. On June 18, 1963, he took influence from Hemingway's solution to the pain and smuggled a gun into his hospital room. He shot himself directly in the chest and died instantly at the age of fifty-one.

Pedro Armendáriz was buried at the Panteón Jardín cemetery in Mexico City. His death was mourned in his home country; most of the attention any American press gave tended to sensationalize his suicide. *From Russia with Love* was released four months later, containing his very last performance; it was critically lauded, with the film itself consistently appearing at the top of the best 007 movie lists.

"I don't blame Pete," John Wayne said to the press after hearing about his friend. "I'd do the same thing he did."

Armendáriz's wife died later that same year; both of their children entered the film industry with Carmen as a producer and Pedro Jr. as an actor (he appeared in the 1989 Bond film *License to Kill* and later died from eye cancer at the age of seventy-one).

John Wayne was more than just a smoker. An urban legend around his habit said that Duke only lit one match in the morning; every new cigarette was ignited by the one that came before it. While an obvious hole in that story is that the actor would have had to extinguish the butt to focus on filming a scene, it doesn't fall too far from the truth.

He chain-smoked since his teenage years and went through five, sometimes six, packs a day. His fingertips were constantly stained black by the nicotine. Wayne loved smoking one brand in particular—he appeared in multiple print advertisements and a series of 1952 television commercials for Camel Cigarettes, shot on the set of *Big Jim McLain.* "If you want to find out how enjoyable a cigarette can be? Do what I did! Smoke only Camels for thirty days," he says, puffing away in a dapper black suit alongside a narrator's flavorful sales pitch. "I think you'll stay with Camels, too."

Another has Wayne in the midst of a fight sequence, with the narrator assuring, "When the camera stops, John Wayne takes time out to enjoy his favorite cigarette." The faux director calls, "Cut!" and sure enough, the actor reaches for his pack. "Well, after you've been making a lot of strenuous scenes, you like to sit back and enjoy a cool, mild, good-tasting cigarette," Wayne casually states, lighting up before taking a seat. "And that's just what Camels are: mild and good tasting, pack after pack. I know. I've been smoking 'em for twenty years. So why don't you try 'em yourself and see what I mean."

A good decade after that batch of advertisements aired alongside countless others—some with "doctors" discussing which brand of cigarettes they prefer—the notion that smoking was bad for your health seemed to gain some traction. The Stanford University School of Medicine noted throat cancer had been deemed "the smoker's cancer" since the nineteenth century, but tobacco companies had retaliated by capitalizing on people's fears with "throat reassurance"—a guarantee that their product was mild and harmless on the most delicate of lymph nodes.

Scientists Ernst Wynder and Evarts Graham linked cigarette smoking with the development of lung cancer through a 1950 study; yet, it wasn't until the US Surgeon General announced cigarette smoking was a health hazard in the United States that the information began to be believed. A statement issued in January

1964 claimed lung cancer risks due to smoking were high and that action was required to reduce harmful effects. Smokers were urged to cut down or quit.

John Wayne's response? "So maybe it'll take six months off my life, but they're not going to kill me."

Duke thought nothing of the persistent cough he'd been dealing with for a good two years. It didn't just come and go, either; the cough had gotten so bad on the set of his Pearl Harbor drama *In Harm's Way*, he would ruin takes because of frequent hacking and wheezing fits. When he was vacationing in Mexico, Wayne attempted to water ski; he found himself unusually out of breath and unable to get himself up out of the water. His solution, once a lengthy coughing fit was dealt with, was vowing to never water ski again.

It was only when Wayne signed up for another Western with pal and frequent costar Dean Martin that his whole life changed. He was set to go straight from *In Harm's Way* to the production of *The Sons of Katie Elder* in the summer of 1964 but found himself with two weeks to spare. The actor apparently hadn't seen a doctor for two years and was told by his wife, Pilar, that he should go in for a checkup before embarking on another project.

Routine X-rays were taken at the Scripps Clinic in the small seaside community of La Jolla, California. Not so routine was that they showed a golf-ball-size tumor on his left lung. America's toughest hero was instantly diagnosed with cancer. He'd described the moment as if "somebody hits you in the belly with an iron pipe."

For many in 1964, lung cancer was just about the same thing as a death sentence. As the leading cause of cancer-related deaths, lung cancer had a mortality rate well over 50 percent—survivors were promised that the disease would return within five years.

By 1964, Wayne's career seemed to reach unflappable heights. Riding off of a successful directorial debut, he and John Ford seemed to chug along like a well-oiled machine; *Rio Bravo*, *Donovan's Reef*, and *The Man Who Shot Liberty Valance* were all bona fide classics. Throw creative ventures into the mix like the comedic *McLintock!* and African poacher adventure *Hatari!* and his star status shot past any atomic test to beyond the stratosphere.

Wayne was due on *The Sons of Katie Elder* set, and he was certain nothing was going to prevent him from sitting down in his makeup chair on the first day of shooting. Casually, he gathered director Henry Hathaway and producer Hal Wallis to break the news. "I'm going to hit you with it. I've got the Big C," Wayne said, assuring no radiation treatments or time off would be necessary. He'd instead opt for the lung to be removed completely, a surgery he was set to undergo the day after sharing the information with his crew.

There was some talk of replacing Wayne with Kirk Douglas, but Wallis had the entire production pushed back by six weeks to give his star time to recover–a respectful act that a very nonchalant Duke deemed unnecessary. Hathaway had survived colon cancer a decade prior and warned that surgery was no piece of cake.

Wayne agreed, rolling up to Dr. John Jones's office at Good Samaritan Hospital on September 16, ready to have the appendage yanked out so he could be on his way. The doctor instead broke the news that the tumor was far too large to attack from the front; he'd have to conduct a far more invasive surgery by going in through Wayne's back.

The press and public were told Wayne was admitted to the hospital for a minor ankle surgery, while in reality, a twenty-eight-inch incision was made from his chest to his back. Two ribs had to be removed with his stomach and diaphragm rearranged for easier access. The six-hour surgery resulted in Dr. Jones snatching the entire upper lobe of his left lung, which contained the egg-sized tumor.

Another six-hour surgery followed a few days later and was performed to rectify broken stitches and take care of severe swelling and fluid collection that rendered Duke helpless. He left the hospital, fresh from three weeks of painful recovery and rigorous breathing exercises; the icon was hardly able to move without help when he set foot out the door.

John Wayne fell into a deep depression on his arrival home. A brush with death tends to bring a person's mortality to the forefront of their mind, but the actor also wondered what exactly the future would hold for him. If he were to survive cancer, would he be able to move like he used to? Ride like he used to? Perform painful stunts like he did?

The question of Duke being able to get insurance on movie sets made him toss and turn during his bedridden stretch. His reduced breathing capacity would surely limit the locations he was allowed to visit, more than likely having to cross dusty southwestern deserts off the list.

That very battle was playing out in Hal Wallis's office with back and forth bargaining between he and Paramount Pictures for the right to keep Wayne attached to *Katie Elder*. The studio didn't want to wait any longer and insisted Wayne couldn't be brought down to Mexico for the shoot; the insurance would be far too high.

Robert Mitchum and William Holden were circled for his part around the time Dr. Jones invited Duke to his office, where they took a fresh set of X-rays. Based on his findings and what the doctor had witnessed from the surgery, there was no evidence that the cancer had spread. Rushed past his wife's protest, Wayne was cleared for production, a bittersweet victory that left the actor triumphant yet nervous to get back in the saddle.

An oxygen tank sat on the sidelines in case Wayne, working in a considerably high altitude, literally needed a breather between takes. Crew members recalled him being hesitant about his first few scenes riding a horse. His line delivery was noticeably more airy. His off-screen banter had changed from politics to death; the actor apparently vented about everything from the pain to his fears about leaving his family behind. He'd show off his scar to anyone who wanted a peek.

Henry Hathaway refused to baby his star and forced him to jump off a bridge into a freezing river during the production's very first week of shooting. After the icy waters knocked the wind out of him, Wayne said he was grateful for the no-nonsense approach. He himself refused to fall behind Dean Martin's antics and began shooting mezcal and smoking double-time to prove he could still live up to his manly image.

The actor had made a few life changes for the better; he seemed to possess a grander consideration for others because of the experience, reaching out to other celebrity acquaintances embarking on their own cancer journeys. Deep down, he felt there was far more work to be done. With the risk of cancer's return still looming in the foreseeable future, Wayne turned to dark humor to keep his spirits up every time he went to get himself examined. He again used his film and Batjac's namesake *The Wake of the Red Witch* to dub his disease: "I'm going down to La Jolla to see if the Red Witch is waiting for me," he'd say.

What weighed on his mind most was the fact that none of his fans–fans and audience members going through the exact same thing–knew about his bout with cancer. Advisor Charles Feldman was absolutely certain the news of cancer would obliterate his image, and quality work would be hard to come by. Doctors felt the positive message of hearing the fact that John Wayne beat cancer could serve as an inspiration.

"I thought to myself, I was saved by early detection. Movie image or not, I think I should tell my story so that other people can be saved by getting annual checkups," Duke explained. Wayne possessed an overwhelming urge to get on with his life and return to normal, but the celebrity began to realize that there was no normal to return to and no sense in hiding the truth. "Every day is precious to me now."

Ten weeks after the surgery, on December 29, 1964, Wayne called a press conference to publicly state that he had "licked the Big C." That phrase quickly spread like the very disease it stood for, with many attributing its first utterance to the actor. "I know the man upstairs will pull the plug when he wants to, but I don't want to end my life being sick," he told the assembled crowd. "I want to go out on two feet–in action. I'm not the sort to back away from a fight. I don't believe in shrinking away from anything. It's not my speed. I never flinched before in my life, so I see no reason to do so now. I'm a guy who meets adversities head on."

*The Sons of Katie Elder* became a financial success, mainly due to the fact people were curious about how Wayne would look from his operation. More than middle-aged at fifty-seven, Wayne had a stiffer stance and far bigger belly–solid signs of getting older, which his masculine worshippers gladly embraced.

The actor found himself pelted with follow-up questions about the cause of his so-called Red Witch. Wayne was a heavy drinker, often struggling to stop at one or two glasses of Wild Turkey bourbon. He dined on a diet of red meats and traveled the globe, getting

down and dirty on movie shoots in the jungles of Third World countries. Wayne must have studied the deaths of Dick Powell and Pedro
Armendáriz for a split second or two before plucking out a common
thread.

Given the surgeon general's announcement, Duke experienced
a change of heart on the matter and quietly believed cigarette smoking caused his lung cancer. Hopelessly addicted, he struggled to stay
on the wagon for the rest of his days, simultaneously vowing to
break his habit and encouraging others to do the same. He switched
back and forth between chewing tobacco and smoking cigars, saving cigarettes for the special moments in his life—for example, an
appointment in 1969. Five years after his surgery, Wayne was officially given the word that he was completely cancer-free.

# 13: Turn of the Times

On a walk through Tinseltown in the 1950s, David O. Selznick told
screenwriter Ben Hecht, "Hollywood's like Egypt, full of crumbled
pyramids. It'll never come back. It'll keep crumbling until finally the
wind blows the last studio prop across the sands."

RKO's demise was by far the loudest crumble of the studio system's fall, and its echo certainly did not go unnoticed. From studio
heads to big-shot producers, actors and screenwriters, the gaffers—
everyone in the industry stood with their mouths agape when the
production giant that had given the world some of the greatest cinematic achievements in film history clawed for dear life yet came
up short.

RKO always was the wobbliest of the Big Five, but its shutdown
still served as a sobering reality check for all those dedicated to
making motion pictures. Not only was it evidence that Hollywood
wasn't made of Teflon, RKO's closure stood as a marker that everything about the way movies were viewed and put together was
about to change.

Selznick was only half right with his Egyptian theory. Hollywood did manage to rebuild, but it took the better part of the 1950s
and '60s to shake off the ancient dust and bridge the gap between
the old and the new. Starting with the block-booking ban when

studio-owned theater chains were forcibly sold off by the mid-1950s, a freer Hollywood arose. Smaller entities like the "Little Three" majors–United Artists, Columbia Pictures, and Universal Studios–could not only compete but thrive with work that finally found a proper audience.

New companies like Walt Disney Studios, thanks to RKO's soiled partnership, took advantage of underutilized markets like family entertainment and animation and surpassed the competition to become a full-fledged world-domineering empire. It was the insubstantial and poorly run ones like John Wayne's old Western stomping grounds, Republic Pictures, who decided to fold their hand; quality seemed to forever elude them.

When it came to the stars, no one was able to control the larger-than-life personalities. Contract deals, similar to what Wayne had going with RKO, where actors were paid a lump sum, given a number of promised roles, and potentially forced into ones they didn't want, were an archaic practice that ended on somewhat of a mutual term. Celebrities, particularly the ones with clout, were hopping from studio to studio for singular projects and battling it out against competitors for the shiniest gigs.

Boiled down to the basics, what you had were the biggest Hollywood players–the giant movie studios that ignited the whole industry with this very system–unable to guarantee where their pictures were shown or what stars were in them. Following decades of growth and unchecked power, that was a crippling handicap to say the least; the only way forward seemed to be an exhausting demand for endless creativity.

The substantial changes in the way studios did business left them weak and susceptible to any attack from a worthy adversary; and what an adversary they had on their hands with television. Movies may have won a battle or two in the 1950s, but TV emerged as the reigning victor of the ongoing war.

Movies took advantage of bigger screens and their access to color; they got Gene Kelly to tap dance and brought in Marilyn Monroe to show off a little . . . okay, a lot of leg! They put actors in chariots, on spaceships, and atop Mount Rushmore; but in the end, it wasn't enough. Audiences grew tired of the onslaught of spectacles and turned on the tube at home, agreeing they could miss the next four or five epic releases because they'd just be the same as the last one or possibly even as unwatchable as *The Conqueror*.

RKO's conclusion resembled one lone lemming stampeding off a cliff to its doom; the others were right behind it, but some managed to dig in their heels in the nick of time. Others figured they could best the cliff (and television) altogether.

MGM pressed on with the exact *Conqueror* mold in hand, headed by a revolving door of producers following Louis B. Mayer's forced exit in 1951 and all of whom insisted on putting all their cash on flashy big-budget musicals that began to flop following the Oscar-winning *Gigi*.

Paramount fumbled its fruitless dealings with the DuMont Television Network and ignorance about the wealth of their film library.

Only Warner Bros. slipped by without suffering much more than bruises and scrapes, and that was due mostly to their diversification into television and record labels.

Speaking of crumbling Egypt, 20th Century Fox famously chose to make *Cleopatra*, a four-hour saga that made *The Conqueror* look like a home movie. Starring Elizabeth Taylor in the title role, tens of thousands of extras filled a total of seventy-nine elaborate sets. Production dragged on for four-and-a-half years, racking up a $31 million ($256 million) budget, plus an extra $12 million for marketing.

*Cleopatra* may have been the highest grossing picture of 1963 but was so expensive, the mismanagement behind the monster forced Fox to lay off the entirety of its staff and sell off the backlot to stay in business. If Howard Hughes entering into a consent decree with the Justice Department is seen as the start of the studio system collapse in 1948 and RKO's closure the tipping point, *Cleopatra*'s elaborate failure is often considered the very end.

Theatrical attendance was next to dwindling in the second half of the 1960s, plummeting from forty-five million American audience members each week in 1965 to nineteen million at the turn of the decade. It's easy to see why: Everyone completely ran out of steam when the sword-and-sandal epics tanked nearly every time.

Hollywood studios in the sixties were essentially on autopilot, offering up nothing more than mindless candy floss as they studied

RKO's wrongdoings. They scratched their empty noggins in search of plans on how to move ahead and overcome the almighty boxes in people's living rooms.

Doris Day jumped from kooky romance to kooky romance. Hound dog Elvis Presley thrust his pelvis in over twenty-five carbon-copy plots. Cheap beach-themed movies with problematic surfing competitions were churned out repeatedly, each one circling around teenage girls named Gidget or people way too old to be playing teenagers, i.e., Frankie and Annette.

Overpacked vehicles like *It's a Mad, Mad, Mad, Mad World* and *The Great Race* crammed in as many stars, crisscrossing each other in different storylines, as they could and often pushed the running time to more than three hours. Heists and buddy robberies and stupefied war battles were all too frequent. Science fiction seemed to require hallucinogens to follow along.

The success of *The Sound of Music* brought 20th Century Fox back from the brink in 1965, perking up the attention of every studio who rushed to replicate the formula and failed on practically every try. They'd sneak in a *Conqueror*-esque epic or family musical every now and then in a bid for more cash, but bloated kid flicks like *Dr. Doolittle* or old-fashioned song-and-dance throwbacks like *Hello, Dolly!* weren't even competing anymore.

Products from the so-called "movie capital of the world" had evolved into hokey, predictable, and stale entertainment; therefore, the job was left to other countries to tackle.

Akin to the rise of the Beatles, the "British invasion" infiltrated moviegoers' minds with James Bond, swinging films starring either Michael Caine or Albert Finney, and anything to do with edgy mod culture. In fact, half of the Best Picture winners at the Academy Awards came from across the pond. David Lean was just about the only one thriving with the epic genre in the sixties with immortal giants like *Lawrence of Arabia* and *Dr. Zhivago*. Foreign influences didn't stop with jolly old England, either.

Audiences forwent the sugary escapism for the darker realities brought to life by the likes of Francois Truffaut and Jean-Luc Godard; film critics turned movie directors were credited with igniting the French New Wave. Their low-budget black-and-white works were unfamiliar, a stark contrast to American cinema, filled with painful human emotion, unconventional narratives, and a downer ending.

From Italy, Federico Fellini's surrealism appeased the dreamers while Sergio Leone's so-called "spaghetti Westerns" gave John Wayne a run for his money thanks to stylized violence and grit emanating from Clint Eastwood.

From Asia, Akira Kurosawa ascended as the master of Japanese cinema while Satyajit Ray gave the world *Pather Panchali* and other Indian stories.

On home turf, daring filmmakers like John Cassavetes were dubbed the "grandfather of the independent movement" with pictures like the free-flowing *Shadows*–made completely without studio backing.

Their works inspired a whole new generation of young faces, the "movie brats," which included the likes of Francis Ford Coppola, Robert Altman, Steven Spielberg, Martin Scorsese, Peter Bogdanovich, Brian De Palma, William Friedkin, George Lucas, Mike Nichols, Paul Mazursky, Woody Allen, Bob Rafelson, John Schlesinger, Arthur Penn, Roger Corman, Michael Cimino, Roman Polanski, Sidney Lumet, Sam Peckinpah, and Hal Ashby to name a few.

Some leaped into the business as the first folks with extensive film degrees in hand. Others seemingly wandered off the street with self-made projects and a deep love for icons like Hitchcock, Wilder, and Bergman that melded with inspiration from worldly cinema of the day.

At the forefront of the fight for film were revolutionaries like Warren Beatty, who brought the blood-soaked *Bonnie and Clyde*, a sexy and violent counterculture "rallying cry" to the screen in 1967. Mike Nichols released his controversial directorial debut, *Who's Afraid of Virginia Woolf?*, only one year prior. It was the first mainstream film to contain such profane language–words like "goddamn" or "screw you"–that a warning was published to notify viewers that the film was suitable for only mature audiences.

By 1970–only four years later–just about every colorful word imaginable could be heard onscreen, as was every body part on full display. The Motion Picture Code, whose mighty grip on movie censorship was challenged time and time again under First Amendment laws in the 1950s, was now completely ignored; with no regard for their approval, the board had no choice but to abandon their wholesome mission.

The likes of edgy Jack Nicholson losing his cool over dry toast in *Five Easy Pieces* and long-haired Dennis Hopper inhaling every drug imaginable shook up the physical norms and brought to the screen an electric energy that saw them fade into a variety of characters; younger viewers were quick to claim that the hammy overacting style of the "old generation" paled in comparison.

Actresses simultaneously broke past roles that demanded only a physical presence and the odd harem-set striptease. With the bubbling women's liberation movement pushing against stereotypes and getting more and more females into the workforce, so, too, did cinema join the wave of change to represent different perspectives.

Stories like *Rosemary's Baby* tackled the pressures and taboos of pregnancy and female sexuality. Elaine May's *A New Leaf* challenged the attributes of leading ladies with a mousy lead. True, more skin than ever was shown, but more frequently with a goal to spark conversation or a connection to the plot.

Washed along with the wave of change, instances of altering an actor's race using makeup were deemed insensitive in the wake of the civil rights movement. The yellowface heyday of the late 1950s burned out like the rest of Hollywood's Golden Age practices and went under the microscope in more than just a casting confusion sense.

Starting with Mickey Rooney squinting and groaning through buckteeth in *Breakfast at Tiffany's*, critics and audiences were divided on the over-the-top performance clearly built on exaggerated stereotypes. "Never in all the more than forty years after we made it—not one complaint," the actor later said in a reflection on the experience. "Every place I've gone in the world people say, 'God, you were so funny.' Asians and Chinese come up to me and say, 'Mickey, you were out of this world.' Had I known people would get offended, I wouldn't have done it."

Alec Guinness made his living by altering his skin to portray Saudi princes, Indian gurus, and Japanese businessmen in dramas. Peter Sellers found humor in East Asian stereotypes, portraying a bumbling Bollywood actor in Blake Edwards's *The Party* and later opting to star in a Fu Manchu remake. Time and time again films with yellowface were released, but as the years progressed, so, too, did attitudes and the criticisms that cried louder in the wake of each instance.

The outcries against altered skin tones weren't always consistent, with dramatic works tending to slip past scrutiny more so than a Sellers comedy; but the commonality and reasoning behind the practice were certainly changing. The Academy would still award Linda Hunt's yellowface performance with a Best Supporting Actress Oscar for *The Year of Living Dangerously* in 1983.

By the time acid-fueled *Easy Rider* hit theaters in 1969–the classic biker road trip made up of orgies, pot, and the counterculture zeitgeist–the so-called "Golden Age" of Hollywood was etched in stone for the history books. Seasoned stars like Jimmy Stewart turned their noses up at the "filth" populating movie houses just as greats like Burt Lancaster and William Holden thrived in grittier roles.

With people behind the camera becoming celebrities in their own right, the auteur theory begged the question that films could be far more than a money-making committee–a personal stamp from a so-called "author" could create a reflective piece of art. The mandate was that a smaller, more contained production with intimate plots was the way forward; stories with modern music, anti-establishment themes, and an examination of the antihero; protagonists with motives that weren't black and white. People wanted to see themselves up onscreen, the polar opposite of million-dollar escapisms cobbled together with crudely portrayed history, desert-set battles, and Genghis Khan–made for nothing more than a mindless thrill and the evident pursuit for cash.

Ideas driving the picture business at the end of the 1960s were radical, fresh, and wildly different than ever before; epic desert-set spectacles looked to be an entertainment form of the past. They were new and, thankfully, managed to save the American motion picture industry.

"Crumbling ancient Egypt" was rebuilt, often described as a moment when "the lunatics took over the asylum." What they created in that flurry of freedom was, like it or not, New Hollywood.

The late 1960s for John Wayne marked a significant shift in both his personal and professional life; a newfound zest seemed to bring out a youthful playfulness in him while a drive to champion charitable causes expunged every remaining drop of energy. His very place in the world as an American icon seemed to sway without effort when moviegoers reveled in the violence and gore that new Clint Eastwood films and Sam Peckinpah's *The Wild Bunch* sought to explore.

Many clapped in the name of art and realism. Wayne shook his head at the cinematic movement and pressed on with more classical pictures, holding firm to his masculine, right-winged image held dear by loyal fans. Duke's staunch traditionalism made him look like a dusty, out-of-touch relic to the youthful left, who began using the movie star and his work as a symbol for the previous generation's perceived unwillingness to move forward. Wayne, on the contrary, seemed to care very little about how he fared with the "hippie" crowd, insisting he was not a political figure although he tirelessly backed Richard Nixon as the Republican presidential hopeful and threw his support behind the Vietnam War.

With the big health scare behind him, Duke threw himself into a string of Western work . . . if you could call it that. Each choice that followed was hardly anything more than an excuse to spend time with friends. Reuniting with Howard Hawks, he starred in *El Dorado* with newfound pal Robert Mitchum and teamed up with Kirk Douglas and Frank Sinatra for *Cast a Giant Shadow*. He made casual returns to directing with supportive behind-the-scenes work on *The Green Berets* and *Big Jake* to flex his creative muscle.

Duke began to see that television was valuable for keeping him in the limelight; he began regularly popping up in cameo appearances, momentarily teaming up with the Clampett family in *The Beverly Hillbillies* and kicking off a ten-episode stint on *Rowan & Martin's Laugh-In*.

"They say I'm tough. They say I'm bossy. But I found a friend in my big, brown horsey," Wayne recited in a reoccurring poetry segment, clutching a giant red, white, and blue flower for each installment. "The sky is blue, the grass is green. Get off your butt and join the marines," he ordered in another, gleefully taunting the counterculture in each appearance. His most famous bit on the show might arguably be when he miserably stomped out in a fuzzy blue bunny outfit for an Easter-themed sketch.

Nothing holds a candle, however, to the success and longevity of his most revered project from this period. *True Grit* encapsulated absolutely everything audiences knew and loved about Duke. The role of Rooster Cogburn was largely humorous, giving Wayne the chance to ham up every scene as a stumbling drunk character, fleshing the character out with his own beloved bravado.

"This is the best script he ever read," screenwriter Marguerite Roberts said Wayne told her, though his taste in source material clearly did not have the greatest track record. In this case, the actor was right on the money in uncovering a plum part–basing his rotund waddle off of the lout-like actor Wallace Beery and paying tribute to his own cantankerous mentor, John Ford, by sporting an eye patch.

Leather-skinned, hoarse-voiced, and scowling along with a smile that constantly tried to fight its way across his face, Duke leaped off the screen in ways he hadn't done in years. No, he may not have appeared very young and agile in *True Grit*, but he made up for his age with a limitless determination to go against type and have an absolute gas with his profession. For a man who claimed time and time again he routinely went from job to job and did what he was told, nowhere in this picture does that seem to ring true.

Directed by Henry Hathaway and costarring satin-voiced singer Glen Campbell as the Texas Ranger who helps Marshal Cogburn and a "tomboy" teenager track down her father's killers, *True Grit* easily entered the top ten grossing films of the year. Reviews were mostly positive, with almost all of the praise going to Wayne's performance. Some criticized the role, saying it fell too closely toward self-parody.

Famed critics like Roger Ebert celebrated the fact that the filmmakers recognized and utilized his "special presence." "I have on occasion disliked his movies," Ebert said, "but Wayne has a way of surmounting even bad movies, and in forty years he has also made a great many good ones. Today there is no actor in movies who is more an archetype."

Wayne hardly paused to celebrate the success, instead tracking down a new partner, one that could help satisfy a gnawing need inside him to help. Cancer weighed heavily on Duke's mind, and holding a clean bill of health, he felt he owed the public more than just a simple recounting of how he triumphed over the disease.

The American Cancer Society (ACS) had been drumming up support for research and funding since 1913, a time when the word *cancer* was unmentionable in public. Decades of spreading awareness and running various donation campaigns had certainly made them well known in the public eye, but the charity was always in need of more funds to continue their fight.

By the late 1960s, actors like Tony Curtis were lending their fame to the "I quit smoking club," a series of commercials that were aimed at showing people the harm of cigarettes. Duke saw an opportunity to make use of his celebrity in a similar vein and approached the society to see if he could be of service. Little did he know that gesture would be the beginning of a series of public service announcements sharing the importance of checkups and ACS support.

From a dusty saloon and wearing a cowboy costume, Wayne addressed the public on the matter for the first time in 1969. "I was just finishing my 199th picture—never felt better in my life. I said to myself, 'When this is finished, I'm going out on my boat,' " he recounts. "And then I got nagged into going for a medical checkup. They found a spot on the X-ray; it was lung cancer. If I had waited a few more weeks, I wouldn't be here now."

Footage of a gun-toting Rooster Cogburn is intertwined, highlighting where treatments and early detection were able to take the actor. "That's me seven years later in *True Grit* 'cause I did myself a favor and got a checkup. So why don't all of you do yourselves a favor and get a checkup. Talk someone you like into getting a checkup. Nag someone you love into getting a checkup. And while you're at it, send a check to the American Cancer Society, too. It's great to be alive."

The PSA proved to be such a hit, shorter bumper-style announcements were quickly spattered throughout the television cycle and aired ad nauseam in the early 1970s. "You know, they may find a cure for cancer even without your help. But if I were you, I wouldn't bet my life on it," Wayne sternly quips in one of the split-second clips. "We're asking you for help again this year; you're lucky, it could be the other way around," he warns in another, keeping each message short and sweet and always directing donation efforts toward the cancer society.

John Wayne had been one of the first celebrities to go public with his cancer, but his vocal follow-up to his fight made him one of the most outspoken faces associated with the disease. Few television aficionados today who grew up in the 1970s can say they don't recall the actor's dead serious mug asking for donations.

They aired everywhere, with the man himself speaking about the whole ordeal on talk shows and during magazine interviews. When the question of the cause came up, namely cigarettes, he'd often shrug his shoulders and claim not to know; his advice was always to opt for checkups and donate what you could spare.

At this newfound height of popularity, he was nominated for his third Academy Award nomination in *True Grit*–his second for an acting performance. He had already picked up a Golden Globe for the performance; but being a Hollywood relic, his chances seemed slim as he had been vocal about many of the works up for other Oscars that year. He had ragged on Jane Fonda's opposition to the Vietnam War and expressed that Hollywood seemed interested in producing "sex pictures" that were "garbage." In a controversial interview with *Playboy* magazine, Wayne named *Easy Rider* and that night's big winner, *Midnight Cowboy,* as examples of the problem.

"Wouldn't you say that the wonderful love of those two men in *Midnight Cowboy*, a story about two fags, qualifies?" he controversially asked. Ironically, the iconic drama and first and only X-rated Best Picture winner had a scene discussing whether or not Wayne himself was a homosexual.

The revolutionary picture earned three Oscars on April 7, with its stars Jon Voight and Dustin Hoffman both up for Best Actor. Veterans Richard Burton and Peter O'Toole were also part of the nominated company.

Duke joked that he'd have better luck staying at home since he had often scooped up statues for his friends not in attendance. Luckily, the actor attended that night where the sins of making *The Conqueror* were forgiven and a bright pink Barbra Streisand, teasing that she wouldn't tell, called out his name.

"Wow. If I'd known that, I'd have put that patch on thirty-five years earlier," he quipped, wiping a tear and offering a small bow to the crowd. His profuse thanks to Academy members and fans and an assurance he was humbled caused naysayers to go on the attack. Critics and Oscar buffs were quick to say the win acted as more of an honorary award that celebrated the summation of his career rather than the Rooster Cogburn performance.

Soured, some nitpicked the character, calling the role lazy and underwhelming. Others insisted he should have won for *Sands of Iwo Jima* twenty years earlier. People suggested his earlier cancer diagnosis swayed more emotional voters into choosing him. Whether or not Wayne was a "good" actor was widely up for debate.

Whatever the case, Wayne finally had his statue; and it seemed to stand for more than just an honor for a job well done. With New Hollywood films about drugs, free love, prostitution, realistic violence, and homosexuality, and then one of the businesses most iconic and long-standing forces getting his due for the genre he was known for, that particular Oscar ceremony marked the mishmash sign of the times and the accelerated changeover between the past and future.

With the sins of *The Conqueror* washed away, it was almost as if a very old friend had come to speak at the "funeral" for the Golden Age.

Miles away in the far less glamorous St. George, Utah, an increase of adult cancers and childhood leukemias failed to decline during the latter part of the 1960s; they were on the rise and few were willing to take notice. Dr. Harold Knapp's findings of high iodine-131 levels in Washington County milk had gone sour; after the failed publication, he dropped his research and accepted work with the Institute for Defense Analysis.

Few others batted an eye at any similar data. Being a sparsely populated Mormon state, hardly any residents drank alcohol or smoked tobacco—Utah, on paper, had some of the lowest cancer rates in the United States. An investigation to dive further into the problem looked to be unnecessary.

At the same time as Knapp discovered the traces of iodine-131, German-born professor Ernest J. Sternglass began to follow the work of Oxford University preventive medicine department head Alice Stewart. Her research on radiation exposure in England led to her theory that any radiation exposure to the fetus could double the child's chances of developing cancer. Sternglass began to research similar ideas in the United States throughout the 1960s, expanding his view far past the borders of Nevada and Utah.

Testifying before a congressional committee about another radioactive isotope, strontium-90, Sternglass declared in 1963 that the dangerous byproduct could in fact cause leukemia in children. Baby teeth samples from as far east as St. Louis, Missouri, contained traces of the substance, giving cause for claims that fallout potentially touched every corner of the US mainland.

By 1969, he concluded that four hundred thousand American infants had died because of medical problems caused by fallout and cited low immune systems and smaller birth weights as the most common defects. An additional phrasing framed his findings as "one in three children who died before their first birthday in America in the 1960s died because of peacetime nuclear testing."

People grew panicked, even furious, with the Atomic Energy Commission and flooded them with complaint letters, calling on their constituencies to act. The AEC, in turn, routinely dismissed Sternglass's claims and stuck with the mantra that exploding neutrons were the source of nuclear harm, not gamma rays and airborne particles.

While Sternglass's findings could have hit a dead end the way Knapp's did, a string of unfavorable strikes against the AEC left the agency with more than just wounds to lick. In 1966, scientists from the National Academy of Sciences and the National Research Council criticized their waste-disposal procedures, suggesting economics were put ahead of environmental concern. Again, the AEC refused to publish the report without edits, but their blockage was widely publicized, making it seem that the agency did indeed have secrets to hide.

When the consideration for nuclear energy was on the rise and the AEC's decree that "one thousand reactors would be producing electricity for homes and businesses across the United States," John Gofman and Arthur Tamplin stepped in with studies on the health of Hiroshima and Nagasaki bomb survivors. They concluded federal safety guidelines for low-level exposures should be reduced by 90 percent, subsequently adopting the Linear No-Threshold (LNT) model to officially estimate cancer risks from low-level radiation. Met with more dismissal from the Atomic Energy Commission, they called for a massive agency overhaul and the abandonment of power plants in their book *"Population Control" Through Nuclear Pollution*.

On a more human level, AEC response letters to residents inquiring about nuclear safety had a growing distastefulness about them as more and more children began to pass away. Issued and signed by former chair Lewis Strauss, they quoted former President Truman as saying, "The dangers that might occur from the fallout of our tests involve a small sacrifice compared to the greater evil of the use of nuclear bombs in war."

The daughter-in-law of Norris Bradbury, former director of Los Alamos laboratory, said he told the public there was no danger but quietly urged her and her husband to move away when she became pregnant. They had lived at the foot of Zion National Park, some forty miles east of St. George.

As for the safety video about that very community the AEC had released about Upshot-Knothole Harry and atomic testing becoming a routine aspect of the community? A handful of the residents that had been prominently featured in that very film were reported to have also died from cancer.

If that wasn't enough to exterminate any fanfare for the AEC, the 1970 Baneberry shot (of Operation Emery) in Area 8 of the Nevada Test Site raised sweat-dripping eyebrows after its nine-hundred-foot detonation underground went awry. The soil unexpectedly cracked, sending a plume of flames and dense fallout over the crew and exposing more than eighty-six workers with much of the residue carried by winds across the northwest United States. While there were no immediate fatalities, it was seen as one of the worst nuclear disasters on American soil.

The days of atomic-themed cocktails and cutesy duck-and-cover sing-along videos were long over, leaving behind a nasty hangover throbbing with shame, anger, pain, and confusion. In a time when government popularity was at a record low, the AEC was seen as an oligarchy with far too much power and countless conflicts of interest.

The green movement under the Nixon Administration ultimately packed the final punch when the widespread conversation across the nation pondered whether or not an expansion into nuclear power could have an everlasting effect on the environment. President Nixon additionally signed the Anti-Ballistic Missile Treaty in May 1972 with Soviet leader Leonid Brezhnev in a further bid for nuclear arms control and peace.

Antipollution attitudes and a lowered public opinion ultimately led to the Energy Reorganization Act of 1974, shutting down the Atomic Energy Commission; regulative and promotional duties were split between the newly formed Nuclear Regulatory Commission and the Energy Research and Development Administration (later folded into the US Department of Energy). The hope was that nuclear development would be overhauled, and the government would keep a closer eye on its atomic capabilities.

With no one to dispute research and bury reports, the works of Gofman, Tamplin, Sternglass, and Harold Knapp prevailed. Inspired by the latter, Dr. Joseph Lyon of the University of Utah began to study death certificates to prove the radiation and cancer link in his home state; he determined the rates were indeed four times higher when compared to others.

Lab tests on mice in 1961, at the very least, had shown that the whole-body exposure to the radioactive isotope caesium-137, a plentiful byproduct from nuclear fission, killed the animals within a thirty-day period; dogs given a half-body dose in 1972 died within twelve months.

Underground testing pressed on at the Nevada proving grounds amid a widening realization that the AEC misjudged and lied about fallout dangers. The correlation between nuclear fallout and cancer was becoming clear; all that was missing now was action and a plea for some kind of justice before it was too late.

# 14: Life Can Never Last

The early 1970s were not kind to *The Conqueror*'s supporting cast. The picture's crowing antagonist, Thomas Gomez, had succumbed from injuries sustained during a car crash in Santa Monica. Nearly a month in the hospital, he passed in June 1971 at the age of seventy-five.

Ted de Corsia soon followed in 1973 by dying of a heart attack at age sixty-nine, and the actor who played Targutai, Leslie Bradley, passed at sixty-six in 1974. Given the three men's diverse careers and unrelated deaths, family members shed tears, but no one else batted an eye. It became somewhat of an inside joke that the film was cursed; nothing much about that notion was ever mentioned publicly.

Agnes Moorehead found steady work in the early 1960s, reuniting with Wayne for John Ford's *How the West Was Won*, pairing up with Bette Davis for the heavily intense *Hush . . . Hush, Sweet Charlotte*, and appearing as Sister Cluny in the original iteration of *The Singing Nun*. To the surprise of many—apparently including herself—Moorehead accepted a supporting role on a television series that she expected to be a short-lived job that would most likely fail.

*Bewitched* was anything but a failure; the campy sitcom became an instant family classic, running for eight seasons on ABC from 1964 to 1972. The first three seasons hovered across the top ten spots of the Nielsen ratings, pulling in an average of twenty-five million viewers per week and earning twenty-two Emmy nominations throughout its run.

Centered around the marriage of mortal Darrin Stephens (Dick York and later Dick Sargent) and magical nose-wiggling Samantha (Elizabeth Montgomery), Moorehead was cast as the upper-crust witch of a mother-in-law, Endora—the sitcom's flaming redheaded antagonist determined to break up the couple. It would quickly become the most popular and associated role of her career.

"I've been in movies and played theater from coast to coast, so I was quite well known before *Bewitched*, and I don't particularly want to be identified as a witch," Moorehead told the *New York Times*. To *TV Guide*, she called the program's writing "hack" and expressed dismay for the farfetched storylines and "unchallenging" material.

She did later express some appreciation for the experience and her costars, except Dick York, who referred to her as a "tough old bird," so it was worked into her contract early on that Moorehead had to appear in only eight out of every twelve shows.

With 254 credited episodes in total, she earned six Emmy nominations and entered the pop culture lexicon thanks to the nasty nicknames she bestowed on her unfortunate son-in-law, such as "Derwood," "Darwin," and "what's-his-name."

The actress's devout Christian upbringing seemed to creep its way into her belief system, setting her apart in Hollywood as a detractor of everything from the 1960s' youth movement to Marlon Brando and method acting. Fans and feminists celebrated her independence and lauded her success as an actress working past the age of fifty; Moorehead rarely indulged in any praise that came from fame. "You have to keep on developing and maturing and being sincere in your work, and just go right on whether audiences or critics are taking your scalp off or not," she explained.

A major setback to her career's momentum came just a year and a half after the sitcom wrapped; Moorehead was diagnosed with uterine cancer. Friend and costar Sandra Gould recalled Moorehead specifically agonizing over her time spent in the Utah desert during *The Conqueror* shoot. She told Gould that she had grown paranoid from learning of the nearby nuclear testing and even spotted "radioactive germs" on set. "Everybody in that picture has gotten cancer and died," she insisted, pointing to Dick Powell, Pedro Armendáriz, and a growing number of crew members as proof and fearing she'd be next on that growing list.

The actress was hospitalized at the Methodist Hospital in Rochester, Minnesota, in early April. Amid her pain and struggles, she reportedly said, "I should never have taken that part." Agnes Moorehead died on April 30, 1974, at the age of seventy-three. With no spouse or heirs, her money and belongings were inherited by her 106-year-old mother, Mary, with some of the funds getting dispersed to Muskingum University students and awarded in her name.

Fears about the culminating number of deaths related to *The Conqueror* amounted to nothing more than chitchat between friends; the public remained in the dark while only a handful of people associated with the film began to wonder if a dark inside joke was cause for panic. Moorehead's death was ironically attributed to another conspiracy theory altogether: the *Bewitched* curse.

Because of the occult nature of the show, some began to speculate that some sort of bad juju had been cast over its stars. The premature deaths of cast members Alice Pearce and Marion Lorne, not to mention the sudden replacement of an ill Dick York with Dick Sargent, fueled the rumor mill. Plummeting ratings for the final seasons and then Moorehead's death only furthered the lore, snowballing over later decades with each publicized misfortune of an associated actor.

Few had reason to know the names of the behind-the-scenes crew who worked on *The Conqueror*, meaning the quiet deaths of cinematographers Carroll Clark, Leo Tover, and Harry J. Wild; makeup artists Web Overlander and Mel Berns; art director Albert S. D'Agostino; set decorator Al Orenbach; sound designer Terry Kellum; stuntman Cliff Lyons; and associate producer Richard Sokolove, all went relatively unnoticed and meant very little in the way of public productions curses.

Susan Hayward's long-awaited Oscar win served as a distinct marker between public and private life; the world saw very little of the star in her later years. She wore out movie screens with a stream of releases in 1961, popping up in the political thriller *Ada* with Dean Martin, the romance *Back Street*, and the Swedish-themed sex comedy *The Marriage-Go-Round*. Then there was hardly anything at all. Some called it a career slump. Others supported Hayward's decision to take a step back from what had been a roller coaster of a Hollywood life.

Any squabbles or tensions were left up onscreen in her mid-1960s' work. Unofficially capping her career with the 1964 courtroom drama *Where Love Has Gone* costarring Bette Davis, Hayward embraced farm life at Floyd Eaton Chalkley's Georgia ranch, declining roles to raise her boys, Tim and Greg, into adulthood. "It's a great place," she told reporters. "No telephones ringing all day long, no big deals being made, no smog. People down there really know how to live and relax."

In a more reflective mood as she approached the age of fifty, the once-promiscuous star quietly converted to Catholicism with her husband in 1964 and ditched her widely mocked interest in astrology (Hayward had previously sought the advice of Carroll Righter, otherwise known as "the Gregarious Aquarius").

Days were spent wandering the ranch, caring for cattle, and galloping atop horses. The couple donated thirteen acres of adjacent land to the church and lent a hand in constructing a new place of worship called Our Lady of Perpetual Help. As Hayward enjoyed such a shockingly different–almost unimaginable–life, misfortune seemed to make a point of seeking her out.

With nine years of marriage behind them, Chalkley suddenly passed away from hepatitis in January 1966. He was fifty-six years old and had worked as an attorney, owner of an automobile agency, and an FBI agent before meeting Hayward and retiring outside the town of Carrollton. The semiretired actress mourned the loss of her husband and moved away from their country home to Florida to again construct a new life for herself.

She accepted a role in her first film in three years, a swinging crime-comedy called *The Money Pot* with Rex Harrison; the Joseph L. Mankiewicz–directed romp failed to make an imprint during the revolutionary turn in Hollywood productions. Hayward then took a small supporting role in the *Valley of the Dolls*, a psychedelic, sexually charged adaption of Jacqueline Susann's novel about actresses battling it out for meaningful show biz careers.

Again, the actress disappeared from the big screen–and this time for longer than before. Hayward turned to the stage, starring in a production of the bohemian musical satire *Mame* at Caesars Palace in Las Vegas, occasionally appearing as a guest on television programs like the *Joey Bishop Show*.

Chalkley's death and a seemingly stunted career sent Hayward back to the bottle; after more than a decade of sobriety, she found comfort in drinking and smoking several packs of cigarettes a day. Son Tim only added to her woes when he underwent an operation to have a benign tumor removed from his mouth. An annual checkup in 1972 failed to lift the actress's spirits; a tumor of her own was also found to be growing on one of her lungs.

Hayward had always been a smoker, previously advocating for the "far milder" Chesterfield brand. Fearful of any sort of surgery and what that might mean for her life in pictures, she refused treatment and fled to Hollywood under immense protest from her doctor.

Hayward did her best at hiding her ailment, accepting any sort of work she could get her hands on to distract her mind and keep up the illusion all was normal. She managed to tag along with William Holden and Ernest Borgnine in the gritty Western *The Revengers*; but by the time she got to *Say Goodbye, Maggie Cole*–a TV movie about a widowed doctor working at an inner-city clinic–her health was deteriorating.

Hayward was drinking profusely and began suffering from what she figured were terrible hangovers. When the pounding headaches failed to stop, even without alcohol in her system, she could no longer bear the agony. Hayward sought further medical examination and found the tumor was indeed cancerous and had metastasized to her brain.

Thin and pale, her condition immediately halted the Maggie Cole project. The program was intended to evolve into a weekly series, but the diagnosis put a stop to any further consideration. Still refusing medical attention, Hayward attended a Hollywood party in April 1973. There, she suddenly lost all control of her body, writhing and jerking all over the floor until she finally entered an unconscious state. Taken to the hospital, the actress had suffered a seizure from the growing tumor; not only that, the cancer was spreading rapidly with no less than twenty new tumors discovered on her brain. With available options slimming by the day, Hayward decided it was time to finally undergo chemotherapy treatments.

Longtime physician Dr. Lee Siegel called Hayward's cancer "a very rare case," estimating that she would live for only another six weeks to three months. "She had a tremendous desire to live," Siegel said. "She was a terrific fighter." He attributed her strong will against the disease to her fighting spirit and Catholic faith.

Unlike costars John Wayne and Dick Powell, Hayward did not intend to go public with the cancerous battle for her life. Chemo had decimated her iconic red hair and shriveled her body down to eighty-five pounds. Hollywood found out on its own through the use of slippery reporters determined to get a glimpse of the fading star.

The tumors responded to the treatments and shrank down enough to put the actress in remission and give the tabloids a positive scoop. It was at that moment Hayward received an invite from the Motion Picture Academy, asking if she'd make a glamorous and celebratory appearance to present Best Actress at the 1974 Oscars ceremony. Hayward didn't hesitate for a second.

Suffering from seizures, broadcasters were panicked that the star could potentially–and horrifically–crumble to the stage on live television. The other side of the coin was a boost in ratings with fans tuning in to see how Hayward was doing. It was to be her first public appearance since presenting at the Emmy Awards two years prior, and now with a skeletal frame, Hayward knew she had her work cut out for her to dazzle the crowd.

She instantly enlisted famed costume designer Nolan Miller to comb up a "Susan Hayward" wig and a custom-fit black dress that sparkled in the spotlight. Growing more and more paralyzed on the left side of her face as the days went on, she forged ahead with her duties by slathering herself in makeup and taking an extra couple hits of her Dilantin medication before the big moment. Clinging to the arm of Charlton Heston, Hayward entered the stage to a stunned audience, keeping their noise levels low in fear of triggering a reaction.

The actress leaned heavily on the podium but spoke the nominees' names in her commanding, classic Hollywood voice. Hayward had succeeded, radiating beauty and fooling the bulk of viewers at home that she was fine.

Moments after director Melvin Frank bounded up to accept the award on behalf of winner Glenda Jackson, Hayward suffered a powerful seizure backstage and left the ceremony on a stretcher. It would be her last public appearance.

The positive reactions from fans and costars fooled Hayward into believing she was on the mend if not completely cured of cancer. She dispatched her sons to tell the press she was fine–never sick in the first place. For Tinseltown duties, she hired producer Jay Bernstein to spread the news she was ready to work. The actress thumbed through TV pilots while her seizures became all the more frequent.

The Barker brothers said their mother became less independent than a small child as 1974 dragged on. Tim described her as often being crumpled up in the fetal position, unable to swallow. She would slip in and out of comas as permanent paralysis set in on her left side.

On March 14, 1975, a massive seizure shook Hayward's entire body, causing her to bite off a piece of her tongue. Violently thrashing in her Beverly Hills home, Susan Hayward (born Edythe Marrenner) passed away at the age of fifty-seven. Golden Age film fans mourned the loss of the star who was buried in her Oscar dress at Our Lady of Perpetual Help in Georgia right next to Floyd Eaton Chalkley.

Howard Hughes blew his RKO days out of the water with the collection of "projects" he chose to tackle in the 1960s and tearing through businesses like the economy was a roll of toilet paper. Forced out of TWA, Hughes was made to sell off his shares, scooping up the wealth of a small country, $500 million ($3 billion today) in the process. Not too shabby, considering the original investment was $80 million.

With that kind of freedom, Hughes leisurely nabbed a controlling interest in Northeast Airlines (later merged into Delta Airlines) in 1962 but sold the company two years later. Three local service airlines merged to form Air West at the end of the decade, which Hughes then snapped up to form Hughes Airwest in 1970. The international all-jet airline serviced much of the American Southwest throughout the decade before it was acquired by Republic Airways.

The billionaire spent his free days outside of the plane game hiding from Hughes Tool Company lawsuits, forcing them into limbo until the Supreme Court finally just overturned them. He lent his name and eccentric image to the CIA as a cover to retrieve a sunken Soviet submarine off the coast of Hawaii and sent a $205,000 loan to Richard Nixon's brother Donald, stirring up speculations his money was somehow the sole motivation behind the Watergate scandal.

There was the time he rode the train to Las Vegas on November 14, 1966, checked into the Desert Inn, and refused to leave the high-roller suite once he had reached the ten-day limit. Instead of switching casinos or hotel rooms, Hughes's answer to the eviction was to abruptly purchase the entire building for thirteen million dollars.

A "nerve center" was quickly constructed on the Desert Inn's eighth floor; it was a place for Hughes to conduct all of his wheeling and dealing and was operated by a team that belonged to the Church of Jesus Christ of Latter-Day Saints. Hughes refused to trust anyone who smoked, drank, or gambled, which gave the press cause to dub his employees the "Mormon Mafia."

The ninth-floor penthouse became the billionaire's home, a place few were allowed to enter. Clothing with any dirtying potential was barred. It was there he demanded his staff bring 350 gallons of a discontinued Baskin-Robbins banana-nut ice cream to the casino, only to decide his cravings had changed the moment the shipment arrived.

At night, he would drift off watching films broadcast on a station he purchased and then forced to play his favorite pictures without advertisements, sometimes requesting the shows to be switched midmovie.

From his windows (which were taped and draped shut to seal out the potential for germs), he had another '60s-era casino, the Silver Slipper, in plain view. Rumor has it that the bright neon sign bothered him at night when he slept, so he bought that building, too, just so he could have the sign relocated.

The Landmark, the Sands, the Castaways, and the New Frontier fell under Hughes's ownership within months of each other, as did most of the vacant lots on the infamous Vegas Strip and twenty-five thousand acres of land west of the city.

"I like to think of Las Vegas in terms of a well-dressed man in a dinner jacket and a beautifully jeweled and furred female getting out of an expensive car," Hughes proclaimed.

District Attorney George Franklin felt Hughes was a welcome breath of fresh air compared to the chokehold gangsters and mafiosos held on anything gambling or nightlife related. "This is the best way to improve the image of gambling in Nevada by licensing an industrialist of his stature," he said, assuring that the playboy planned to clean the water supply, open a medical school, and construct a high-speed train.

While Hughes operated his many airline and manufacturing ventures, he forwent public service installations in favor of a far bigger battle. Of all the possible grievances he could have tackled, he decided to wage war on nuclear testing. Long gone were the days when tourists flocked to feel the atomic rumbles from Vegas cocktail bars; people were fearful and tourism was at risk of diminishing as a result. With the impending underground Boxcar test of 1968–a 1.3-megaton blast that was set to shake Nevada like no other bomb before–the billionaire felt it was his duty to act if his desert empire was to continue.

"Has anybody ever tried to compute the price paid . . . for the privilege of laying waste, mutilating, and contaminating for all the days to come millions of acres of good, fertile, vegetated Nevada earth . . . through the damage wrought by these explosions?" Hughes asked in a memo to his aide, Robert Maheu. Negotiating with the Atomic Energy Commission to move the test site farther away proved unsuccessful.

In a letter sent directly to President Lyndon Johnson, he said, "I think Nevada has become a fully accredited state now and should no longer be treated like a barren wasteland that is only useful as a dumping place for poisonous, contaminated nuclear waste material." Johnson agreed to lend an ear to Hughes's pleas and invited him to his Texas ranch to discuss what could be done. Hughes deployed Maheu in his place, armed with a one million dollar check and strict instructions to bribe the president and put a stop to further detonations.

Maheu consciously left the bribe out of the conversation, and testing continued, causing Hughes to turn his attention–and cash– to presidential candidates Hubert Humphrey, Robert Kennedy, and Richard Nixon. None of them acknowledged that they would so much as consider an atomic testing halt, either, prompting Hughes to finally drop the whole crusade by the decade's end.

Hughes himself didn't seem worried about the health effects of fallout anyway. He took plenty of trips to the Nellis Air Force Base before his self-confinement days and was discovered lying in a ditch after doing god-knows-what just off a stretch of Route 95 about a hundred miles northeast of the proving grounds. As legend has it, a blue-collar milkman by the name of Melvin Dummar found Hughes disheveled and was asked to drive him to the Sands. He later appeared in Hughes's will, inheriting $156 million of Hughes's vast fortune—a contested fact Dummar was never successfully able to prove.

In the midst of his antinuclear war, Hughes was asked about that old dud of a picture he had produced years back at RKO, the one where John Wayne played Genghis Khan. He had allowed production to occur downwind of the Nevada Test Site, and a few key players had now seemed to have passed from cancer. What did he have to say in response to that? Did he feel responsible? Was there anything he felt could have been done?

All Howard ever mentioned about the making of *The Conqueror* was that he felt "guilty as hell about the whole thing," and nothing more.

The eccentric businessman still held control over his Nevada empire—all lumped together under what was called the Summa Corporation. Any move made was done over the telephone or through a memo from an array of hotel suites across North America, including Beverly Hills, Vancouver, Managua, and Acapulco to name a few.

The final years of Hughes's hotel-based phase were spent in a psychotropic isolation that inched him further and further toward madness as the days went on. Jean Peters, Hughes's wife since the late fifties, hadn't seen her husband since he jaunted off to Vegas and had been apparently communicating with him through scattered telephone calls. She finally filed for divorce in 1970 and was awarded seventy thousand dollars every year in alimony for the rest of her life, and she refused to dredge up her marriage for the media or through any book deals.

Hughes's desire for partners of any kind had greatly diminished in his later years as his obsessive-compulsive disorder and all-encompassing fear of germs pushed away any chance at meaningful human contact. His dependency on the pain medication codeine, which had been escalating since his Beverly Hills plane crash in 1946, took the top spot of priorities and hit its highest plateau when he ordered the drug to be injected multiple times a day. Hughes made sure to follow the shots with an additional twenty to thirty tablets of aspirin.

Loaded with medication, Howard chose to stay bedridden and refused to eat anything more than candy bars. Afraid of human contact or any contamination from items like scissors or razors, he let his hair and beard grow out into a long, tangled mess. His fingernails and toenails were not to be touched, growing freely to the point where they extended nearly three inches past his skin. By 1975, with a lanky frame and height of six feet two inches, Hughes's weight dropped below one hundred pounds.

Whether it was to stave off boredom or nurture insanity, Hughes fittingly turned to cinema for comfort at the end. The "Mormon Mafia" unanimously concluded the former mogul's uncontestable favorite film of all time was the 1968 North Pole–set nuclear submarine thriller *Ice Station Zebra* starring Rock Hudson and Ernest Borgnine. His delight in staring at the barren arctic setting and military machines was so great, Hughes had his team play the film on an endless loop.

When he grew tired of the watching the film and wanted to ogle other aircraft, he had them put on *Jet Pilot* in its place. The third film his staff insists Hughes requested to be played at least 150 times was *The Conqueror*. He called the film his own personal favorite, allegedly masturbating to the picture until he grew too weak to do so. Some claimed John Wayne's rippling portrayal appealed to his long-hidden homosexual side; others suggested his self-absorption knew no limits. A few insisted he was just absolutely in awe of the might and power of Genghis Khan.

Barricaded behind an impenetrable wall of employees, the world was rarely granted a glimpse of Howard Hughes in his climactic tumultuous state. The mysterious allure only fattened rumors of what he supposedly looked like or what nasty little tasks he ordered his team to perform. Author Clifford Irving created a media storm when he announced that he had cowritten an autobiography with Howard in 1972; the manuscript was pulled before publication when Hughes dispelled the claim with what would be one of his final telecast appearances.

Most were fascinated by his vast wealth, which was theorized by some to have no definite end. From the early 1960s to late 1970s, Hughes was almost exclusively cited as the richest man in the United States with a fortune amounting to $2.5 billion ($11 billion). "I'm not a paranoid, deranged millionaire," he quoted to the press, who had labeled him as such. "Goddammit, I'm a billionaire."

On April 5, 1976, he was nothing more than a man who reached the end of his life. Onboard a Learjet flying from Acapulco to his childhood home–Houston, Texas–Howard Hughes died from kidney failure at the age of seventy. Claims and lawsuits stemming from his complex last will and testament dragged on for decades. Countless films, books, television shows, and fascinated fans aimed to capture and explore his incomparable time in the world.

The greatest takeaway in terms of Hughes and his involvement with *The Conqueror* is the aforementioned fact that he was the only key player involved to never have stepped foot in St. George or Snow Canyon, Utah. He had an insignificant benign tumor removed, and that was all. Hughes managed to outlive most of the actors and crew members involved and never once received a cancer diagnosis.

John Wayne didn't have to do anything he didn't want to by the time the 1970s rolled around. He seemed financially golden and could have jetted off to favorite destinations like Panama for beachfront weekends far more than he actually did. He was deemed to be in good health and had done his part in attracting new American Cancer Society supporters; there was no binding reason that forced him to appear in any more public service announcements. No, America's most popular actor didn't even have to act if he didn't want to.

Wayne hadn't the need to flip through scripts or exhaust the energy to throw his name behind any political cause. But any reader wondering why he didn't pounce on opportunities to take his "retirement years" easy didn't know John Wayne at all.

The icon seemed to march through the decade with one singular purpose in mind: to fight against the political left. His film *The Green Berets* purposely stirred up controversy with a very pro-war agenda defending the Vietnam War, a topic Wayne argued for time and time again. He backed friend and fellow actor Ronald Reagan as the Republican candidate; he himself became a staple speaker at the Republican National Convention.

Ironically, Duke had been backed by the Texas Republican Party to run for office in 1968, but he felt no one in their right mind would consider an actor for the top job in the White House. Instead, he chose to make his beliefs known by the film projects he chose to tackle or, in most cases, decline.

The actor campaigned for the title role in *Dirty Harry*, but producers felt he was too old and gave it to his Western rival Clint Eastwood. The significantly younger star felt the two of them could still pull off a great picture together and suggested they team up for *High Plains Drifter*–the story of a stranger who murders a town's corrupt law enforcers.

Wayne sent Eastwood a letter about the movie, stating "that wasn't how the Old West really was and not how a real Western should go," putting an end to any further conversation about the two of them partnering.

Next, Duke turned down Gene Wilder's role in *Blazing Saddles*, telling director Mel Brooks the script was too dirty and would hurt his family image. He then turned down working with Steven Spielberg at the height of the icon's career, calling his parody of Pearl Harbor, *1941*, unpatriotic and a subject people shouldn't joke about.

His actual theatrical output ranged from a *True Grit* spinoff lazily titled *Rooster Cogburn* (costarring four-time Oscar winner and admitted fan Katharine Hepburn) to the Irish mob comedy *Brannigan*. Looking back, Wayne figured he never did quite learn how to choose roles with any level of consistency, though he was certain one bomb stood out above the rest.

"*The Conqueror* is one of the worst films I ever made, and it was a massive success," Wayne admitted during an interview late in his life. "I think it was only because epic films were in vogue at the time, and although I thought the film was a sort of Mongolian Western, it was a historical epic, and I guess people like those films. I began to wonder if they'd like Westerns anymore."

He accepted his final role, that of J. B. Books, a dying gray and gravelly gunfighter in the 1976 Western *The Shootist*. There wasn't terribly much that was memorable about the picture except for a gangly Ron Howard and a rare appearance by Lauren Bacall; apart from its placement in Wayne's filmography, its use in an American Cancer Society commercial might be *The Shootist*'s greatest significance when looking back.

Jimmy Stewart appeared as a doctor who diagnoses Wayne's character with an advanced cancer. A snippet of that clip transitions to Wayne, who, in stark contrast to his early Camel commercials, wears a suit and tie in a calm office setting and with old age on full display.

"Before that picture was made, I did the same scene in real life," the actor recalls. "That was twelve years ago. Cost me a piece of lung. We've made real progress with cancer since then. But it costs money. The American Cancer Society is asking you for help again." Sternly, in a tone only Wayne could get away with, he warns, "Pilgrim, if you don't give it to them, I'm going to kick you in the butt."

The man's image, that rare cohesion of surly charm, could not have grown bigger in his elder years. Wayne's own Republican army practically worshipped him as a god, at the very least making Wayne their poster image for whatever cause fit: masculinity . . . classic Hollywood . . . traditional American values. He had the stats to back up the level of devotion shown to him. The American Film Institute ranked him as the thirteenth greatest male star of all time. Duke graced the Top Ten Money Makers Poll of all films from 1949 to 1974, taking first place in 1950, 1951, 1954, and 1971.

When Bruce Dern's character killed Wayne's character in the 1972 film *The Cowboys*, Dern said he received death threats and was hurled insults whenever he walked down the street. What other actor can say their onscreen murder prompted fans to truly loathe their fictional killer?

But the greatest dangers to John Wayne, contrary to his audience's beliefs, were not bandits or bullets or standoffs outside a dusty saloon; undeniably, he was beloved, but no fan could save the star from cancer.

Duke was beginning to look a bit worse for wear in the late '70s– suffering from prostate troubles and heart problems that required a mitral valve replacement (one he delighted in the fact came from a pig). His voice became increasingly raspy due to chronic bronchitis, which also frequently gave him shortness of breath. A daily diet of digitalis, digoxin, allopurinol, potassium, and Lasix pills forced him to tape a chart on his bathroom mirror just to keep the meds straight.

For a sixty-nine-year-old male, the ailments weren't too terribly out of the ordinary, but for an action movie star who mucked around dusty corrals all day, it meant work was nearly impossible to come by. Some studios refused to insure the elderly icon while others proposed scripts that doctors refused to let him touch.

His own Batjac production company puttered along after the release of *The Alamo*, slowing output significantly and turning Wayne's old hits like *Hondo* into short-lived television shows. There was a small boom of pictures produced through the company and distributed through Warner Bros. in the early 1970s. *McQ* in 1974 would unintentionally be their last; Wayne lacked the energy to push projects forward amid the new Hollywood environment. Wayne's son Michael picked up the torch and managed the company, mostly to safeguard his pop's legacy, for another thirty years.

His troubling 1971 *Playboy* interview showed just how out of touch the actor could be; Wayne, in a particularly no-holds-barred mood, attacked everything from socialism to homosexuality, even the Black Panthers. "With a lot of blacks, there's quite a bit of resentment along with their dissent, and possibly rightfully so. But we can't all of a sudden get down on our knees and turn everything over to the leadership of the blacks," Wayne said in the interview. "I believe in white supremacy until the blacks are educated to a point of responsibility. I don't believe in giving authority and positions of leadership and judgment to irresponsible people."

His racial remarks made headlines, but Wayne received no known requests for a public clarification. Son Ethan defended his father when the interview made waves in 2019 by claiming, "It would be an injustice to judge someone based on an interview that's being used out of context."

Without an endless buffet of work ready for the taking, Wayne's boredom got him into trouble. The death of his mentor, John Ford, from stomach cancer in 1973 had pushed him into a bit of a rut of despair and cocktails. Spouse Pilar Pallete actually announced a trial separation in November of that year, complaining about her husband's absences and how they had grown apart. True, Pallete moved out of their house, but the two never officially ended their marriage. Wayne did, however, strike up a relationship with his secretary, Pat Stacy, sometime later, who would become his primary caretaker when the actor started to fall ill.

By January 1979, it had been nearly four years to the day since he had stepped on *The Shootist*'s set when he arrived at the UCLA Medical Center to do what he had always done since his cancer diagnosis and get his body searched for "the Red Witch."

Dr. William Longmire opened Duke to find gastric carcinoma in his stomach and cancer cells in its lymph nodes. The dangerous strain meant almost certain death if not immediately dealt with, so the actor's entire stomach and gall bladder were removed through a nine-and-a-half-hour procedure; his small intestine became a makeshift stomach for the rest of his life.

Radiation treatments blasted away what was left. Duke, as friends and family knew him, diminished through the process, completely losing his appetite and, for the most part, his independence. The actor shriveled down to 180 pounds–tiny for his bulky frame. Any energy he did have was spent trying to dodge the wall of reporters who lurked outside every hospital and clinic he was expected to visit.

Naturally, the rumor mill churned out gossip on how the old cowboy was dealing with the diagnosis. News of his condition spread faster inside his own industry, with friends calling and popping by on an hourly basis and failing to let an exhausted Duke rest. Jimmy Stewart, Ann-Margret, Lauren Bacall, Stacy Keach, Michael Caine, Henry Fonda, Maureen O'Hara, Frank Sinatra, Ronald Reagan, Cary Grant, Laurence Olivier, and Gregory Peck were just some of the well-wishers who came bearing letters and flowers. Anyone who got to actually see Duke in person knew his life was now measured in months.

Leave it to the Academy to rope a sick star into a moment of distinction and publicity. Wayne was asked to present Best Picture at the Oscar ceremony that April; he became adamant about doing the appearance and began practicing his own walk so at the very least he could show up with some physical familiarity. With such a shrunken frame, the actor's suit was specially padded to make him appear bigger than he was and absorbed the river of sweat that poured from every inch of his shivering body.

He began April 9, 1979, by undergoing his daily radiation treatments and then rested for most of the afternoon before it was time to get dressed for the telecast. Wayne made it mere moments before the show began, dodging the red carpet to step out on stage for a standing ovation at the tail end of the evening.

"That's just about the only medicine a fella'd ever really need," Wayne croaked into the microphone. "Believe me when I tell you I'm mighty pleased that I can amble down here tonight. Oscar and I have something in common. Oscar first came to the Hollywood scene in 1928–so did I. We're both a little weather-beaten, but we're here and plan to be around for a whole lot longer."

He announced *The Deer Hunter* as the night's top prize earner, a Vietnam War film the actor likely would have disapproved of. Wayne had little energy, none whatsoever now to raise a stink about pictures at that point in his life. The star posed for a few snapshots when he left the stage and then headed straight for bed. Both he and Hollywood knew it'd be the last time they'd meet.

When dizzying spells led to a collapse at home in early May, Wayne was admitted into UCLA for the final time. He ate through intravenous tubes and rarely got out of his bed, not even for the bathroom. Interferon injections were introduced as a temporary measure, but it didn't help the fight; he was too weak. They, along with radiation and chemotherapy treatments, were stopped and replaced with morphine to help combat his pain.

During his most uncertain of moments, President Jimmy Carter came to pay Wayne a visit, followed by friend and costar Maureen O'Hara. In a bid to cheer the actor up, O'Hara testified before congress to get a Congressional Gold Medal approved–the highest honor for an American citizen alongside the Presidential Medal of Freedom (which Duke would also earn later on). O'Hara cited her reasoning as the simple fact that "John Wayne was the United States of America."

President Carter approved the medal and worked to push the order through at a rapid pace–making John Wayne the eighty-fifth recipient of the honor. Duke received it on May 23–almost forty years since Howard Hughes had received his–and exactly on his seventy-second birthday.

His son Patrick figured the cancer had spread to just about everywhere in his father's body by that time. Duke had slipped in and out of comas for much of his final weeks, battling with lucidity by perking up and being able to hold a conversation one hour and not being able to recognize anyone around him in the next. He requested a Catholic baptism on June 10 and was administered his last rites. On Monday, June 11, 1979, Marion Mitchell Morrison, known to the world as John Duke Wayne, died at the age of seventy-two of respiratory arrest caused by gastric cancer.

When word of Duke's passing got out into the world, newspapers like the *Los Angeles Times* ran it as their front-page story. The Orange County Airport almost immediately renamed its airstrip as the John Wayne Airport, while an elementary school, a marina, and a hundred-mile trail in Washington State adopted his name to pay tribute to the legend. TV stations immediately ran marathons of his movies. People as high up as President Carter stopped to speak publicly about his lasting impact and how this undoubtedly marked the end of an era.

He was buried at Pacific View Memorial Park in Newport Beach under an unmarked grave–an effort by his family to try to limit the traffic from hordes of fans. They finally agreed to mark the actor's final resting place with his name in 1999 and included an inscription that read: "Tomorrow is the most important thing in life. Comes into us at midnight very clean. It's perfect when it arrives and it puts itself in our hands. It hopes we've learned something from yesterday."

# 15: Blast of the Bombshell

The year 1979 began as one of the more hopeful years a person could ask for if they were part of the antinuclear movement or a resident of the American Southwest struggling to care for family members ravaged by cancer. First, James Bridges' dramatic thriller,

*The China Syndrome*, made the word *nuclear* one of the major popular talking points just a mere two months in. Starring Jack Lemmon, Jane Fonda, and Michael Douglas, it was one of the first films to tackle overlooked safety measures at a nuclear power plant, albeit a fictional one.

Released on March 16, *The China Syndrome* hit theaters twelve days before the very real accident at Three Mile Island–a partial reactor meltdown at a plant in Pennsylvania. The event was labeled the most significant nuclear accident in US history; fortunately, it was one without any immediate fatalities. The extensive cleanup effort took thirteen years and one billion dollars to complete; for those with any sort of antinuclear agenda, be it a reactor or a bomb, stark contamination imagery garnered from that accident was absolutely priceless.

Over in the Nevada desert, underground atomic testing had become a fluid routine deep below the earth's surface inside shafts and tunnels. Every year throughout the 1970s, each testing series ran like a television season, sometimes containing up to thirty-four individual shots in a series. External fallout was minimal, but crews were extensive–made up of hundreds of residents who were hired to brave exposure, head down into the dark shaft depths, fill in the holes after underground tests, and get straight to digging another.

Thousands were still grappling with the shots that had been carried out right over their heads during the 1950s and 1960s. Recollections and resettlement saw community members beginning to refer to themselves as downwinders, a name to identify people from states like Nevada, Utah, Arizona, Washington, Idaho, and New Mexico who had lived adjacent to nuclear test sites during the atomic heyday and were now experiencing health problems and significant loss in their families. The radiation-heavy Upshot-Knothole Harry test simultaneously garnered a nickname of its own, "Dirty Harry," to further convey people's displeasure with the messy, contaminated aftermath.

Terms like *downwinder*, a name that unequivocally suggested gusts carrying clouds of harmful nuclear fallout to the homes of unassuming people, were used to instigate a larger push on the government to pay attention, admit their wrongdoings, and help citizens through an unprecedented region-specific struggle. It was this kind of lingo, words that spread quickly throughout public consciousness, that helped illustrate fallout theories in a new era without the use of complex charts, graphs, and dense pages of jargon.

While patriotism was at an all-time low and agency opposition nil, a wave of claims and old Atomic Energy Commission documents had come to light at the end of the decade. A 1965 federal study was released to the public by the Carter administration, showing that unusually high leukemia deaths were in fact occurring in Utah; yet, the AEC's criticisms halted any further action or publication of the findings at that time.

Dr. Joseph Lyon's University of Utah study on soaring leukemia rates was published in the *New England Journal of Medicine* without interference. *Deseret News* reporter Gordon Eliot White began publishing a lengthy article series detailing government ignorance during the days of atmospheric testing. Army sergeant Paul Cooper received widespread coverage when he appealed to the Veterans Administration, arguing that he had contracted cancer from nuclear fallout in 1957.

As for the forty-three hundred sheep that had died in 1953—a freak accident determined in court that all succumbed to chilly weather and natural causes—Dr. Harold Knapp reemerged, arguing that they had absorbed up to a thousand times the maximum amount of radioactive iodine allowed for humans due to fallout from "Dirty Harry."

Utah governor Scott M. Matheson, who served from 1977 to 1985, agreed with Knapp, stating in a *New York Times* interview that "the documents contained some very damning information with respect to the effects of radiation fallout on sheep and the sheep happened to be in the same area where there were, at that time, numbers of people—we have to assume that the exposure on one was also an exposure on the other."

Matheson also recalled seeing "flashes in the sky" when he was growing up; how he was awakened by family members and encouraged to watch the widespread effects from atomic testing; feeling the fine dust settle on his skin. It was these people—those who now wielded power and came of age amid the atomic rumbles; ones who had lost their own kin to cancer and were now awakening to a dizzying amount of similar accounts–they would be the people who held the insight and wherewithal to make all the difference.

"It's so heartbreaking to see these people in southern Utah," Matheson continued in his interview. "They are the most patriotic people and perhaps somewhat naïve. When *The Star-Spangled Banner* plays, you can just see their hearts swell. And this one lady said to me, 'Do you really think the government would lie to us?' "

Governor Matheson met with President Carter and Joseph A. Califano Jr., Secretary of Health, Education, and Welfare, to finally discuss the effects of nuclear fallout; both agreed to fund a new study and go from there. Matheson seemed satisfied with the promise, but others felt the time for restitution was absolutely of the essence.

Former Arizona congressman Stewart Udall had been advocating for the rights of uranium workers for much of the 1970s, particularly compensation for widows and members of the Navajo nation. During his time talking with workers, Udall found himself meeting more and more downwinders along the way. Their pleas for help made the congressman realize the scope of contaminated Americans was far bigger than he ever imagined–a discovery that led him to widen his cause.

Another Utah congressman, Wayne Owens, advocated for both wartime peace and environmentalism; he was ousted from his seat in 1975 but remained a constant voice arguing against nuclear testing and for downwinder justice for years to come. Senator Orrin Hatch was admittedly fearful of USSR and Chinese repercussions if testing ceased, but he did side with his fellow Utahns affected by fallout and began pressing the Senate Labor Committee for compensation around the same time.

The final ingredient to tinder a spark was Senator Ted Kennedy (John F. Kennedy's youngest brother), who found himself a major advocate for clean energy and for halting the development of nuclear power. Though the man was about as far away from Utah as you could get (born, raised, and representing the state of Massachusetts), his bevy of related causes made him the perfect candidate to lead the charge.

Kennedy had fought earlier in the decade for better workplace health care through the Health Maintenance Organization Act as well as the National Cancer Act to help strengthen the nation's resources for research on the disease. On a more personal level, Kennedy's own son Edward Jr. had been diagnosed with bone cancer when he was just twelve years old, a battle he would overcome through a two-year struggle to shape his father's moral determination to help anyone in a similar situation.

Matheson, Udall, Owens, and Hatch brought America's fallout woes to Kennedy, a man who certainly held significantly more congressional clout than they did. The senator held Health and Scientific Research Subcommittee hearings in Salt Lake City to learn from the people directly affected and see what they demanded of their government. He used their backing to introduce the first piece of major legislation advocating for and simply even acknowledging the downwinders.

After its fifth draft, Senator Kennedy officially sponsored the Radiation Exposure Compensation Act of 1979 (RECA), introduced on October 9 to the Ninety-Sixth Congress. The bill summary explained that its purpose was to "hold the United States liable for damages to certain individuals, to certain uranium miners, and to certain sheep herds, due to certain nuclear tests at the Nevada Test Site." The Radiation Exposure Compensation Act failed to gain a single vote and therefore did not move forward. The bill was instead "referred to the Senate Committee on Labor and Human Resources" for further conversations.

The lengthy and convoluted legalities of Howard Hughes's death in 1976 saw puzzled lawyers and court proceedings struggle to decipher the man's last will and testament for the following thirty-three years. Strangers with their hands stretched out marched to any Hughes-related business in droves, claiming they had been one of the billionaire's short-lived spouses or illegitimate offspring and were owed their share.

Howard's Medical Institute insisted they were the obvious beneficiary to inherit his entire estate while prized aircrafts and company stock were all left hanging to scrap over without proper heirs.

The one collection few demanded to battle it out for was Hughes's pile of little-known *Conqueror* copies as well as the exclusive rights to the picture.

Universal Pictures had released *Jet Pilot* and must have looked into purchasing it for their catalogue. When it was discovered that *The Conqueror* had no foreseeable owner and was up for grabs, the studio acquired the Mongol epic for an undisclosed sum in 1979 and officially renewed the rights in 1983. It had not been viewed, aired, or publicly spoken of in any significant manner since its release almost twenty-five years earlier.

The only blip back in the spotlight was in 1974, when *Daily Variety* announced that Paramount Pictures had obtained reissue rights and planned to release *The Conqueror*; Hughes successfully blocked the move with a cease and desist letter.

Universal's purchase was formulated with good fortune and impeccable timing; John Wayne had passed away and the cinemagoing world mourned that loss with touching publications and retrospectives. Movie marathons were displayed in Duke's memory, and honorary awards were offered left, right, and center from groups such as the Directors Guild of America. Statues were erected and mosaics commissioned—that's how much the actor was beloved.

The legacy of John Wayne was on many minds in 1979, so when a long-forgotten film that had faded from memory for most and risen into mythic lore for younger fans suddenly became available, *The Conqueror* was once again the talk of Hollywood.

At the time, a reporter by the name of Peter Brennan happened to work for the *Star*, a tabloid magazine that spun wild yarns and spread trashy Hollywood gossip. Features about Wayne and glossy pictures of the icon splashed over every magazine one could think of—including the *Star*. Hard news about the plight of America's downwinders simultaneously covered more reputable publications.

Brennan sought to do a simple story on the return of Wayne's legendary portrayal of Genghis Khan. Cross-examination in the magazine aisle, and some later fact-checking, revealed the film had been shot in the desert where St. George and other Utah communities were dealing with the brunt of all this fallout aftermath; Brennan realized he had stumbled on a massively wilder scoop.

All Brennan had to do was pick up on the link appearing in both John Wayne obits and downwinder stories: the word *cancer*. A quick glance at *The Conqueror* cast list would certainly show cancer was an abundantly common theme. The spectacle's hook became simple: "Radiation from nuclear bomb testing may have killed John Wayne!" Brennan drove home the point that the government, an institution the Republican actor (and many of the tabloid's readers for that matter) unequivocally believed in, could have been responsible for the icon's demise.

It was timely. It was controversial. For supermarket gossip, it was perfect. And after the story's publication in early August, it was carried by a slew of major publications including the *New York Post*, *Los Angeles Times*, and *Times* in London—each using Brennan's article as their source. Unbeknownst to them, the reporter had made no connections with anyone involved in the production and wrote the piece as a completely speculative idea.

To actress Jeanne Gerson, the cancer claims weren't so pie in the sky. Gerson had taken a bit part as a "slave girl" in *The Conqueror*, one of her very first roles, which required several weeks of shooting in Snow Canyon. She had contracted skin cancer in 1965 (subsequently cured through surgery) and was then diagnosed with breast cancer ten years later. A mastectomy and chemotherapy effectively put the actress in remission, but the trauma of her health problems and time spent in and out of hospitals completely froze her modest career.

Gerson emerged as one of the only cast members who had beaten their disease—twice—and stood painfully aware of the pattern stemming from the RKO production. As Brennan's article took over newsstands, Gerson took to television programs like NBC's *Prime Time* with Tom Snyder to confirm that it was true, and she acted as somewhat of a poster child for the cause and gave legitimacy to the rumor.

In the wake of John Wayne death theories, Gerson interviews, and all the *Conqueror* exposure, magazines and newspapers were rushing out to collect "human stories" and profile any actual downwinder willing to share their atomic experience. In October 1979, *People* magazine spoke with elderly St. George resident Irma Thomas and published a detailed recounting of the family she had lost and war she had waged to get the government's attention, going so far as banding together 442 victims to sue the feds for $230 million. A very small mention about the controversy surrounding *The Conqueror* production was shoehorned in following Brennan's article.

Karen G. Jackovich and Mark Sennet recognized *People* magazine's medley of celebrity news and human interest stories and saw an opportunity to appeal to both sides with the *Conqueror* rumor. The magazine was in its sixth year when the writer/photographer duo began contacting family members and authorities. They spent well over fourteen months to piece together what would become the November 1980 bombshell titled "The Children of John Wayne, Susan Hayward and Dick Powell Fear That Fallout Killed Their Parents."

In it, Jackovich and Sennet tallied the *Conqueror* cast and crew—a total of 220 members—and claimed that, as of 1980, 91 of them had contracted cancer since 1954. Furthermore, 46 of the 91, including the more familiar names of Wayne, Powell, Armendáriz, Hayward, and Moorehead, had died.

The saddened children of the celebrities got their space in the article to chime in and share their suspicions over the fallout fears. Tim Barker detailed Hayward's horrendous final months and wondered what the future would hold for him and his brother since they had lived with their mother for the duration of the shoot.

Pedro Armendáriz Jr. recalled that his father had to be frequently hosed down due to "heavy dust," while Norman and Ellen Powell lent their concern and well wishes to the people of St. George.

Jeanne Gerson received another chance to rally for a lawsuit and again express that she had long been convinced that it was all more than a coincidence.

To provide context, a brief background of Upshot-Knothole Simon and "Dirty Harry's" radiation deposits were included along with mention of the spin and suppression committed by the Atomic Energy Commission throughout the testing process. With scientific backing, the article claimed undeterred fallout isotopes such as strontium-90 and cesium-137 would have blown northeast during the wind shift when the Harry shot was conducted.

Fallout allegedly concentrated in the deep dunes of Snow Canyon, spaces referred to as "hot spots." Radioactive material within those isotopes would have been ingested through the consumption of locally grown food, the water they drank, and all of the airborne sand, thus contacting susceptible soft tissue and increasing the risk of cancer.

"The government definitely had a complete awareness of what was going on," claimed Harold Knapp in the article. "To a trained professional, the information contained in some of their once-confidential reports is most shocking."

Dr. Robert Pendleton, director of radiological health at the University of Utah, insisted that "with ninety-one, I think the tie-in to their exposure on the set of *The Conqueror* would hold up even in a court of law."

In an attempt to strike balance, unsupportive views–particularly from John Wayne's son Michael–were also included in the piece. "Suing the government isn't going to bring my father back," Michael insisted, adding that his father had remained cheerful and positive until the very end. Duke's eldest son emerged as one of the most outspoken critics of the radiation rumor, attributing the actor's cancer contraction to his smoking habit and nothing more. Ex-wife Pilar Pallete joined the conversation a little later on to dismiss the article, claiming she, too, had been on set in St. George but had not gotten cancer. Michael, who played a minuscule role in *The Conqueror* as a Mongol guard, passed away from lupus two decades later at the age of sixty-eight.

The *People* story cast a bright spotlight while creating more of a public stir than any other publication had before. It has since remained as the pinnacle detailing and most frequently cited source on *The Conqueror* controversy.

A gamut of publicized opinions instantly batted the story in and out of public consciousness like a balloon tossed across all angles in the wind. Readers seemed eager to poke holes in the article, citing a handful of other productions including *Run of the Arrow* in 1957, *They Came to Cordura* in 1959, and more recently Sydney Pollack's *The Electric Horseman* in 1979 that had all shot in Snow Canyon, Utah, and its participants had emerged cancer-free.

Dick Hammer, the local restaurateur who catered *The Conqueror*, called up the *Deseret News* to inform them that none of the local fifty-five staff members he had employed during film production had been diagnosed with any form of cancer.

Lynn Anspaugh, research professor of radiobiology at the University of Utah, challenged Dr. Pendleton's claims in the *People* article and found through her own research that the cast and crew only would have received one to four millirems of radiation, which was considered a less than normal dose.

Jackovich and Sennet's math was also called into question, seeing as how there were 108 official credits on *The Conqueror* and the claim of 220 cast and crew members more than doubled that number. While no comment was given and no records released, aspects like catering, wrangling, and construction have been offered up as suggestions for where that total may have come from, plus all of the St. George residents who had a hand in the shoot—people now virtually impossible to track down given their absence in the credits.

The vast majority of readers knew the commonality of smoking in the 1950s, its connection with lung cancer and other diseases, and Wayne's lifetime struggle to kick the habit. The paraphrased definition of Occam's razor, "the simplest solution is most likely the right one," was enough to satisfy the most rational or disinterested minds—cigarettes were the only other common thread in *The Conqueror* crew's lives. Those same people also took issue with  the fact that most of the deaths were occurring twenty-five years after exposure.

On the opposite side of the spectrum, others feared the fates of the hundreds of Shivwits band of Paiute members who had served as extras in the film. They had not been included in Jackovich and Sennet's cast and crew count, and the tribes were seemingly being left out of the downwinder conversations altogether.

Others, much like many of Agnes Moorehead's *Bewitched* fans, truly believed that *The Conqueror* was cursed, claiming Navajo burial ground disturbances were to blame.

The recent death of Howard Hughes led some to believe that, as producer, he was well aware of the nuclear dangers and felt guilty before anyone started falling ill. His buyout of and protection over *The Conqueror* lent itself to the claim that Hughes knew all along what would happen and tried to make the film vanish from public memory.

The federal government remained tightlipped as the congressional push for downwinder compensation dragged on. The only acknowledgment was from an undisclosed Pentagon Nuclear Defense Agency spokesperson, who, upon receiving a request from *People* magazine to comment, apparently uttered, "Please, God, don't let us have killed John Wayne."

Jeanne Gerson's avocation did eventually lead her to Stewart Udall, who was then serving as secretary of the interior and in the midst of preparing a class action lawsuit on behalf of the downwinders. Udall heard the actress out, feeling skeptical since filming of *The Conqueror* hadn't actually commenced during a physical bomb test, and told Gerson "short-term" and "long-term" resident cases should not be mixed at that time. Without backing or successfully rallying the children of her costars, Gerson stopped attempting to file lawsuits and publicly speaking on the matter for good.

The actress's obstacle was not isolated by any means; the largest hurdle to bring forth a lawsuit of any kind for people who worked on *The Conqueror* was the scientific community's belief in the nonstochastic effect—a theory that health effects would be developed only after reaching an exposure threshold. With the accepted impression that radiation potency decayed within twenty-four hours of an atomic blast, many, like Udall, claimed radiation exposure could not have been significant enough at the point of film production to cross that threshold.

When in doubt, opponents clung to the National Cancer Institute's 1980 statistics, which plainly showed that 41 percent of people would contract cancer in their lifetime and 21.7 percent would die from the disease. Jackovich and Sennet's numbers aligned exactly, almost to the decimal, of those cancer rates, signifying that, if there was radiation fallout to blame, the death toll was still nothing out of the ordinary.

The year that followed *People*'s publication seemed to be nothing more than a table tennis match between skeptics and believers, slinging facts back and forth in the name of science, justice, pure infatuation with the oddity of it all. A piece of good news managed to emerge in 1981, when Michael Wayne founded the John Wayne Cancer Center at UCLA with friend and renowned doctor Donald Morton to "promote leading-edge cancer research and the education of the next generation of cancer physicians."

The center later moved to Saint John's Hospital and Medical Center in Santa Monica and became John Wayne Cancer Institute, where comprehensive research and treatments are conducted and a foundation was established to fund research, education, awareness, and support under the direction of son Ethan.

At the same time as the announcement, the Howard Hughes Medical Institute's annual budget also skyrocketed from $4 million each year to $200 million when its founder passed. Most of the anticipated annual revenue for the institute had instead been filtered for Hughes Aircraft developments, but new trustees and the sale of the aircraft division led to a dramatic growth in the mid-1980s.

The Medical Institute's possibilities blossomed, allowing for a wider focus on research in cell biology, genetics, immunology, neuroscience, and structural biology to occur, much of it relating to the prevention and understanding of cancer.

With the news of these institutions' goals—particularly the announcement of Wayne's foundation—many felt a positive outcome had emerged from controversy. Duke's work and image as a cancer icon would live on, and, therefore, an unspoken conclusion had been reached: There was no need to take anything to the courts.

*The Conqueror* received less and less attention as the weeks went on, and the debate whether or not it was just another conspiracy theory or a workplace tragedy seemed to become a silent stalemate; despite the hype, the movie never actually played on any theater screen.

With no consensus, government sympathy, reparations, or apologies for those associated with *The Conqueror*, and with Hughes and his incarnation of RKO both long gone, there was no one left to take the fall for any negligence during production anyway. The problem with the whole quieting down was that any coverage given or momentum gained for downwinders and families left in communities adjacent to the Nevada Test Site, like St. George, went away with it.

The Radiation Exposure Compensation Act had grown cold, and in one single snap, both *The Conqueror* and desert-dwelling families reeling from radiation exposure were dropped as the tabloid flavor of the month.

# 16: Myth in the Making

Yet again, Hollywood found itself falling into the moviemaking motions, similar to the 1950s, when pricey eye candy dominated cinema screens. At least the folks responsible for this go-round had the good sense not to include Mongols, Shakespearian-influenced dialogue, or much of anything set in the desert.

The blockbuster era ignited with whiz kids Steven Spielberg and George Lucas releasing special effects–driven thrills like *Jaws*, *Star Wars*, *Raiders of the Lost Ark*, and *E.T.* at the cusp of summer–a treat that soon morphed into an annual expectation as the decade rolled on.

What the 1980s also changed in the way of cinema was both the access to films and the overall culture surrounding people's passion for the medium. With the invention of home video and the dawn of rental stores, VHS tapes battled it out with Betamax cassettes for space on the shelves while people wandered in to pick up a copy of something new or something they had seen long, long ago and never gotten the chance to revisit.

Home video gave older films and initially unsuccessful releases a new life, backing a pastime built on fanaticism and conversations that could reach far past sticky theater seats. It was there–in the depths of those rental stores–where bits of trivia would be shared and film legends passed along down the line–albeit much akin to the telephone game where facts often get replaced with one's own personal spin or misinformation.

*The Conqueror*'s atomic association did not live and evolve through film theory classes or media sensationalism–it was the staunch audiences who carefully shaped the narrative, offering knowledge up to customers as a free-of-charge tidbit that came with their rental and spread through word of mouth. True or not, the production stories made good conversation. Everyone, at the very least, had a basic understanding of who John Wayne was. And they were probably popping in to pick up something nuclear-related to boot! In a new, more hostile and cynical treatment of yet another phase in the Cold War and atomic era, Hollywood explored the growing technical advancements in nuclear weapons, mostly the probable catastrophes from their use.

In 1983, *WarGames* tackled the technology through a stylized teen sci-fi thriller. Made-for-television movie *The Day After* looked at nuclear repercussions through the lives and experiences of small-town Kansas folk. You had your radiation conspiracies like *Ground Zero* and your cheesy sci-fi stories like *The Manhattan Project*. There were apocalypse horrors like *Dead Man's Letters* and *Threads* along with sappy family dramas like *Testament*.

Gamers also had their chance to fire off ballistic weaponry and thwart (or cause) an atomic doomsday through plenty of Cold War–themed video games like *Missile Command* and *Raid over Moscow*. Readers could soak up hypothetical nuclear holocaust fiction in every genre—most oddly in *The Butter Battle Book* written by Dr. Seuss. Three decades later, atomic everything was back—and with a very alarming vengeance.

*The Atomic Café*, an experimental 1982 documentary stylishly composed of the most campy nuclear test site training films, AEC propaganda clips, Upshot-Knothole newsreels, and Bert the Turtle's duck and cover instructions, attempted to examine the ridiculousness of the atomic heyday and challenge the United States' increasingly offensive measures. The small niche film failed to make a thunderous impression but thrived because of individual tastes that possessed the power to seek the film out or stumble across it in the aforementioned video stores.

Low-budget nuke thrillers tapered off in the early 1990s, but their popularity was unmistakable during the Reagan realm. The shift in cinema production allowed for smaller, more independently produced movies to find audiences, meaning unique ventures like *The Atomic Café* and these dime-a-dozen cousins of the B picture were a safer, potentially more profitable endeavor than a risky blockbuster.

Old habits seemed to have died hard for one studio in particular, a studio that had made a living—or in their case, failed to make a living—through its reminiscent block-booking model. As studios started looking to distribute and actually develop low-budget pictures for a quick side dime, this one saw an opportunity to capitalize on the video market and churn out smaller, more slapdash motion pictures for yet another shot at relevancy. That studio was RKO.

Yes, RKO had lain dormant from the late 1950s to the tail end of the 1970s, but parent company RKO General, which had etched out a respectable television and radio broadcasting empire, decided to reconstitute the production sector and give film production another try. A subsidiary called RKO Pictures Inc. was announced in 1978, with its first project, a comedy about a white executive who discovers he has an illegitimate black son called *Carbon Copy*, hitting theaters in 1981.

The film (notable as Denzel Washington's first role) was a coproduction with the Herndale Film Corporation. While the racially charged movie was a critical and commercial dud, RKO's new foray allowed for a variety of distribution partnerships with two of the old Big Five studios, Paramount and 20th Century Fox. This time, there would be no charismatic studio head to bark flamboyant orders like a god—oddly, one of the reasons creative risks and mold-breaking releases would be nil.

Thomas O'Neil remained as the head honcho until his official retirement in 1985 with son Shane beginning to take the reins several years before. The film production subsidiary was skimpily manned and instead welcomed outside producers like Tony Richardson and Paul Schrader to bring projects to them, most of which would play to empty theaters but become hits with renters.

The new incarnation of RKO chose to foster a slow-burning Jack Nicholson drama called *The Border*, an erotic remake of its own 1940s' horror classic *Cat People*, and an eyebrow-raising Dolly Parton/Burt Reynolds musical romp called *The Best Little Whorehouse in Texas*—all released by Universal in 1982.

Then, starting with the very small Meryl Streep film *Plenty* in 1985 and followed by the sexual drama *Half Moon Street* starring Michael Caine and Sigourney Weaver, plus the well-received

Vietnam War film *Hamburger Hill*, RKO was back in the saddle and independently producing motion pictures for the first time since *The Conqueror*.

The company's future as a picture producer looked brighter than it had since the days of *King Kong* and Ginger Rogers, but alas, the short-lived return was not meant to last. By the latter part of the decade, the newly formed parent company, GenCorp, was having money trouble; the film subsidiary was still turning out a handful of pictures each year–mostly gross-out teen comedies and campy Australian coproductions that often got buried in the depths of video rental stores.

Licensing disputes and a mass company shuffle led to the sale of RKO Picture's trademark and remake rights to Wesray Capital Corporation in 1987 and a complete exit from the broadcast business in 1991. At the time, Wesray was the owner of Six Flags and purchased RKO for thirty-one million dollars with hopes of possibly incorporating the studio's historic content into its amusement parks. Ultimately, nothing came of their ownership, and no further films were produced.

Actress and Post Cereals heiress Dina Merrill swooped in with her husband, Ted Hartley, to purchase a majority stake in 1989 and merge what was essentially RKO's name with their own Pavilion Communications; Turner Entertainment had previously snagged the worldwide rights to eight hundred of RKO's classics months before.

RKO Pictures LLC, the studio's official title since 1990, remains in operation under Hartley's quiet ownership. About fifteen projects have intermittently seen the light of day over the past thirty years (the most significant being a remake of RKO's 1949 gorilla picture *Mighty Joe Young*, an ironic coproduction with Disney given their strained history together).

Aside from the grim reality that RKO's stake in movie making is all but the size of a crumb, the former Hollywood giant's contributions to the world are aired on Turner Classic Movies and discussed ad nauseam by film fans. Historian Richard B. Jewell authored a 1982 retrospect *The RKO Story*, which detailed the studio like no other in the business so lovingly received. Its logo, perhaps rivaled only by Leo the MGM lion, stands as the iconic emblem of classic cinema.

Or, golden legacies are just wishful thinking and what people really remember RKO for is that one insane cinematic blunder in particular. At the very least, *The Conqueror* keeps the RKO Radio Pictures name alive, as it's often referred to in the business as an "RKO Radioactive Picture."

The nuclear arms race had reached abruptly dangerous heights in the 1980s as the Reagan administration pushed Cold War measures to levels even the greatest science fiction writers could never have dreamt up. Scrapped peace talks with the Soviet Union and a more offensive approach led to a new boom in atomic development, with the Strategic Defense Initiative announced in 1983.

Nicknamed "Star Wars" by its critics, an antiballistic missile system was proposed to defend the United States from an outer space battle station, widening the risk for catastrophe on an unfathomable global scale.

At a cost of burdening their agriculture and manufacturing sectors, the USSR surpassed the US's military arsenal, mounting fears that their atomic stockpile was additionally larger and more advanced. Nervous chatter in Washington, DC, led to fear in America's Southwest that atmospheric testing might occur in order to best the Soviets; underground shots were still actively underway at the Nevada Test Site.

The people of southern Utah had grown tired waiting for any kind of reintroduction of the Radiation Exposure Compensation Act and took action when radiation hazards again loomed on the horizon. More than eleven hundred residents (both current and former) banded together to file claims against the government nuclear fallout with a requested settlement of two billion dollars–a massive movement that would actually get its day in court.

A high-profile trial, beginning in September 1982, brought in doctors, scientists, national defense employees, and witnesses– most testifying that cancers can absolutely be linked to radiation. Suppressing years of pent-up frustration, people like Harry Butrico, a retired public health service engineer, shared their experiences.

Adamant St. George residents were asked by the AEC to wash the fallout off their cars but not themselves. John Wayne's death was even brought to the discussion table from time to time only to be routinely dismissed.

Again, the Energy Department officials repeated their automatic response that "radiation released from aboveground nuclear testing posed no significant threat to people living downwind from the Nevada Test Site." Acknowledging cancer and leukemia rates were higher than normal, Energy Department assistant manager Bruce Church successfully argued that Utah still had one of the lowest cancer rates as a whole in the entire country (due to such a sparse population).

The acceptable tolerance dose of radiation that a typical human could theoretically come in contact with each year was a shifting concept that revealed a very fine line. While five rems (Roentgen equivalent man) of radiation had been deemed by scientists to be a safe annual amount, readings immediately after the Harry shot had measured six rems.

A radioactive substance's half-life was also established to indicate its level of potency, specifically an estimated timeframe that radiation levels were expected to fall by half. A UN Scientific Committee looked at the effects of atomic radiation and determined that out of the most significant cancer-causing radionuclides, strontium-90 had a half-life of twenty-eight years, caesium-137 a half-life of thirty years, and carbon-14 had a half-life of fifty-seven hundred years. Iodine-131 was found to have an eight-day half-life, but exposure still posed a risk of cancer. Following Harry, scientific estimates pegged the amount of iodine-131 to be as much as five hundred times higher than normal in some spots.

The committee's reports determined "the highest exposure was found to be due to long-lived radioactive material that causes radiation exposures over many years," meaning anyone in the vicinity, including *The Conqueror* crew, would have come in contact with any of those radionuclides.

Appeal after appeal and individual lawsuits bore no fruit. Twenty-four plaintiffs were chosen to represent the twelve hundred individual victims in 1984, when Judge Bruce Sterling Jenkins ruled that "fallout caused human deaths and the federal government was negligent in failing to warn residents." On yet another appeal, the government argued grounds of national security and won.

The public response was not a quiet one; more than thirty-seven thousand southern Utahns and Nevadans immediately gathered for protests and demonstrations at the gates of the Nevada Test Site to voice their frustrations over the never-ending saga. In March 1988, the American Peace Test organization sponsored twelve days of more than eight thousand protestors demanding an end to testing at the Nevada Test Site gate; three thousand attendees were arrested. Attorneys, meanwhile, flocked to St. George and knocked on doors like traveling salesmen to inquire if anyone had contracted cancer and wished to file another claim.

On Capitol Hill, Senator Kennedy's RECA bill landed itself a place in the history books—a footnote marking the first commendable attempt in getting some kind of reparation for people exposed to radiation. Without much traction, it seemed that's all it or any recognition for the downwinders was going to be.

Utah senator Orrin Hatch had taken over the reins chairing the resulting committee shortly after the bill was introduced, with Kennedy placing his efforts in an onslaught of other causes. Hatch held about a dozen hearings in Utah throughout the early 1980s, turning to the National Cancer Institute to provide backing on the health effects of radiation. Yet, another introduction—this time as an amendment to an existing compensation bill for Pacific Islanders— failed to get enough votes.

Bothered by the hypocrisy that inhabitants of the Marshall Islands were to receive compensation from the testing done at Bikini Atoll but American citizens went home empty-handed, Senator Hatch took the Treaty of Peace and Friendship "hostage" and successfully argued to the Reagan administration that action also needed to be taken for fallout victims near the Nevada Test Site.

Support for Hatch's argument remained mixed; Utah's second senator, Jake Garn, was in favor of national security and meandered around the issue of compensation. Stewart Udall had exited politics and began penning books about Spanish gold-seekers and Western legends (though he would publish *The Myths of August* in 1994, which examined American atomic history). Governor Scott Matheson battled multiple myeloma and died from the disease in 1990. Many believed the rare cancer was in fact caused by nuclear testing fallout.

The revamp of RECA was happening, mind you, in the midst of Soviet leader Mikhail Gorbachev's arrival with a more peaceful agenda in tow. Gorbachev ushered in a unilateral testing moratorium in 1986, with a promise from President Reagan to do the same in America and ban nuclear testing once and for all. A stabilized relationship was finally developing between the two superpowers with Reagan's "Star Wars" project scrapped and George H. W. Bush voted in as president. A failed coup against Gorbachev and the fall of the Berlin Wall signaled that the Iron Curtain was lifting and Communist governments were falling out of fashion in the East.

Former congressman Wayne Owens recognized the power of timing and jumped to keep a radiation compensation aspect in the conversation. More than a decade had passed when he took back his congressional seat in 1987. Owens's determination and unwavering passion for the cause proved to be the missing ingredient for a successful attempt. RECA was given yet another introduction, with the bill authored by Senator Hatch and Owens sponsoring in May 1989 to the 101st Congress. The Radiation Exposure Compensation Act was officially passed by Congress on October 5, 1990, and signed into law by President George H. W. Bush on October 15.

The "one-time" benefit payments could now be accessed by "persons who may have developed cancer or other specified diseases after being exposed to radiation from atomic weapons testing." Personnel who worked on an atmospheric shot for the Nevada Test Site would receive seventy-five thousand dollars in compensation while residents of a rectangular twenty-two-county area surrounding NTS, covering Nevada, Utah, and a small part of Inyo County, California, and the northern portions of Mohave and Coconino Counties in Arizona, could get fifty thousand dollars.

A morose chart listed the variety of eligible cancers and when people should have been diagnosed. It included nineteen different forms of cancer such as brain, thyroid, stomach, breast, and lung—all of which had to have been contracted at least five years after radiation exposure. The final stipulation was by far the most limiting—an evident design to shrink applicant numbers. To be considered a downwinder, someone had to have set foot in the designated area between January 21, 1951, and October 31, 1958, and then June 30, 1962, to July 31, 1962; those eligible "must have been physically present for a period of at least 24 consecutive months." It meant any cast or crew member who worked on *The Conqueror* would be ineligible to apply for RECA payments and would not be recognized as downwinders.

Residents of the allotted southwestern states reported years of struggle following RECA's introduction—predominately excessive wait times for payments to come, mountains of paperwork to sign, and legal hoops to jump through to prove their residency or just be accepted if they were family of the deceased.

Amendments had been made along the way—most significantly in 2000, which saw the zone of eligibility expand. Some residents expressed that the bill still did not go far enough and was only implemented to quiet the downwinder conversation and appear as a silent admission of error rather than to actively help lives stricken by cancer.

Specialty groups such as the National Association of Atomic Veterans and downwinder advocate Jay Truman's Utah-based organization have endlessly fought for further compensation and awareness and have used *The Conqueror* controversy as an attention-grabbing hook to get people interested in their cause.

According to the Radiation Exposure Compensation Act information package, RECA has awarded more than $2.3 billion in benefits to more than thirty-six thousand claimants since its inception in 1990.

A unanimous victory for both downwinders and all citizens of the world happened with a moratorium order, signed by President Bush, that mandated a nine-month halt on US nuclear weapons testing. With no more ideological enemy to fend off, the moratorium was extended, with the final underground atomic test—code-name "Divider" under the Operation Julin series—taking place at the Nevada Test Site on September 23, 1992.

The United States and 183 countries signed the Comprehensive Nuclear Test Ban Treaty on September 10, 1996, to confirm that no further nuclear test should ever occur under any power. In total, 1,054 American atomic tests had been conducted since 1945 with 928 of them at the Nevada Test Site, making it the most bombed place on planet Earth.

Finally, capping a near thirty-year gap, *The Conqueror*–in full–was offered to audiences when it was officially released on VHS in 1983. Curiosity about the movie increased during the home video boom, and now people had a chance to revisit it, even if just to glimpse John Wayne as Genghis Khan.

Sadly, at the time RECA was being implemented and more and more tapes hit rental shops, the last of the principal cast and crew were in the process of passing on, pushing the crew member death toll higher and inadvertently stirring up radiation rumors each time another one died.

Leathery Lee Van Cleef, typecast as outlaws, henchmen, and Western gang goons passed away of a heart attack in December 1989, battling throat cancer at the same time. Chameleonic John Hoyt popped up on just about every television show a person could think of, including sci-fi soft-core porn; he died of lung cancer in 1991 at the age of eighty-five. Poor Jeanne Gerson was diagnosed with cancer for a third time and officially passed away from pneumonia in February 1992; she was eighty-seven years old.

Oscar Millard, on the contrary, retired from writing scripts in the late 1970s to travel and hammer out editorials for the *Los Angeles Times*. The man never commented on *The Conqueror*, instead crusading throughout the 1980s to rid people's stereotyped image of Hollywood screenwriters typing beside swimming pools. Being one of the only people who worked on the Mongol movie who didn't visit the set, Millard died of natural causes at the age of eighty-two.

Those who stampeded straight for the dated motion picture expecting to somehow catch a glimpse of radioactive waves wafting in the background or bomb tests rocking the set were crestfallen. For all the allure and mystique *The Conqueror* had surrounding it in the way of production woes, people drawn to its sensationalism quickly discovered that the Mongol epic was in fact exactly what they were told it was all along–a very bad movie. Viewers had certainly been given fair warning: John Wilson, creator of a yearly tradition that honors the very worst in cinema called the Golden Raspberry Awards, or "Razzies" for short, included *The Conqueror* in his list of "100 Most Enjoyably Bad Movies Ever Made."

Film critic Michael Medved awarded John Wayne–one year after his death–a "Golden Turkey Award" for worst casting choice of all time, previously including the film in his 1978 book *The Fifty Worst Films of All Time (and How They Got That Way).*

*Complex* magazine named the picture as "the worst biopic of all time," while David Wallechinsky stuck it in his ten worst movies list in his novelty publication *The Book of Lists.*

Cinephiles with background knowledge of what they were looking at when they rented *The Conqueror* could get a tad more mileage out of the watch. Taking pleasure in ungodly onscreen messes was a pastime–usually with tastes that circled toward the lowest-grade Ed Wood feature or schlock horror. The Mongol movie began showing up at viewing parties and niche film festivals to purposely celebrate its many foibles.

Anyone grabbing the film as a John Wayne fan or period piece lover, blindly unaware of its scholarly rankings, would have probably shut the movie off before getting halfway. *The Conqueror* absolutely has its defenders–those who insist "it's not as bad as they say" or praise the film's production values. But even the very best material Hollywood has to offer struggles to appeal to casual audiences. Why would they waste their time with something knowingly repugnant?

Somewhere along the way, VHS copies fell out of the classic section and landed in specialty nooks labeled "enjoyably bad" or "campy cinema." Additionally released on two separate VHS editions in 1992 and 1999, the labels made sure to reference the fact that this was "one of John Wayne's most unusual roles." One forwent a plot summary and mentioned how Howard Hughes managed to keep it out of public reach until the 1990s, while the other edition used the nuclear controversy as a selling feature by stating that the film was "shot on locations in Utah near an atomic testing site, and in a tragic aftermath, many of the film's cast and crew later contracted cancer."

When VHS began to fall by the wayside with the rise of DVDs in the early 2000s, GoodTimes Entertainment issued the first disc release. Universal dumped *The Conqueror* into a five-film package called *John Wayne: An American Icon Franchise Collection* in May 2006. The set was meant to offer Duke's lesser-known work, which included *Seven Sinners*, *The Shepherd of the Hills*, *Pittsburgh*, and *Jet Pilot*.

*The Conqueror* wouldn't get its own Universal DVD release until 2012, when it was made available through the company's Vault series: a manufactured-on-demand selection consisting of 285 other Golden Age films meant to make unpopular or obscure releases available in some purchasable form or another. Because it was mostly buyable online for collectors specifically looking to own a copy, very few consumers stumbled across it in department store entertainment sections or bargain bins unless it was secondhand.

High-priced DVD and Blu-ray copies, many of them issued in other countries, are floating around for sale online if people hunt hard enough; it has occasionally aired on Turner Classic Movies.

Through the influx of blogging, instantaneous platforms to reach readers, and limitless interaction with others from around the globe, the World Wide Web has provided *The Conqueror* with a whole new and entirely separate life, one of aggrandizement in the name of clicks.

Google the movie's title, and you'll infinitely scroll through pages and pages of lists and videos, recountings of the ill-fated production in publications including the *Guardian*, the *Telegraph*, the *New York Times*, *Variety*, *Hollywood Reporter*, or film fans placing the picture among the "Worst Movies of All Time" and rehashed write-ups with titles claiming John Wayne's Mongol movie is "the Most Dangerous Film Ever Made."

One could probably argue, given the amount of homemade videos, posts, and passionate ramblings, that *The Conqueror*'s most dominant role in modern day is as a source of debate, pitting people against each other about whether or not the atomic tests could have actually been responsible for the death of John Wayne. Pick a source, any source, and you'll be able to back up whatever belief you wish to hold, using entertainment fodder to squabble over radioactive toxicity levels and how many Camels Duke puffed in a day.

The problem for intrigued gossip column readers and diehard conspiracy enthusiasts is that there is no concrete ending wrapped up with a bow. The government has never officially acknowledged the nuclear controversy associated with the film; no movement has ever been made—at least to public knowledge—to prove or dispel the cancer claims.

Entities like the Discovery Channel dedicated an entire episode of their program *Best Evidence* to get to the bottom of the production, determining there was never enough of the hazardous isotope cesium-137 in the soil to have killed anyone who worked on the film. Any downwinder would tell you different.

Some pledge allegiance to the theory that cigarettes were to blame for at least a few of the deaths, seeing as how that theory came from Duke's own mouth. Others believe statistics tell a different story, figuring far higher death tolls would have occurred for every Golden Age film, given the amount of smokers back then. *The Conqueror*'s death toll is too much of a coincidental oddity to dismiss on something so common. At its very least, the surrounding controversy has acted as a window into the far bigger and very real problem plaguing the residents of southern Utah.

With the days of production so far gone in the past, almost nobody can speak on their experience. It's impossible to account for the casual employees who worked on the production and accurately document everyone who developed cancer in later years. Without an official proclamation, something coming straight from the people at the top, speculations and arguments won't ever reach a satisfied conclusion. Then again, after everything uttered by the AEC, would people have cause to believe them?

So, instead we are left wondering if a beyond cringe-worthy 1950s' period picture about Genghis Khan could really have been the catalyst to kill the Hollywood studio system, RKO, and the most iconic movie star of all time.

Carleton Young's quote from John Wayne's classic 1962 Western *The Man Who Shot Liberty Valance* often gets associated with *The Conqueror* to illustrate how its story has been spun over the years: "When the legend becomes fact, print the legend."

If its controversies were dispelled by every scientist and government official on earth, Duke and his costars would not be brought back to life, nor would *The Conqueror* be any better of a movie than it is today; so the whole "legend" aspect has become a moot point.

Murphy's Law doesn't work, either. Whatever can go wrong will go wrong is an appealing attribution to give when looking back at the production, but saying it would only let those who were in positions of high power off the hook.

Millions of motion pictures have been made in such a short amount of time, but most of what has been released throughout the past century and a half has fallen off the face of the earth; only a handful are steadily rewatched. None of them have a story quite like what a forgettable Mongol sword-and-sandal picture does—one that will endure as a Hollywood classic in its own right and that perhaps deserves a movie of its own.

Coincidence or calamity, a blinding overdose of fame, power, negligence, patriotism, sex, and money most certainly killed *The Conqueror*. If atomic testing didn't kill him, then to satisfy our desire for a conclusion, would it be a stretch to say those very same culprits were what killed John Wayne?

# Epilogue

Robert Downey Jr. zips through the skies inside his iconic Iron Man armor, leading both his team of Avengers and the trends of twenty-first-century cinema. Leonardo DiCaprio spins his totem top to check if he's entered a dream or awakened in reality. A red-faced Daniel Day Lewis screams at the top of his lungs from the altar of a church that he's abandoned his boy. Gosling and Stone hearken back to the studio musical with an ode to the dreamer, while the boy who lived gets whisked away aboard the Hogwarts Express to learn the world of witchcraft and wizardry. Tom Hanks cries at the loss of his inanimate volleyball companion.

A quick glance at modern cinema proves nothing remotely close to *The Conqueror* gets anywhere near a green light. It is a foreign relic that feels alien in practically every way; younger generations seem unable to comprehend that sword-and-sandal cinema was once intended as entertainment. But dated trends be damned, so many lessons have been indirectly taken from that one production to educate filmmakers—educate them on what never, ever to do.

Budgets for modern-day movies are bigger than ever—Marvel blockbusters come in at costs quadrupling what it took to make *The Conqueror*—yet productions have actually shrunk in size. Hundreds of millions go toward superstar paychecks and cutting-edge technologies instead of sustaining sweaty crew circuses in the desert.

Epic period pieces shot on location have ebbed and flowed, but nothing has compared to what was produced in the days of *The Conqueror*. It was always risky—far too dangerous, even without mismanagement, inexperience, and atomic bomb testing mucking up due process. These types of undertakings had become so overwhelming that the health and safety of celebrities, let alone countless extras and wranglers, became far too uncertain. It's a miracle more deaths didn't occur.

Scaled back to save unnecessary costs and travel, the popularization of chroma key techniques has allowed for everything from medieval wars to Mongol battles to be digitally created through the use of green-screen backdrops. Seas of crowds, whether soldiers on horses or throngs of audience members in coliseums, can be digitally added, saving studios millions and sparing mass amounts of bit-part actors from spending long, hot days in potential danger.

Quentin Tarantino, Christopher Nolan, and Paul Thomas Anderson are some of the notable names who have criticized its use and the growing reliance on special effects as an assault on the purity and art form of cinema, but the shift to digital filmmaking has absolutely allowed for greater control. Lazy or not, *The Conqueror*'s weather woes, possibly its entire existence, would not have occurred if RKO had these now rudimentary resources at their disposal.

The entertainment world is also starting to see a shift in terms of the way women are treated within the industry, moving past exploitation and sexualized pigeon holes that *The Conqueror*'s crafters were all too happy to indulge in. The #MeToo movement brought to light the global issue of sexual assault and harassment that women have endured in the workplace and their daily lives. No place seemed to be shaken more than the entertainment world when accusations brought down a plethora of powerful men who made a living preying on others.

Howard Hughes's predatory behavior as he lorded over aspiring actresses would forever go unpunished, feeding a stereotype that many producers, particularly Harvey Weinstein, subscribed to. More than eighty women came forward with stories of sexual assault and abuse in 2017, leading to Weinstein himself being found guilty of rape in the third degree and sentenced to twenty-three years in prison. The revelation has since promoted an overdue examination of power and misconduct that has long plagued Hollywood since the days Hughes arrived without a moral in hand.

In a more socially conscious and racially sensitive era, bloggers and entertainment writers have often focused on Wayne's casting, criticizing the practices of yellowface makeup and whitewashing Hollywood roles–most of them completely behooved by the decision and listing *The Conqueror* as a benchmark low for discrimination in the motion picture business.

Countdown video publisher *WatchMojo*, for instance, ranked John Wayne playing Genghis Khan as the number one "worst movie casting choice," "most controversial casting choice," and "worst whitewashed movie role."

Yellowface makeup in any mainstream entertainment medium almost never goes unchecked in the twenty-first century, with just about any race-altering performance receiving rounds of heavy scrutiny from pundits and the online community. That doesn't mean instances are completely eradicated; Rob Schneider was heavily slammed for his role as an Asian minister in the 2007 Adam Sandler comedy *I Now Pronounce You Chuck and Larry*. Smaller occurrences, like actress Emma Stone playing a character with one-quarter Chinese background in *Aloha*, caught media flack.

The larger argument today seems to be the practice of whitewashing roles to replace characters of color with Caucasian actors (Scarlett Johansson's involvement with *Ghost in the Shell* comes immediately to mind). So, at the very least, it would seem the consensus in Hollywood is that certain uses of makeup can be an insensitive choice, with very few exceptions squeaking by atop a tight rope.

Genghis Khan is a role that Hollywood just could never seem to do quite right in any era. Beyond Duke, Egyptian actor Omar Sharif played the ruler in the panned 1965 period piece *Genghis Khan* shortly after Rolando Lupi portrayed him in the 1961 Italian epic *The Mongols*. You also have American actor Richard Tyson taking the role in an unfinished Soviet Union–produced biopic, and strangest of all, Marvin Miller (forever known as the nasal voice of Robby the Robot in *Forbidden Planet*) portraying Khan in *Golden Horde*.

It's actually a little saddening to note that the first time an Asian actor portrayed the conqueror in a major release was Al Leong in the 1989 teen comedy *Bill and Ted's Excellent Adventure*. Several

Chinese productions have since fared well, notably *Mongol* from 2007, which earned an Oscar nomination for Best Foreign Language film, and *Genghis Khan: To the Ends of the Earth and Sea.* You'd think casting wouldn't be that hard, seeing as how scientists have estimated that one in every two hundred people carries the real Genghis Khan's lineage.

Really, the only aspect that *The Conqueror* has in common with the cinema of today is the surplus of big-budget blockbusters hogging movie screens. Television has shot ahead by leaps and bounds in its battle with film; the popularization of binge watching and the introduction of the limited series have all stolen away most viewers looking for an immersive experience. What remains that drives people off their couches and into theaters are strings of superhero movies, most based on comic books that have interconnecting stories and an already built-in legion of fans—a new version of the spectacle film.

History is doing what it knows it has always been good for: repeating itself, as Hollywood cycles into a new batch of old mistakes. Giants like Spielberg and Lucas have theorized that sooner or later the love for repetitive blockbusters will dry up along with studio bank accounts. Fingers are crossed that another revolution akin to the New Hollywood movement in the late 1960s will save the movies, but again, never has the theatergoing experience been so threatened by entities like Netflix in its entire existence.

You might not see Universal or Paramount shudder like RKO, but instead their whole mandate is completely shifting to the newest leader in the war for viewership: online streaming platforms.

Outside epic action movies and the film industry, present day has unfortunately more in common with *The Conqueror* than most would have hoped. After Pakistan and India carried out several nuclear tests in May 1998, the world had actually seen a complete halt in known atomic weapons development until the late 2010s. A threat that loomed for decades became a sobering reality when North Korea officially announced in 2016 that they had successfully developed a long-range rocket capable of carrying a nuclear warhead; a hydrogen bomb test caused a 6.3 magnitude earthquake in September 2017.

Because of the hostile developments, the metaphorical Doomsday Clock–a symbol used since 1947 to illustrate how close the
world is to an atomic catastrophe–was moved ahead by the *Bulletin of the Atomic Scientists* to "100 seconds to midnight." North
Korea's efforts, a worsening US–Russia relationship, and the effects
of climate change–which they theorize could have unintentional
and disastrous effects on nuclear weapons–were all cited as reasons
why.

The clock has been updated twenty-four times in three-quarters
of a century, but the 2020 announcement marked the closest it's
ever been to doomsday. The second closest the clock has ever been
to that position was in 1953–the year of the Upshot-Knothole series,
"Dirty Harry," and the very beginning of *The Conqueror.*

What does that mean for America's Nevada Test Site? The
Comprehensive Nuclear Test Ban Treaty of 1996 may have aided
in world peacekeeping for several decades, but the fact of the matter is that the United States remains as one of five nations that has
not ratified their signature. The powers in Washington never fully
agreed to the treaty's terms, meaning there is and always has been
intent that nuclear testing could be reimplemented through a simple command.

Waiting for the go-ahead, the former bombing grounds were
renamed the Nevada National Security Site (NNSS) in 2010 and
are used for defense programs, National Environmental Research
experiments, and radiological emergency response training. The
odd group of protestors still gather to storm the gates, instead
hoping to unveil the alleged interstellar secrets kept in the mythic
high-security facility, Area 51, rather than vie for nuclear justice;
the desert has seemingly shifted into a hokey tourist trap for road
trippers, conspiracy theorists, and alien aficionados.

St. George has inadvertently become a recreation hub for
extraterrestrial tourism in southwest Utah, rising above its contamination hardships to become the seventh-largest community in
the state with a metropolitan population of over 170,000. In 2018,
the Census Bureau named St. George the fastest-growing city in
America. With a close proximity to Zion National Park, Red Cliffs
National Conservation Area, and the Escalante Desert, it's easy

to see why interest in visiting the area as a tourist destination has increased over time.

Its closest attraction, nestled at the junction of the Mojave Desert, Great Basin, and Colorado Plateau, attracts more than 350,000 hikers, bikers, campers, and picnickers each year. Officially open to the public since 1962, the seventy-four-hundred-acre area contains more than thirty-eight miles of hiking trails, paved biking paths, and equestrian routes. Yes, beautiful Snow Canyon State Park is open to the public year-round.

For those looking for more of an educational holiday, a monument marks the spot where the first bomb–Trinity–was detonated in the nearby Jornada del Muerto desert of New Mexico.

The Atomic Heritage Museum can also be enjoyed in the city of Las Vegas, where guests can learn all about the bomb and join free monthly tours to visit the proving grounds and step foot onto America's historic nuclear test site.

# Bibliography

Allyson, June. *June Allyson*. New York: Berkley Publishing Group, 1983.

*American Cancer Society*. https://www.cancer.org/, accessed 5 February 2020.

*American Film Institute*. https://www.afi.com/, accessed 19 November 2019.

Andersen, Christopher. *A Star, Is A Star, Is A Star!: The Lives and Loves of Susan Hayward*. New York: Doubleday, 1980.

*Atomic Heritage Foundation*. https://www.atomicheritage.org/history, accessed 31 March 2020.

Back, Steven, and Thomas Schatz. *The Genius of the System: Hollywood Filmmaking in the Studio Era*. Minneapolis: University of Minnesota Press, 1988.

Ball, Howard. "Downwind From the Bomb." *New York Times*, February 9, 1986.

Barlett, Donald L., and James B. Steele. *Howard Hughes: His Life and Madness*. New York: WW Norton, 2004.

Bell, Chris. "The Movie So Toxic It Killed John Wayne: The Tragedy of The Conqueror." *Telegraph*, January 17, 2017. https://www.telegraph.co.uk/films/0/movie-toxic-killed-john-wayne-tragedy-conqueror/.

Biskind, Peter. *Easy Riders, Raging Bulls*. New York: Simon & Schuster, 1998.

Broeske, Pat H., and Peter Harry Brown. *Howard Hughes: The Untold Story*. New York: Viking Press, 1996.

Carroll, Rory. "Hollywood and the Downwinders Still Grapple with Nuclear Fallout." *Guardian*, June 6, 2015.

D'Arc, James. *When Hollywood Came to Town: A History of Movie-making in Utah*. Layton, UT: Gibbs Smith, 2010.

Doyle, Jack. "Wayne for Camels, 1950s." *The Pop History Dig*, January 29, 2010, https://www.pophistorydig.com/topics/tag/john-wayne-camel-cigarettes/.

Dreyfuss, Randy, and Harry Medved. *The Fifty Worst Films of All Time*. Robbinsdale, MN: Fawcett Columbine Books, 1978.

Drosin, Michael. "The Secret World of Howard Hughes." *Macleans*, February 4, 1985, 16–33.

Editors of the Official John Wayne Magazine. *Duke in His Own Words: John Wayne's Life in Letters, Handwritten Notes and Never-Before-Seen Photos Curated from His Private Archive*. New York: Media Lab Books, 2016.

Eliot, Marc. *American Titan: Searching for John Wayne*. New York: Dey Street Books, 2014.

Esson, Dylan. "Did 'Dirty Harry' Kill John Wayne? Media Sensationalism and the Filming of The Conqueror in the Wake of Atomic Testing." *Utah Historical Quarterly* (Summer 2003): 250–65.

Esterow, Milton. "R.K.O. Sale Takes a Dramatic Turn." *New York Times* (January 6, 1956).

Eyman, Scott. *John Wayne: The Life and Legend*. New York: Simon & Schuster, 2015.

Eyman, Scott. *Print the Legend: The Life and Times of John Ford*. New York: Simon & Schuster, 2015.

*Film Reference*. http://www.filmreference.com/encyclopedia/Romantic-Comedy-Yugoslavia/Star-System-THE-STUDIO-SYSTEM-AND-STARS.html.

*Filmsite*. https://www.filmsite.org/epicsfilms.html.

Fuller, John. *The Day We Bombed Utah*. New York: Signet, 1981.

Gallagher, Carole. *American Ground Zero: The Secret Nuclear War*. Cambridge, MA: MIT Press, 1993.

Gillians, Peter. "Atomic Documents Debate Over Government's Utah Atom Tests." *United Press International*. August 5, 1984.

Goldman, Michael. *John Wayne: The Genuine Article*. San Rafael, CA: Insight Editions, 2013.

Gomery, Douglas. *The Hollywood Studio System: A History*. British Film Institute, 2005.

Hack, Richard. *Hughes: The Private Diaries, Memos and Letters: The Definitive Biography of the First American Billionaire*. Beverly Hills, CA: Phoenix Books, 2009.

*Hollywood the Golden Years: The RKO Story*. BBC-TV, 1987.

*Howard Hughes Medical Institute*. https://www.hhmi.org/about, accessed 29 March 2020.

*Howard Hughes: The Man and the Madness*. Directed by Nick Millard. Maljack Productions, 1993.

*Internet Movie Database*. https://www.imdb.com/title/tt0049092/.

Jackovich, Karen G., and Mark Sennet. "The Children of John Wayne, Susan Hayward and Dick Powell Fear That Fallout Killed Their Parents." *People* (November 10, 1980).

Jewell, Richard B. *RKO Radio Pictures: A Titan Is Born*. Oakland: University of California Press, 2012.

Jewell, Richard B. *The RKO Story*. New York: Random House Value Publishing, 1985.

Jewell, Richard B. *Slow Fade to Black: The Decline of RKO Radio Pictures*. Oakland: University of California Press, 2016.

*John Wayne*. https://www.johnwayne.com/, accessed 29 March 2020.

*John Wayne: American Legend*. Directed by Kerry Jensen. A&E Network, 1998.

*John Wayne Cancer Institute*. https://www.saintjohnscancer.org/, accessed 29 March 2020.

Kelly, Cynthia C., and Richard Rhodes. *Manhattan Project: The Birth of the Atomic Bomb in the Words of Its Creators, Eyewitnesses, and Historians*. New York: Black Dog & Leventhal, 2009.

Kirkham, Pat, and Jennifer Bass. *Saul Bass: A Life in Film and Design*. London: Laurence King Publishing, 2011.

Landesman, Fred. *The John Wayne Filmography*. Jefferson, NC: McFarland Publishing, 2007.

Lasky, Betty. *RKO: The Biggest Little Major of Them All*. Warwick, NY: Roundtable Press, 1989.

Linet, Beverly. *Susan Hayward: Portrait of a Survivor*. New York: Atheneum, 1980.

Lippman, Thomas W. "'50s Nuclear Tests Prove to Be a Time Bomb for 'Downwinders.'" *Los Angeles Times* (May 30, 1993).

Longworth, Karina. *Seduction: Sex, Lies, and Stardom in Howard Hughes's Hollywood*. New York: Custom House, 2018.

Marrett, George J. *Howard Hughes: Aviator*. Annapolis, MD: Naval Institute Press, 2016.

Mason, Aiden. "How the Film "The Conqueror" Is Responsible for John Wayne's Death." *TV Overmind*, 2018, https://www.tvover mind.com/film-conqueror-responsible-john-waynes-death/.

McGivern, Carolyn. *John Wayne: A Giant Shadow*. Berkshire, UK: Reel Publishing, 2000.

McKenna, Kristine. "ART: The Real Death Valley: Nobuho Naga-sawa Has Created 'The Atomic Cowboy'—An Exhibition That Addresses the Fatal Consequences of Using Former Atomic Test Sites as Locations for '50s Films." *Los Angeles Times* (January 19, 1992).

Miller, Richard L. *Under the Cloud: The Decades of Nuclear Testing*. The Woodlands, TX: Two-Sixty Press, 1986.

Moon, Krystyn R. *Yellowface: Creating the Chinese in American Popular Music and Performance, 1850s–1920s*. New Brunswick, NJ: Rutgers University Press, 2004.

Munn, Michael. *John Wayne: The Man Behind the Myth*. New York: Berkley, 2005.

Norman, Neil. "Did Howard Hughes Kill John Wayne?" *Express.co.uk* (January 29, 2010). https://www.express.co.uk/expressyour self/154848/Did-Howard-Hughes-kill-John-Wayne/.

*The Numbers*. https://www.the-numbers.com/, accessed 30 December 2019.

Oberhansly, Curtis, and Dianne Nelson Oberhansly. *Downwinders: An Atomic Tale*. Salt Lake City, UT: Black Ledge Press, 2001.

Oldradioshows. "Atomic Consequences of 'The Conqueror': Howard Hughes Big Budget Film Flop." *OldRadioShows.org*, June 17, https://www.oldradioshows.org/2012/06/atomic-consequences-of-the-conqueror-howard-hughes-big-budget-film-flop/.

Pallete, Pilar, and Alex Thorlseifson. *John Wayne: My Life with the Duke*. New York: McGraw-Hill, 1987.

Parish, James Robert. *The Hollywood Book of Death: The Bizarre, Often Sordid, Passings of More Than 125 American Movie and TV Idols.* New York: McGraw-Hill Education, 2001.

Porter, Darwin. *Howard Hughes Hell's Angel: America's Notorious Bisexual Billionaire.* New York: Blood Moon Productions, 2005.

Porter, Jeff. *Oppenheimer Is Watching Me: A Memoir.* Iowa City: University of Iowa Press, 2007.

*RKO.* http://rko.com/company/legacy/, accessed 6 March 2020.

Staff Reports. "Magazine Notes High Cancer Rate Among Actors at Utah Site." Associated Press (November 2, 1980).

Stringham, Paige. Brigham Young University. "The Production and Legacy of The Conqueror (1956)." *Intermountainhistories.org,* last updated on May 29, 2019. https://www.intermountain histories.org/items/show/144/.

*Susan Hayward: The Brooklyn Bombshell.* A&E Network, 1998.

"Susan's Illness and a Final Grand Performance." *Chicago Tribune* (June 27, 1985).

Thomas, Tony. *The Dick Powell Story.* Burbank, CA: Riverwood Press, 1992.

Thomas, Tony. *Howard Hughes in Hollywood.* New York: Citadel Press, 1985.

Titus, Constandia A. *Bombs in the Backyard: Atomic Testing and American Politics.* Reno: University of Nevada Press, 2001.

Tranberg, Charles. *I Love the Illusion: The Life and Career of Agnes Moorehead.* Albany, GA: BearManor Media, 2007.

*Turner Classic Movies.* http://www.tcm.com/tcmdb/title/71427/ The-Conqueror/notes.html, accessed 11 April 2020.

United States, Congress, House, Public Health and Social Welfare. *Radiation Exposure Compensation Act.* 101st United States Congress, 1990.

*Variety* staff. "The Conqueror." *Variety* (December, 31, 1955), https://variety.com/1955/film/reviews/the-conqueror -1200418011/.

Von Tunzelmann, Alex. "The Conqueror: Hollywood gives Genghis Khan a Kicking He Won't Forget." *Guardian* (May 3, 2013).

Weiler, A.H. "Screen: 'The Conqueror'; John Wayne Stars in Oriental 'Western.'" *New York Times* (March 31, 1956).

Wilson, John. *The Official Razzie Movie Guide: Enjoying the Best of Hollywood's Worst.* New York: Grand Central Publishing, 2005.

# Index